-A Hartsfield and Hillsbeth book

Copyright 2006, 2017 Thomas J. Rico

ISBN 978-0-692-8-8019-7

Manufactured in the United States

Oxford, MS

handhpub@gmail.com

For the seeker; may this map be a guide and your own heart the southern star leading you home.

1) Natural Man
15) Knowledge
31) Tradition
42) Regulation
51) The World as Seen and Reality
73) The Tempter, Desire, Sin
89) Reality of Deeds Done: Karma
110) Pride, Vanity, and Hypocrisy: Attachment
115) Punishment and Tribulation, Judgment
124) Duty
127) Charity
134) Love, Kindness and Compassion
141) Humility
153) Faith and Action
163) Non-Judgment, Non-Attachment
172) Mercy and Grace
179) Life
183) Truth
187) Self-knowledge
198) Unity
217) Atman
221) Patience, Confidence and Contentment, Perseverance
238) Inner Peace and Harmony
244) Love
252) Worship
258) Realization, Discrimination, and Watchfulness: Metanoia
278) The Way of the Word
325) Historical Glossary

Natural Man

What do I mean by a True Man? The True Man of ancient times did not rebel against want, did not grow proud in plenty, and did not plan his affairs. Being like this, he could commit an error and not regret it, could meet with success and not make a show. Being like this, he could climb the high places and not be frightened, could enter the water and not get wet, could enter the fire and not get burned. His knowledge was able to climb all the way up to the Way like this. The True Man of ancient times slept without dreaming and woke without care; he ate without savoring and his breath came from deep inside. The True Man breathes with his heels; the mass of men breath with their throats. Crushed and bound down, they gasp out their words as though they were retching. Deep in their passion and desires, they are shallow in the workings of Heaven. The True Man of ancient times knew nothing of loving life, knew nothing of hating death. He emerged without delight; he went back in without a fuss. He came briskly, he went briskly, and that was all. He didn't forget where he began; he didn't try to find out where he would end. He received something and took pleasure in it; he forgot about it and handed it back again. This is what I call not using the mind to repel the Way, not using the man to help out Heaven. This is what I call the True Man.
Chuang Tzu

Man has received from heaven a nature innately good, to guide him in all his movements. By devotion to this divine spirit within himself, he attains an unsullied innocence that leads him to do right with instinctive sureness and without any ulterior thought of reward and personal advantage.   Hexagram 25, I Ching

The Perfect Way is difficult only to those who pick and choose; do not like, do not dislike; all will then be clear. Make a hairbreadth of difference, and Heaven and Earth are set apart; if you want the truth to stand clear before you, never be for or

against. The struggle between for and against is the minds worst disease...The more you talk about It, and the more you think about It, the further from It you go; stop talking, stop thinking, and there is nothing you will not understand... There is no need to seek Truth; only stop having views. The ultimate Truth about both Extremes is that they are One Emptiness...Whether we see it or fail to see it, it is manifest always and everywhere.
Seng Tsan (third Chinese patriarch)

As is the use of a well of water or a pond when the whole countryside is flooded, such is the use of all the scriptures to the self-realized man.   Bhagavad Gita 2:46

If only your mind doesn't harbor particulars what place isn't still and clear?   *Hanshan*

A Zen student came to Bankei and complained: "Master, I have an ungovernable temper. How can I cure it?" "You have something very strange", replied Bankei. "Let me see what you have." "Just now I cannot show it to you", replied the other. "When can you show it to me?" asked Bankei. "It arises unexpectedly", replied the student. "Then", concluded Bankei, "it must not be your own true nature. If it were, you could show it to me at any time. When you were born, you did not have it, and your parents did not give it to you. Think that over."

Colors blind the eye. Sounds deafen the ear; flavors numb the taste. Thoughts weaken the mind. Desires wither the heart. The Master observes the world but trusts his inner vision. He allows things to come and go. His heart is open as the sky.
Tao Te Ching 12

The Master gives himself up to whatever the moment brings. He knows that he is going to die, and he has nothing left to hold on to: no illusions in his mind, no resistance in his body. He doesn't think

about his actions; they flow from the core of his being. He holds nothing back from life; therefore, he is ready for death, as a man is ready for sleep after a good day's work.
Tao Te Ching 50

Open yourself to the Tao, then trust your natural responses; everything else will fall into place.
Tao Te Ching 23

The ancient Masters were profound and subtle. Their wisdom was unfathomable. There is no way to describe it; all we can do is describe their appearance. They were careful as someone crossing an iced-over stream. Alert as a warrior in enemy territory. Courteous as a guest. Fluid as melting ice. Shapeable as a block of wood. Receptive as a valley. Clear as a glass of water.
Tao Te Ching 15

Be in this world as though you were a stranger or a traveler.
Hadith of the Prophet Mohammad

And so in the days when natural instincts prevailed, men moved quietly and gazed steadily. At that time, there were no roads over mountains, nor boats, nor bridges over water... You could climb up and peep into the raven's nest. For then man dwelt with birds and beasts, and all creation was one. There were no distinctions between good and bad men. Being all equally without knowledge, their virtue could not go astray. Being all equally without evil desires, they were in a state of natural integrity, the perfection of human existence. But when the sages appeared, tripping people over charity and fettering them with duty to one's neighbor, doubt found its way into the world. And then with their gushing over music and fussing over ceremony, the empire became divided against itself. Horses live on dry land, eat grass and drink water.... Thus far only do their natural dispositions carry them. But bridled and bitted, with a plate of metal on their foreheads, they learn to cast vicious looks, to turn the head to bite, to resist, to get the bit out of the mouth or the bridle in it. And thus their natures become depraved... In the days of Ho Hsu, the people did nothing in particular when at rest, and went nowhere in particular when they moved about. Having food, they rejoiced; having full bellies, they strolled about. Such were the capacities of the people. But when the sages came to worry them with ceremonies and music in order to rectify the form of government, and dangled charity and duty to one's neighbor before them in order to satisfy their hearts- then the people began to develop a taste for knowledge and to struggle one with the other in their desire for gain. This was the error of the sages.   *Chuang Tzu*

But what is the secret of finding this treasure? - There isn't one. This treasure is everywhere. It is offered to us all the time and wherever we are.... This is true spirituality, which is valid for all times and for everyone. We cannot become truly good in a better, more marvelous, and yet easier way than by the simple use of the means offered us by God: the ready acceptance of all that comes to us at each moment of our lives.   *Jean Pierre de Caussade*

The Prophet said that Truth has declared: 'I am not hidden in what is high or low nor in the earth nor skies nor throne. This is certainty, O beloved: I am hidden in the heart of the faithful. If you seek me, seek in these hearts.'   *Jalaludin Rumi*

There is something nearer to us than Scriptures, to wit, the Word in the heart from which all Scriptures come.
William Penn on the doctrine of *Inner Light*

Goodness needs not to enter into the soul, for it is there already, only it is unperceived.
Theologia Germanica

If you wish to tranquilize the mind and restore it to its original purity, you must proceed as you would do if you were purifying a jar of muddy water. You first let it stand, until the sediment settles at the bottom, when the water becomes clear which corresponds with the state of the mind before it was troubled by defiling passions. Then you carefully strain off the pure water...When the mind becomes tranquilized and concentrated into perfect unity, then all things will be seen, not in their separateness, but in their unity, wherein there is no place for the passions to enter, and which is in full conformity with the mysterious and indescribable purity of Nirvana.   *Surangama Sutra*

The difference between a good and bad man does not lie in this, that the one wills that which is good and the other does not, but solely in this, that the one concurs with the living inspiring spirit of God within him, and the other resists it, and can be chargeable with evil only because he resists it.   *William Law*

The Father uttered one Word; that Word is His Son, and he utters Him forever in everlasting silence; and in silence the soul has to hear it.   *St. John of the Cross*

A sannyasin must speak only those words that ring with truth, and always act according to conscience.
Uddhava Gita *13:16*

The ultimate way is without difficulty; those who seek it make their own hardship. The true mind is originally pure; those who exercise it make their own defilement.   *Hui-kung*

Everyone has a torch giving off great light: originally it spontaneously illumines heaven and earth; there is no distance to which it does not reach. It is no different from the Buddha's and Zen masters, but when it gets covered by false ideas and material toils, so that it cannot come out, it is therefore necessary to use effort in study to polish it.   *Yuan-Hsien*

Fish are born in water; man is born in Tao. If fish, born in water, seek the deep shadow of pond and pool, all their needs are satisfied. If man, born in Tao, sinks into the deep shadow of non-action to forget aggression and concern, he lacks nothing, his life is secure. Moral: All fish need is to get lost in water. All man needs to do is to get lost in Tao. *Chuang Tzu*

Chui the draftsman could draw more perfect circles freehand than with a compass. His fingers brought forth spontaneous forms from nowhere. His mind was meanwhile free and without concern with what he was doing. No application was needed; his mind was perfectly simple and knew no obstacle. So, when the shoe fits the foot is forgotten, when the belt fits the belly is forgotten, when the heart is right for and against are forgotten. No drives, no compulsions, no needs, no attractions: then your affairs are under control. You are a free man. Easy is right. Begin right and you are easy. Continue easy and you are right. The right way to go easy is to forget the right way and forget that the going is easy.
Chuang Tzu

The man of spirit is neither very intimate with anyone, nor very aloof. He keeps himself interiorly aware, and he maintains his balance so that he is in conflict with nobody. This is your true man! He lets the ants be clever. He lets the mutton reek with activity. For his own part, he imitates the fish that swims unconcerned, surrounded by a friendly element, and minding its own business. The true man sees what the eye sees, and does not add to it something that is not there. He hears what the ears hears, and does not detect imaginary undertones or overtones. He understands things in their obvious interpretation and is not busy with hidden meanings and mysteries. His course is therefore a straight line. Yet he can change his direction whenever circumstances suggest it."
Chuang Tzu

And if anyone obeys his own impulse to Good- be sure that Allah is He who recognizes and knows.   Quran 2:158

He Who has made everything which He created Most Good: He began the creation of man with nothing more than clay (...)   Quran 32:7

By the Soul, and the proportion and order given to it; and its enlightenment as to its wrong and its right; - truly he succeeds that purifies it and he fails that corrupts it.   Quran 91:7-10

Ananda: "I take it, therefore, that this mind is the power by which I investigate." Buddha replied: "No, no, Ananda, this is not your mind. This is but the perception of vain and false qualities, which, under the guise of your true nature, has from the first deceived you."   Surangama Sutra

Friends, all of you, each single one, possesses the nature of a Buddha. The good friends (the Bodhisattvas) do not take the bodhi of the Buddha and hand it out to you, nor do they settle things for you. Why? The Nirvana Sutra says that the Buddha has already foretold your destination, namely, that all the Beings are from the beginning in Nirvana; from the beginning they are endowed with the gift of immaculate wisdom. Why do they not recognize this fact Why do they wander in Samsara and cannot attain salvation? Because their view is obstructed by the dust of evil passions. They need the direction of a good friend; then they will recognize that they are Buddhas, cease to wander and attain salvation. (...) Friends, listen attentively as I speak to you of self-deception. What does self-deception mean? You, who have assembled at this place today, are craving for riches and the pleasures of intercourse with males and females; you are thinking of gardens and houses. This is the course form of self-deception. To believe that it must be discarded is the fine form of self-deception. That you do not know. What is the fine form of self-deception? When you hear one speaking of bodhi you think you must have that bodhi; and so when you hear someone speaking of Nirvana, of emptiness, of purity, of samadhi, you think you must have that Nirvana, that emptiness, that purity, that samadhi. These are all self-deception; these are fetters, heresies. With that deception in mind you cannot attain salvation. If unaware of the fact that you are saved, that you are guiltless from the very beginning without anything additional required- you think of leaving the world and abiding in Nirvana, this Nirvana becomes a fetter binding you to this life; in the same way purity, emptiness, samadhi, become fetters. Such thoughts impede your progress to bodhi. (...) Get conscious of the fact that in the natural state your mind is tranquil and pure, completely blank; then it is also unsupported and unattached, unbiased like empty space, reaching everywhere, that is, identical with the tathata-kaya (true-substantial essence) of the Buddhas. Tathata is the quality inherent in the absence of self-deception. Because we understand this fact we preach freedom from self-deception or attachment. One who looks at things free from self-deception, though fully seeing, hearing, feeling and knowing, is always blank and unconcerned about this or that and tranquil; in one act he practices sila, samadhi, and prajna simultaneously and fulfills the ten thousand conditions of virtue. Then he possesses the wisdom of the Tathagata which is wide and large, profound and far-reaching.   *Shen Hui*

Those who know don't talk. Those who talk don't know. Close your mouth, block off your senses, blunt your sharpness, untie your knots, soften your glare, settle your dust. This is the primal identity. Be like the Tao. It can't be approached or withdrawn from, benefitted or harmed, honored or brought into disgrace. It gives itself up continually. That is why it endures.
                              Tao te Ching

Confucius went to see Lao Tzu and talked with him about benevolence and righteousness. Lao Tzu said, "If you get grit in your eye from winnowing chaff, then Heaven and Earth and the four directions get mixed up. A mosquito or gadfly which stings you can keep you awake all night. And benevolence and righteousness, when forced upon us, disturb your heart and produce great distress. You, Sir, if you want to stop everything below Heaven from losing its original simplicity, you must travel with the wind and stand firm in Virtue. Why do you exert yourself so much, banging a big drum and hunting for a lost child? The snow goose doesn't need a daily bath to stay white, nor does a crow need to be stained every day to stay black. Black and white comes from natural simplicity, not from argument. Fame and fortune, though sought after, do not make people greater than they actually are. When the waters dry up and the fish are stranded on the dry land, they huddle together and try to keep each other moist by spitting and wetting each other. But wouldn't it be even better if they could just forget each other, safe in their lakes and rivers?"   *Chuang Tzu*

    Don't do anything whatsoever with the mind- abide in an authentic, natural state. One's own mind, unwavering, is reality. The key is to meditate like this without wavering; experience the great reality beyond extremes. In a pellucid ocean, bubbles arise and dissolve again. Just so, thoughts are no different from ultimate reality, so don't find fault; remain at ease. Whatever arises, whatever occurs, don't grasp- release it on the spot. Appearances, sounds, and objects are one's own mind; there's nothing except mind. Mind is beyond the extremes of birth and death. The nature of mind, awareness, although using the objects of the five senses, does not wander from reality. In the state of cosmic equilibrium there is nothing to abandon or practice, no meditation or post-meditation. Just this.   *Niguma*- Buddhist nun

    The Void needs no reliance; Mahamudra rests on naught. Without making an effort, but remaining natural, One can break the yoke thus gaining liberation.   Song of Mahamudra- *Tilopa*

    Even as a mirror of gold, covered by dust, when cleaned well shines again in full splendor, when a man has seen the Truth of the Spirit he is one with him, the aim of his life is fulfilled and he is ever beyond sorrow. Then the soul of a man becomes a lamp by which he finds the Truth of Brahman. Then he sees God, pure, never-born, everlasting; and when he sees God he is free from all bondage.   Svetasvatara Upanishad

This mind of yours is inseparable luminosity and emptiness in the form of a great mass of light, it has no birth or death, therefore it is the Buddha of Immortal Light. To recognize this is all that is necessary. When you recognize this pure nature of your mind as the Buddha, looking into your own mind is resting in the Buddha-mind.   Tibetan Book of the Dead

O son of noble family, when your body and mind separate, the dharmata will appear, pure and clear yet hard to discern, luminous and brilliant, with terrifying brightness, shimmering like a mirage on a plain in spring. Do not be afraid of it, do not be bewildered. This is the natural radiance of your own dharmata, therefore recognize it. A great roar will come from within the light, the natural sound of dharmata, like a thousand thunderclaps simultaneously. This is the natural sound of your own dharmata, so do not be afraid or bewildered. You have what a mental body of unconscious tendencies, you have no physical body of flesh and blood, so whatever sounds, colors, and rays of light occur, they cannot hurt you and you cannot die. It is enough simply to recognize them as your projections. Know this to be the bardo state.
     Tibetan Book of the Dead

The yellow light of the skandha of feeling in its basic purity, the wisdom of equality, brilliant yellow, adorned with discs of light, luminous and clear, unbearable to the eyes, will come towards you from the heart of Ratnasambhava and his consort and pierce your heart so that your eyes cannot bear to look at it. At the same time, together with the wisdom light, the soft blue light of human beings will also pierce your heart. At that time, under the influence of pride, you will be terrified and escape from the sharp, clear yellow light, but you will feel an emotion of pleasure and attraction towards the soft blue light of human beings. At that moment do not be afraid of the yellow light, luminous and clear, sharp and bright, but recognize it as wisdom. Let your mind rest in it, relaxed, in a state of non-action, and be drawn to it with longing. If you recognize it as the natural radiance of your own mind, even though you do not feel devotion and do not say the inspiration prayer, all the forms and lights and rays will merge inseparably with you, and you will attain enlightenment.   Tibetan Book of the Dead

All substances are my own mind, and this mind is emptiness, unarisen and unobstructed. Thinking this, keep your mind natural and undiluted, self-contained in its own nature like water poured into water, just as it is, loose, open and relaxed.
Tibetan Book of the Dead

Then God said, "Let Us make man in Our image, according to Our likeness." (...) Then God saw everything that He had made, and indeed it was very good.   Genesis 1:26, 31

Truly, this only I have found: that God made man upright, but they have sought out many schemes.
Ecclesiastes 7:29

Now let me sing to my Well-beloved a song of my Beloved regarding his vineyard: my Well-beloved has a vineyard on a very fruitful hill. He dug it up and cleared out its stones, and planted it with the choicest vine. He built a tower in its midst, and also made a winepress in it; so He expected it to bring forth good grapes, but it brought forth wild grapes. And now, O inhabitants of Jerusalem and men of Judah, judge, please, between Me and My vineyard, what more could have been done to My vineyard that I have not done in it? Why then, when I expected it to bring forth good grapes, did it bring forth wild grapes? And now, please let Me tell you what I will do to My vineyard: I will take away its hedge, and it shall be burned; and break down its wall, and it shall be trampled down. I will lay it waste; it shall not be pruned or dug, but there shall come up briars and thorns. I will also command the clouds that they rain no rain on it.   Isaiah 5:1-6

Holy, Holy, Holy is the Lord of hosts; the whole earth is full of His glory!   Isaiah 6:3

Prayer of Azariah- In our day we have no ruler, or prophet, or leader, no burnt offering, or sacrifice, or oblation, or incense, no place to make an offering before you and to find mercy. Yet with a contrite heart and a humble spirit may we be accepted. Such may our sacrifice be in your sight today, and may we unreservedly follow you, for no shame will come to those who follow you. And now with all our heart we follow you; we fear you and seek your presence. Do not put us to shame, but deal with us in your patience and in your abundant mercy. Deliver us in accordance with your marvelous works and bring glory to your name, O Lord.

Though I proclaim Nirvana, it is not real extinction; all things from the beginning are ever of Nirvana nature.
Lotus of the Wonderful Law

Though the heavenly mansions are unobstructed, few are those who go there; for people take the three poisons (greed, hatred and delusion) as their family wealth.   *Wonhyo* (617-686)

Out of the mouth of babes and sucklings you have established strength, Because of your adversaries, That you might still the enemy and the avenger.   Psalm 8:2

What profit has he that works where he labors? I have seen the travail which God has given to the sons of men to be exercised therewith. He has made everything beautiful in its time: also he has set eternity in their heart, yet so that man cannot find out the work that God has done from the beginning even to the end.
Ecclesiastes 3:9-11

Sirs, why do you these things? We also are men of like passions with you, and bring you good tidings, that you should turn from these vain things unto a living God, who made the heaven and the earth and the sea, and all that in them is: who in the generations gone by suffered all the nations to walk in their own ways. And yet He left not himself without witness, in that He did good and gave you from heaven rains and fruitful seasons, filling your hearts with food and gladness.   Acts 14:15-17

For the wrath of God is revealed from heaven against all ungodliness and unrighteousness of men, who hinder the truth in unrighteousness; because that which is known of God is manifest in them; for God manifested it unto them. For the invisible things of him since the creation of the world are clearly seen, being perceived through the things that are made, his everlasting power and divinity; that they may be without excuse: because that, knowing God, they glorified him not as God, neither gave thanks; but became vain in their reasonings, and their senseless heart was darkened. (...) Wherefore thou art without excuse, O man, whosoever you art that judgest: for wherein you judge another, you condemn yourself; for you that judge practice the same things. (...) For as many as have sinned without law shall also perish without the law: and as many as have sinned under the law shall be judged by the law; for not the hearers of the law are just before God, but the doers of the law shall be justified: (for when Gentiles that have not the law do by nature the things of the law, these, not having the law, are the law unto themselves; in that they show the work of the law written in their hearts, their conscience bearing witness therewith, and their thoughts one with another accusing or else excusing them; in the day when God shall judge the secrets of men, according to my gospel, by Jesus Christ.
Romans 1:18-21, 2:1, 12-16

A hunter, walking through the woods, came upon a notice. He read the words: stone-eating is forbidden. His curiosity was stimulated, and he followed a track which led past the sign until he came to a cave at the entrance to which a Sufi was sitting. The Sufi said to him: The answer to your question is that you have never seen a notice prohibiting the eating of stones because there is no need for one. Not to eat stones may be called a common habit. Only when the human being is able similarly to avoid other habits, even more destructive than eating stones, will he be able to get beyond his present pitiful state.   *Sufism*

    If you correct your mind, the rest of your life will fall into place. This is true because the mind is the governing aspect of a human life. If the river flows clearly and cleanly through the proper channel, all will be well along its banks. The Integral Way depends on decreasing, not increasing: to correct your mind, rely on not-doing. Stop thinking and clinging to complications; keep your mind detached and whole. Eliminate mental muddiness and obscurity; keep your mind crystal clear. Avoid daydreaming and allow your pure original insight to emerge. Quiet your emotions and abide in serenity. Don't go crazy with the worship of idols, images, and ideas; this is like putting a new head on top of the head you already have. Remember: if you can cease all restless activity, your integral nature will appear.   *Hua Hu Ching 45*

    I never saw any lamp shining more brilliantly than the lamp of silence.   *Bayazid Bistami*

Knowledge

I teach the Integral Way of uniting with the great and mysterious Tao. My teachings are simple; if you try to make a religion or science of them, they will elude you. Profound yet plain, they contain the entire truth of the universe.
Hua Hu Ching 1

It is essential for you to abandon all previously held knowledge, opinions, interpretations and understandings. It is not accomplished by stopping the mind; temporary relinquishment is not the way- it fools you into wasting body and mind, without accomplishing anything at all in the end. I suggest that nothing compares to emptying yourself. There is nowhere for you to apply your mind. Just be like an imbecile twenty-four hours a day. You have to be spontaneous and buoyant, your mind like space, yet without any measurement of space. You have to be beyond light and dark, no Buddhism, body, or mind, year in and year out. If anything is not forgotten, you've spent your life in vain. That is why it is said, even if you learn things pertaining to buddhahood, that too is a misuse of mind. You have to be free of preoccupations; you have to be natural. *Ch'eng-ku*

Sell your cleverness and buy bewilderment; cleverness is mere opinion, bewilderment is intuition.
Jalal-uddin Rumi

Knowledge puffs up, but love builds up. Anyone who claims to know something does not yet have the necessary knowledge; but anyone who loves God is known by him.
1st Corinthians 8:1-3

Seek the knowledge that is essential; pay no heed to non-essential knowledge. And when you have the knowledge you need, think only of putting it into practice. The Lord Buddha then warned Subhuti, saying, Subhuti, do not think that the Tathagata ever considers in his own mind:

I ought to enunciate a system of teaching for the elucidation of the Dharma. You should never cherish such a thought. And why? Because if any disciple harbored such a thought he would not only be misunderstanding the Tathagata's teaching, but he would be slandering him as well. Moreover, the expression '"a system of teaching" has no meaning; for Truth (in the sense of Reality) cannot be cut up into pieces and arranged into a system. The words can only be used as a figure of speech.   Diamond Sutra

He who loves discipline loves knowledge; foolish is the person who hates correction. The wise are grateful for a rebuke.
Proverbs

Do not deceive yourselves. If you think that you are wise in this age you should become fools so that you may become wise. For the wisdom of this world is foolishness with God. For it is written, "He catches the wise in their craftiness, and then again. "The Lord knows the thoughts of the wise, that they are futile."
1st Corinthians 3:18-20

Being a Sufi is to put away what is in your head- imagined truth, pre-conceptions, conditioning- and to face what may happen to you.   *Abu Said*

One who knows does not speak; one who speaks does not know. Block the openings; shut the doors. Blunt the sharpness; untangle the knots; soften the glare; let your wheels move only along old ruts.   Tao Te Ching

Dongshan once taught the assembly, "Concerning realization-through-the-body of going beyond Buddha, I would like to talk a little." A monk said, "What is this talk.?" The master said, "When I talk you don't hear it." The monk said, "Do you hear it, sir?" The master said, "Wait till I don't talk, then you hear it."

Even as fire without fuel finds peace in its resting-place, when thoughts become silence the soul finds peace in its own source.   Maitri Upanishad

Zhaozhou asked Nanquan, "What is the way?" Nanquan said, "Ordinary mind is the way." Zhaozhou asked, "Shall I try for that?" Nanquan said, "If you try you will miss it." Zhaozhou asked, "How do I know it's the way if I don't try?" Nanquan said, "The way has nothing to do with knowing or not knowing. Knowing is an illusion; not knowing is ignorance. If you penetrate the way of no-trying, it will be wide open- empty and vast. What need is there to affirm or deny it?" Zhaozhou was suddenly enlightened upon hearing this.
From: "Gateless Barrier", Case 19

Subhuti was Buddha's disciple. He was able to understand the potency of emptiness, the viewpoint that nothing exists except in its relationship of subjectivity and objectivity. One day Subhuti, in a mood of sublime emptiness, was sitting under a tree. Flowers began to fall about him. "We are praising you for your discourse on emptiness", the gods whispered to him. "But I have not spoken of emptiness", said Subhuti. "You have not spoken of emptiness, we have not heard emptiness", responded the gods. "This is the true emptiness." And blossoms showered upon Subhuti as rain.

In this world of dreams, dozing off still more; and again speaking and dreaming of dreams. Just let it be.   *Ryokan*

The meaning is not in words. Inquiring students seek further. Moving forward creates pitfalls. Avoidance leads to a standstill. Faced with a great wall of fire, turning your back on it and touching it are both wrong. Expressing it in colorful words only stains it. Midnight is bright, dawn brings no dew. Things are truth itself to be used for removing delusion. This is not created and yet not inexpressible. As form and image face each other in a bright mirror, you are not it but it is you. It is like a baby perfectly possessing five freedoms: Not coming, not going, not rising, not staying and goo goo wa wa- words that are not words. In the end nothing is grasped because speech is not precise. (...) Conceal your practice, work inside. Be ignorant, look foolish. Just keep on doing it.   This is called host with host.   *Dongshan*

    Sentient beings are in essence buddhas. It is like water and ice. There is no ice without water, there are no buddhas outside sentient beings. What a shame, sentient beings seek afar, not knowing what is at hand. It is like wailing from thirst in the midst of water, or wandering lost among the poor, although born a rich man's child.   *Hakuin*

    Eliminate the sage, abandon knowledge, and the people will benefit a hundredfold; Exterminate benevolence, abandon duty, and the people will again be filial; Eliminate ingenuity, discard profit, and there will be no more thieves and bandits. These three, being false adornments, are not enough and the people must have something to which they can attach themselves: Exhibit the unadorned and embrace the uncarved block, have little thought of self and as few desires as possible.   Tao Te Ching

    When dharma does not fill your whole body and mind, you think it is already sufficient. When dharma fills your body and mind, you understand that something is missing. For example, when you sail out in a boat to the middle of an ocean where no land is in sight, and view the four directions, the ocean looks circular, and does not look any other way. But the ocean is neither round nor square; its features are infinite in variety. It is like a palace. It is like a jewel. It only looks circular as far as you can see at that time. All things are like this. Though there are many features in this dusty world and the world beyond conditions, you see and understand only what your eye of practice can reach. In order to learn the nature of the myriad things, you must know that although they may look round or square, the other features of oceans and mountains are infinite in variety; whole worlds are there. It is not only around you, but also directly beneath your feet, or in a drop of water.   *Dogen*

The Sixth Ancestor Huineng came across two monks who were arguing about a banner flapping in the wind. One said, "The banner is moving." The other said, "The wind is moving." They went back and forth without coming to an agreement. The Sixth Ancestor said, "It is not the banner or the wind but your minds that are flapping."

Without stirring abroad one can know the whole world; without looking out the window one can see the way of heaven. The further one goes the less one knows. Therefore, the sage knows without having to stir, identifies without having to see, accomplishes without having to act.
          Tao Te Ching

Jesus said, "Woe to the Pharisees, for they are like a dog sleeping in the manger of oxen, for neither does he eat nor does he let the oxen eat."   Gospel of Thomas

A way can be a guide, but not a fixed path; names can be given, but not permanent labels.
          Tao Te Ching

Into deep darkness fall those who follow action. Into deeper darkness fall those who follow knowledge. One is the outcome of knowledge, and another is the outcome of action. Thus have we heard from the ancient sages who explained this truth to us. He who knows both knowledge and action, with action overcomes death and with knowledge reaches immortality. Into deep darkness fall those who follow the imminent. Into deeper darkness fall those who follow the transcendent. One is the outcome of the transcendent, and another is the outcome of the imminent. Thus have we heard from the ancient sages who explained this truth to us. He who knows both the transcendent and the imminent, with the immanent overcomes death and with the transcendent reaches immortality.
          Isa Upanishad

Proliferating systems of ritual and philosophy attempt to throw dust into the eyes of the eternal wisdom that abides in every soul. How can any system transcend the play of relativity?
Ramprasad

All such dualistic concepts such as "ignorant" and "Enlightened", "pure" and "impure", are obstructions. It is because your minds are hindered by them that the Wheel of Law must be turned. Just as apes spend their time throwing things away and picking them up again unceasingly, so it is with you and your learning. All you need to do is give up your learning, your ignorant and Enlightened," pure and impure, great and little, your attachment and activity. Such things are mere conveniences.... So just discard all you have acquired as being no better than a bed spread for you when you were sick. Only when you have abandoned all perceptions, there being nothing objective to perceive; only when phenomena obstruct you no longer; only when you have rid yourself of the whole gamut of dualistic concepts of the ignorant and Enlightened category, will you at last earn the title of Transcendental Buddha.... Every grain of matter, every appearance is one with Eternal and Immutable Reality! Wherever your foot may fall, you are still within the Sanctuary of Enlightenment, though it is nothing perceptible. I assure you that one who comprehends the truth of "nothing to be attained" is already seated in the sanctuary where he will gain his Enlightenment.   *Huang Po*

However much you study, you cannot know without action. A donkey laden with books is neither an intellectual or wise man. Empty of essence, what learning has he- whether upon him is firewood or books.   *Saadi of Shiraz*

I grew up among the sages. All my life I listened to their words. Yet I have found nothing better than silence. Study is not the goal, doing is. Do not mistake talk for action. Pity fills no stomach.

Compassion builds no house. Understanding is not yet justice. Whoever multiples words causes confusion. The truth that can be spoken is not the Ultimate Truth. Ultimate Truth is wordless, the silence within the silence. More than the absence of words, Ultimate Truth is the seamless being-in-place that comes with attending to Reality.   Pirke Avot 1:17

A certain man was believed to have died, and was being prepared for burial, when he revived. He sat up, but was so shocked at the scene surrounding him that he fainted. He was put in a coffin, and the funeral party set off for the cemetery. Just as they arrived at the grave, he regained consciousness, lifted the coffin lid and cried out for help. "It is not possible that he has revived", said the mourners, "because he has been certified dead by competent experts." "But I am alive!" shouted the man. He appealed to a well-known and impartial scientist and jurisprudent who was present. "Just a moment," said the expert. He turned to the mourners, counting them. "Now, we have heard what the alleged deceased has had to say. You fifty witnesses tell me what you regard as the truth." "He is dead," said the witnesses. "Bury him!" said the expert. And so he was buried.   The Chishti Order of Sufism

"Learning is in activity. Learning through words alone is minor activity."- *Maghribi*

There are many trees: not all of them bear fruit. There are many fruits: not all of them may be eaten. Many, too, are the kinds of knowledge: yet not all of them are of value to men.
Jesus, according to the Book of Amu-Darya

The knowledge of ordinary people is imitative; learned through the training of instructors; thought to be real, though it is not.   *Mohammed Ali El-Misri*

Ma-tsu was then residing in the monastery continuously absorbed in meditation. His master, aware of his outstanding ability...asked him: "For what reason are you sitting in meditation?" Ma-tsu replied, "I want to be a Buddha." Thereupon the master picked up a tile and started rubbing it on a stone. Ma-tsu asked, "What are you doing, Master?" "I am polishing this tile to make a mirror," Huai-jang replied. "How can you make a mirror by rubbing a tile?" exclaimed Ma-tsu. "How can you become a Buddha by sitting in meditation?" countered the Master.

Confucius said, "Yu, shall I teach you what knowledge is? When you know a thing, to recognize that you know it, and when you do not know a thing, to recognize that you do not know it. That is knowledge."

In pursuit of knowledge, every day something is added. In the practice of Tao, every day something is dropped. Less and less do you need to force things, until finally you arrive at non-action. When nothing is done, nothing is left undone. True mastery can be gained by letting things go their own way. It can't be gained by interfering.   Tao Te Ching 48

Therefore, the Master takes action by letting things go their own way. He remains as calm at the end as at the beginning. He has nothing, thus has nothing to lose.   Tao Te Ching 64

This is the nature of the unenlightened mind: the sense organs, which are limited in scope and ability, randomly gather information. This partial information is arranged into judgments, which are usually based on someone else's foolish ideas. These false concepts and ideas are then stored in a highly selective memory system. Distortion upon distortion: the mental energy flows constantly through contorted and inappropriate channels, and the more one uses the mind, the more confused one becomes. To eliminate the vexation of the mind, it doesn't help to do something;

this only reinforces the mind's mechanics. Dissolving the mind is instead a matter of not-doing: simply avoid becoming attached to what you see and think. Relinquish the notion that you are separated from the all-knowing mind of the universe. Then you can recover your original pure insight and see through all illusions. Knowing nothing, you will be aware of everything. Remember: because clarity and enlightenment are within your own nature, they are regained without moving an inch.
Hua Hu Ching 44

Don't imagine that you'll discover it by accumulating more knowledge. Knowledge creates doubt, and doubt makes you ravenous for more knowledge. You can't get full eating this way.
Hua Hu Ching 38

Nan-in, a Japanese master during the Meiji era (1868-1912), received a university professor who came to inquire about Zen. Nan-in served tea. He poured his visitor's cup full, and then kept on pouring. The professor watched the overflow until he could no longer restrain himself. "It is overfull. No more will go in!" "Like this cup,"" Nan-in said, "you are full of your own opinions and speculations. How can I show you Zen unless you first empty your cup?""

Some men love knowledge and discernment as the best and most excellent of all things. Behold, then knowledge and discernment come to be loved more than that which is discerned; for the false natural light loves its knowledge and powers, which are itself, more than what is known. And were it possible that this false natural light should understand the simple Truth, as it is in God and in truth, it still would not lose its own property, that is, it could not depart from itself and its own things.   Theologia Germanica

Who are the learned? They who practice what they know.
Hadith of The Prophet Mohammad

Wishing to entice the blind, the Buddha playfully let words escape from his golden mouth; heaven and earth are filled, ever since, with entangling briars.   *Dai-o Kokushi*

The Self is not realizable by study nor even by intelligence and learning. The Self reveals its essence only to him who applies himself to the Self. He who has not given up the ways of vice, who cannot control himself, who is not at peace within, whose mind is distracted, can never realize the Self, though full of all the learning in the world.
                    Katha Upanishad

If someone is well versed in the scriptures but does not have knowledge of the Self, then that one is not wise. Indeed, that one can be likened to a man that tends a cow that yields no milk.
                    Uddhava Gita 6:18

Those who don't feel this Love pulling them like a river, those who don't drink dawn like a cup of spring water or take in a sunset like supper, whose who don't want to change, let them sleep. This Love is beyond the study of theology, that old trickery and hypocrisy. If you want to improve your mind that way, sleep on. I've given up on my brain. I've torn the cloth to shreds and thrown it away. If you're not completely naked, wrap your beautiful robe of words around you, and sleep.   *Rumi*

The Devil keeps hammering his subtle persuasions until the learned man becomes convinced that he should set about teaching people. Then the Devil intimates to the scholar, "You should embellish your thoughts with pretty language and impressive conceits. Also play up your qualifications. Otherwise your words won't have as much effect; they won't reach people's hearts and they will not succeed in attaining the truth."   *al-Ghazzali*

As long as you have not accomplished the great task and are not in communion with the bloodline of the source, you must avoid memorizing sayings and living inside conceptual consciousness. Has it not been said, "Concepts act as robbers, consciousness becomes waves?" Everyone has been swept away and drowned. There is no freedom in that. If you have not mastered the great task, nothing compares to stopping, in the sense of quiet cessation, the purifying and quieting of the body and mind. At all times avoid dwelling obsessively on things, and it will be easy to unveil this.
Ku-shan (d. ca. 940)

An ancient said, "Buddha and Dharma are constructed teaching methods; the terms Zen and Tao are talk for pacifying children." The names have no relation to actualities; actualities have no relation to names; if you cling to names, you will be blocked from the mystery. That is why I have told you that sayings do not correspond to potential, words do not set forth actualities. Those who accept words perish; those who linger over sayings get lost. When you have caught the fish, you forget the trap; when you have gotten the meaning, you forget the words. We use a net to catch fish; the fish are not the net. *Ku-shan*

This thing cannot be learned, cannot be taught, cannot be transmitted: it can be attained by individual realization. Once you've attained realization, you are content, unpreoccupied, thoroughly lucid, clear and at ease. All spiritual capacities are completely natural and need not be sought elsewhere. *Chen-ching*

No true Brahmin attains the goal by mere research; no partisan is he, nor brother secretary; all vulgar theories which others toil to learn he knows, but heeds them not. From earthly trammels freed, aloof from party broils, at peace where peace has fled, the unheeding sage ignores what others toil to learn. From will some cankers purged, with no fresh growths afoot, from lusts and dogmas free, quit too of theories, he goes his stainless way, devoid of self-reproach.
Sutta Nipata

It is as if a man had been wounded by an arrow thickly smeared with poison, and his friends and kinsmen were to get a surgeon to heal him, and he were to say, I will not have this arrow pulled out until I know by what man I was wounded, whether he is of the warrior caste, or a Brahmin, or of the agricultural, or the lowest caste. Or if he were to say, I will not have this arrow pulled out until I know of what name of family the man is -or whether he is tall, or short or of middle height ... Before knowing all this, the man would die. Similarly, it is not on the view that the world is eternal, that it is finite, that body and soul are distinct, or that the Buddha exists after death that a religious life depends. Whether these views or their opposite are held, there is still rebirth, there is old age, there is death, and grief, lamentation, suffering, sorrow, and despair.... I have not spoken to these views because they do not conduce to an absence of passion, to tranquility, and Nirvana. And what have I explained? Suffering have I explained, the cause of suffering, the destruction of suffering, and the path that leads to the destruction of suffering have I explained. For this is useful.   *Buddha*

Reasoning is related to attachment. When attachment arises, wisdom is shut out.   *Buddha*

Regarding this Dhyana Sect of ours, since the doctrine was first transmitted, it has never been taught that people should seek empirical knowledge or look for explanations of things. We merely talk about studying the Way using the phrase simply as a term to arouse people's interest. In fact, the Way cannot be studied. If concepts based on factual study are retained, they only result in the Way being misunderstood."   *Hsi Yun*

If now you will and at all times, whether walking, standing, sitting, or lying, only concentrate on eliminating analytic thinking, at long last you will inevitably discover the truth.   *Hsi Yun*

The Tao gives rise to all forms, yet it has no form of its own. If you attempt to fix a picture of it in your mind, you will lose it. This is like pinning a butterfly: the husk is captured, but the flying is lost. Why not be content with simply experiencing it?
        Hua Hu Ching 6

I confess that there is nothing to teach: no religion, no science, no body of information which will lead your mind back to the Tao. Today I speak in this fashion, tomorrow in another, but always the Integral Way is beyond words and beyond mind. Simply be aware of the oneness of things. Hua Hu Ching 8

The tiny particles which form the vast universe are not tiny at all. Neither is the vast universe vast. These are notions of the mind, which is like a knife, always chipping away at the Tao, trying to render it graspable and manageable. But that which is beyond form is ungraspable, and that which is beyond containing is unmanageable. There is, however, this consolation: she who lets go of the knife finds the Tao at her fingertips. Hua Hu Ching 13

Similarly, there are two kinds of wisdom. The first is worldly wisdom, which is a conceptual understanding of your experiences. Because it follows after the events themselves, it necessarily inhibits your direct understanding of truth. The second kind, integral wisdom, involves a direct participation in every moment: the observer and the observed are dissolved in the light of pure awareness, and no mental concepts or attitudes are present to dim that light. Hua Hu Ching 26

Why scurry about looking for the truth? It vibrates in everything and every not-thing, right off the tip of your nose. Can you be still and see it in the mountain? The pine tree? Yourself? Don't imagine you'll discover it by accumulating more knowledge. Knowledge creates doubt, and doubt makes you ravenous for more knowledge. You can't get full eating this way. The wise person dines on something more subtle: he eats the understanding that the named was born from the unnamed, that all being flows from non-being, that the describable world emanates from an indescribable source. He finds this subtle truth inside his own self, and becomes completely content. So who can be still and watch the chess game of the world? The foolish are always making impulsive moves, but the wise know that victory and defeat are decided by something more subtle. They see that something perfect exists before any move is made. This subtle perfection deteriorates when artificial actions are taken, so be content not to disturb the peace. Remain quiet. Discover the harmony in your own being. Embrace it. If you can do this, you will gain everything, and the world will become healthy again. If you can't, you will be lost in the shadows forever.   Hua Hu Ching 38

With all this talking, what has been said? The subtle truth can be pointed at with words, but it can't be contained by them. Take time to listen to what is said without words, to obey the law too subtle to be written, to worship the Unnamable and to embrace the unformed. Love your life. Trust the Tao. Make love to the invisible subtle origin of the universe, and you will give yourself everything you need.   Hua Hu Ching 81

The Tao that can be told is not the eternal Tao. The name that can be named is not the eternal Name. The Unnamable is the eternally real. Naming is the origin of all particular things. Free from desire, you realize the mystery. Caught in desire you see only the manifestations. (...) Therefore the master acts without doing anything and teaches without saying anything. Things arise and she lets them go. She has but doesn't possess, acts but doesn't expect. When her work is done, she forgets it. That is why it lasts forever.
Tao te Ching 1-2

When you have names and forms, know that they are provisional. When you have institutions, know where their functions should end. Knowing when to stop, you can avoid any danger.
Tao te Ching 32

In the pursuit of knowledge, every day something is added. In the practice of Tao, every day something is dropped. Less and less do you need to force things, until finally you arrive at non-action. When nothing is done, nothing is left undone. True mastery can be gained by letting things go their own way. It can't be gained by interfering.   Tao te Ching 48

My teachings are easy to understand and easy to put into practice. Yet your intellect will never grasp them and if you try to, you'll fail. My teachings are older than the world. How can you grasp their meaning? If you want to know me, look inside your heart.   Tao te Ching 70

Not-knowing is true knowledge. Presuming to know is a disease. First realize that you are sick; then you can move toward health. The Master is her own physician. She has healed herself of all knowing. Thus she is truly whole.   Tao te Ching 71

Fish can live in water quite contentedly, but if people try it, they die, for different beings need different contexts which are right and proper for them. This is why the ancient sages never expected just one response from the rest of the creatures nor tried to make them conform. Titles should not be over-stretched in trying to capture reality and ideas should be only applied when appropriate, for this is not only sensible, it will bring good fortune.   *Chuang Tzu*

Your search among books, word upon word, may lead you to the depths of knowledge, but it is not the way to receive the reflection of your true self. When you have thrown off your ideas as to mind and body, the original truth will fully appear.   *Dogen*

This gentle Lord Varuna gives wisdom to the simple: the wiser God leads on the wise to riches.   Rig Veda

The Spirit comes to the thought of those who know him beyond thought, not to those who imagine he can be attained by thought. He is unknown to the learned and known to the simple.
     Kena Upanishad

As a flaming fire consumes logs into ashes, so wisdom consumes karma. There is no purifier like spiritual wisdom in this world: restraining his senses, the man who lives in self harmony sees the truth of this as he perfects his discipline in yoga. The devoted man, commander of his self, gains wisdom and grows in faith; with this wisdom he finds the final peace resting in his true Self within.   Bhagavad Gita 4:37-39

Behold, the fear of the Lord, that is wisdom, and to depart from evil is understanding.   Job 28:28

The fear of the Lord is the beginning of knowledge, but fools despise wisdom and instruction.   Proverbs 1:7

Be astonished, O heavens, at this, and be horribly afraid; be very desolate, says the Lord. For My people have committed two evils: they have forsaken Me, the fountain of living waters, and hewn themselves cisterns- broken cisterns that can hold no water.
     Jeremiah

Tradition

You hypocrites! Isaiah prophesied rightly about you when he said: "This people honor me with their lips, but their hearts are far from me; in vain do they worship me, teaching human precepts as doctrines. "And he called to him the multitude, and said unto them, Hear, and understand: Not that which enters into the mouth defiles the man; but that which proceeds out of the mouth, this defiles the man. (...) Do you not perceive, that whatsoever goes into the mouth passes into the belly, and is cast out into the draught? But the things which proceed out of the mouth come forth out of the heart; and they defile the man. For out of the heart comes forth evil thoughts, murders, adulteries, fornications, thefts, false witness, railings: these are the things which defiles the man; but to eat with unwashed hands defiles not the man. (...) And Jesus said unto them, "Take heed and beware of the leaven of the Pharisees and Sadducees".
Matthew 15:7-9, 10-11, 17-20, 16:6

The Oath- A man who was troubled in mind once swore that if his problems were solved he would sell his house and give all the money gained from it to the poor. The time came when he realized that he must redeem his oath. But he did not want to give away so much money. So he thought of a way out. He put the house on sale at one silver piece. Included with the house, however, was a cat. The price asked for this animal was ten thousand pieces of silver. Another man bought the house and the cat. The first man gave the single piece of silver to the poor, and pocketed the ten thousand for himself. Many people's minds work like this. They resolve to follow a teaching; but they interpret their relationship with it to their own advantage.   from the Chishti Order of Sufism

You abandon the commandment of God and hold to human tradition.   Mark 7:8

For I desire mercy and not sacrifice; and the knowledge of God more than burnt offerings.   Hosea 6:6

The Sabbath was made for man, and not man for the Sabbath.
Mark 2:27

While he was speaking, a Pharisee invited him to dine with him; so he went in and took his place at the table. The Pharisee was amazed to see that he did not first wash before dinner. Then the Lord said to him: "Now you Pharisees clean the outside of the cup and of the dish, but inside you are full of greed and wickedness. You fools! Did not the one who made the outside make the inside also? So give in alms those things that are within; and see, everything will be clean for you. But woe to you Pharisees! For you tithe mint and rue and herbs of all kinds, but neglect justice and the love of God; it is these you ought to have practiced, without neglecting the others.""   Luke 11: 37-42

Circumcision is nothing and uncircumcision is nothing; but obeying the commandments of God is everything.   Let each of you remain in the condition in which you were called.
1st Corinthians 7:19-20.

Two monks were walking down a road and came upon a beautiful girl unable to cross a ford in the road without ruining her silk kimono and sash. At once one of the monks lifted her and carried her over the mud. A little while later the other monk said, "We monks don't go near females. You have acted out of line with your brothers. Why did you do this?" The other monk replied, "I set the girl down a long time ago, but you are still carrying her."

His disciples said to him, "Is circumcision beneficial or not?" Jesus said to them, "If it were beneficial, their father would beget them already circumcised from their mother. Rather, the true circumcision in spirit has become completely profitable."   Gospel of Thomas 53

What need have I of all your sacrifices? says the Lord. I am sated with burnt offerings of rams, and suet of fatlings, and blood of bulls; your new moons and fixed seasons fill Me with loathing; they are a burden to Me, I cannot endure them. And when you lift up your hands, I will turn My eyes away from you; though you pray at length, I will not listen. Your hands are stained with crime- wash yourselves clean; put your evil doings away from My sight. Cease to do evil; learn to do good. Devote yourselves to justice; aid the wronged. Uphold the rights of the orphan; defend the cause of the widow.   Isaiah

Spare me the sound of your songs, I cannot endure the music of your lutes. But let justice roll on like a river, and righteousness like an ever-flowing stream.   Amos

When a man follows the way of the world, or the way of the flesh, or the way of tradition, knowledge cannot arise in him.   *Shankara*

When a man lacks discrimination, his will wanders in all directions, after innumerable aims. Those who lack discrimination may quote the letter of the scripture; but they are really denying its inner truth. They are full of worldly desires and hungry for the rewards of heaven. They use beautiful figures of speech; they teach elaborate rituals, which are supposed to obtain pleasure and power for those who practice them. But actually, they understand nothing except the law of Karma that chains men to rebirth. Those whose discrimination is stolen away by such talk grow deeply attached to pleasure and power. And so they are unable to develop that one-pointed concentration of will, which leads a man to absorption in God.   Bhagavad Gita

Now, if you continue to believe that the multiplicity of forms, the diversity of activities and those engaged in them for the sake of momentary pleasure, within a defined time and space, are the sole reality; or that performing the duties which the scriptures require will lead to the perpetuation of the individual soul, or bring some earthly benefits in this world of objects, then, my dear friend, you will remain bound to this cycle of birth, disease, death and rebirth.   Uddhava Gita *5:14-16*

One can be cleansed of impurity by bathing: by acts of charity; through austerities; by fulfilling your duties; by acts of ritual purification; or by remembrance of me. The above six will lead to purity and their opposites to impurity. The purity of a mantra depends on the understanding of one has of it. The purity of actions depends on their being offered to the supreme Self. According to the Vedas that which appears to be pure can in reality be impure, while that which appears impure can in reality be pure. Thus the words of the Vedas cut off at the root categorical judgment of what is pure and impure.   Uddhava Gita *16:14-16*

Ceremonies in themselves are not sin; but whoever supposes that he can attain to life either by baptism or by partaking of bread is still in superstition. *Hans Denk*

Austerities, pilgrimages to holy places, repetition of prayers and mantras, and generous acts of charity, amount to nothing compared to that knowledge gained from the experience of Self-realization.   Uddhava Gita *14:4*

Those injunctions of the Vedas that promise a reward for good actions are meant to entice people towards good- like promising sweets to a child being asked to swallow bitter medicine. This is because human beings are inherently attached to the idea of reward. Think about it, Uddhava: how else could the Vedas persuade people wandering aimlessly towards certain death to do what ought to be done and move towards enlightenment? Only ignorant people who do not understand the true teaching of the Vedas insist on these injunctions and speak of reward and punishment for actions done. Those who know the Vedas do not speak of these things. Those who are caught in the darkness of passion, greed and miserliness are blinded by the light of the fire of the Vedas; heedlessly they indulge in ritualistic acts- only to choke on the smoke of their own ignorance. A strict adherence to ritual will be their only theme: they will not even recognize me dwelling in their own heart and in the heart of this entire creation. At the end of their lives, with their vision clouded by the fog of ignorance, they will not see that which is close at hand. These people committed as

they are to the world of objects and its rewards, and to violence by means of ritual, cannot understand the words of the Vedas that I am now imparting. In sacrificial rituals these cruel people will slaughter innocent animals in order to make offerings to ancestors, gods and spirits all for the gratification of their own desires. Such violence has never been an instruction of the Vedas. They fantasize in their own minds about a heavenly world that comes after this one, and then imagine that like merchants in a market they can trade rituals for a place in such a heaven.
    Uddhava Gita *16:23-31*

    When it is said to them: Follow what Allah has revealed: they say: "Nay! We shall follow the ways of our fathers. "What! Even though their fathers were void of wisdom and guidance.
    Quran 2:170

    It is not righteousness that you turn your faces towards the East or West; but it is righteousness- to believe in Allah and the Last Day, and the Angels, and the Book, and the Messengers; to spend of your substance, out of love for Him, for your kin, for orphans, for the needy, for the wayfarer, for those who ask, and for the ransom of slaves; to be steadfast in prayer, and practice regular charity; to fulfill the contracts which you have made; and to be firm and patient, in pain (or suffering) and adversity and throughout all periods of panic. Such are the people of truth, those who fear Allah.
    Quran 2:177

    They ask you concerning the New Moons. Say: They are but signs to mark fixed periods of time in (the affairs of) men, and for Pilgrimage. It is no virtue if you enter your houses from the back: it is virtue if you fear Allah. Enter houses through the proper doors: and fear Allah: that you may prosper.
    Quran 2:189

The Master said, "Surely when one says: The rites, the rites. It is not enough merely to mean presents of jade and silk. Surely when one says: Music, music, it is not enough merely to mean bells and drums."   Analects 17:11

Thoughtless ones, even if they can recite many sacred verses but do not follow them, have no claim to a religious life, but are like cow herders counting the cows of others.   Dhammapada

When the Tao is lost, there is goodness. When goodness is lost, there is morality. When morality is lost, there is ritual. Ritual is the husk of true faith, the beginning of chaos. Therefore, the Master concerns himself with the depths and not the surface, with the fruit and not the flower. He has no will of his own. He dwells in reality, and lets all illusions go.   Tao te Ching 38

People do not become Brahmans by virtue of their matted locks, their lineage, or their birth. Those in whom there is truth and righteousness- they are blessed, they are Brahmans. (...) The ones I call indeed Brahmans do not cling to sensual pleasures, like water on a lotus leaf, like a mustard seed on the point of a needle. (...) The ones I call indeed brahmans are bright like the moon, pure, serene, and undisturbed- in whom all unseemly conduct is extinct. The ones I call indeed brahmans have traversed this miry road, the impossible world, difficult to travel, with all its vanities- who have gone across and reached the other shore, who are thoughtful, steadfast, free from doubts, free from attachments, and content.
                              Dhammapada

Even a man who has a longing for Yoga is superior to the performer of mechanical rituals. (...) Better is knowledge than mechanical, habitual practice. Better than knowledge is meditation. But better still is surrender in love of attachment to the fruits of action, because there follows immediate peace.
                        Bhagavad Gita 6:44, 12:12

Losing wholeness and naturalness (Tao), man comes to particularize his view. Losing the particular applications of virtue, he comes to a theoretical concept of goodness. Losing the ideal of goodness man's highest value becomes righteousness. When he loses even that he sinks to the level of ceremony. Now ceremony is evidence that conscientiousness and sincerity (hsia) have worn thin and that moral breakdown is imminent.   Tao te Ching 38

Has the Lord as great delight in burnt offerings and sacrifices, as in obeying the voice of the Lord? Behold! To obey is better than sacrifice, and to heed than the fat of rams.
1 Samuel 15:22

Sacrifice and offering You did not desire; my ears You have opened. Burnt offering and sin offering you did not require. Then I said, Behold, I come; in the scroll of the book it is written of me. I delight to do Your will, O my God, and Your law is written within my heart. (...) For you do not desire sacrifice, or else I would give it; you do not delight in burnt offerings. The sacrifices of God are a broken spirit, a broken and contrite heart- these, O God, You will not despise.
Psalms 40:6-8, 51:16-17

Cry aloud, spare not; lift up your voice like a trumpet; tell My people their transgression, and the house of Jacob their sins. Yet they seek Me daily, and delight to know My ways, as a nation that did righteousness, and did not forsake the ordinance of their God. They ask of Me the ordinances of justice; they take delight in approaching God. "Why have we fasted," they say, "and You have not seen? Why have we afflicted our souls, and You take no notice?" In fact, in the day of your fast you find pleasure, and exploit all your laborers. Indeed, you fast for strife and debate, and to strike with the fist of wickedness. You will not fast as you do this day, to make your voice heard on high. Is it a fast that I have

chosen, a day for a man to afflict his soul? Is it to bow down his head like a bulrush, and to spread out sackcloth and ashes? Would you call this a fast, and an acceptable day to the Lord? Is this not the fast that I have chosen: to loose the bonds of wickedness, to undo the heavy burdens, to let the oppressed go free, and that you break every yoke? Is it not to share your bread with the hungry, and that you bring to your house the poor who are cast out; when you see the naked, that you cover him, and not hide yourself from your own flesh? Then your light shall break forth like the morning, your healing shall spring forth speedily, and your righteousness shall go before you; the glory of the Lord shall be your rear guard. Then you shall call, and the Lord will answer; you shall cry, and He will say, "Here I am." If you take away the yoke from your midst, the pointing of the finger, and speaking wickedness, if you extend your soul to the hungry and satisfy the afflicted soul, then your light shall dawn in the darkness, and your darkness shall be as the noonday. The Lord will guide you continually, and satisfy your soul in drought, and strengthen your bones; you shall be like a watered garden, and like a spring of water, whose waters do not fail. Those from among you shall build the old waste places; you shall raise up the foundations of many generations; and you shall be called the Repairer of the Breach, The Restorer of Streets to Dwell In.
                              Isaiah 58

    Thus says the Lord of hosts, the God of Israel: Add your burnt offerings to your sacrifices and eat meat. For I did not speak to your fathers, or command them in the day that I brought them out of the land of Egypt, concerning burnt offerings or sacrifices. But this is what I commanded them, saying, "Obey My voice, and I will be your God, and you shall be My people. And walk in all the ways that I have commanded you, that it may be well with you."'
                              Jeremiah 7:21-23

I hate, I despise your feast days, and I do not savor your sacred assemblies. Though you offer Me burnt offerings and your grain offerings, I will not accept them, nor will I regard your fattened peace offerings. Take away from Me the noise of your songs, for I will not hear the melody of your stringed instruments. But let justice run down like water, and righteousness like a mighty stream.   Amos 5:21-24

With what shall I come before the Lord, and bow myself before the High God? Shall I come before Him with burnt offerings? With calves a year old? Will the Lord be pleased with thousands of rams, ten thousand rivers of oil? Shall I give my firstborn for my transgression, the fruit of my body for the sin of my soul? He has shown you, O man, what is good; and what does the Lord require of you but to do justly, to love mercy, and to walk humbly with your God? The Lord's voice cries to the city- wisdom shall see Your name.   Micah 6:6-9

Brahmin: "Why have men always performed religious sacrifices and rites if what you say is true?" Buddha: "If the person who receives the offering is at the moment of the offering perfect in understanding, fulfilled and accomplished, then, I would say the offering will be successful."   Puralasa Sutta, Sutta Nipata

And it came to pass, that he was going on the Sabbath day through the grain fields; and his disciples began, as they went, to pluck the ears. And the Pharisees said unto him, "Behold, why do they on the Sabbath day that which is not lawful?" And he said unto them, "Did you never read what David did, when he had need, and was hungry, he, and they that were with him? How he entered into the house of God when Abiathar was high priest, and ate the showbread, which it is not lawful to eat save for the priests, and gave also to them that were with him?" And he said unto them, "The Sabbath was made for man, and not man for the Sabbath: so that the Son of man is lord even of the Sabbath." And he entered

again into the synagogue; and there was a man there who had his hand withered. And they watched him, whether he would heal him on the Sabbath day; that they might accuse him. And he said unto the man that had his hand withered, "Stand forth." And he said unto them, "Is it lawful on the Sabbath day to do good, or to do harm? to save a life, or to kill?" But they were silent. And when he had looked round about on them with anger, being grieved at the hardening of their heart, he said unto the man, "Stretch forth your hand." And he stretched it forth; and his hand was restored.
Mark 2:23- 3:5

And there come his mother and his brethren; and, standing without, they sent unto him, calling him. And a multitude was sitting about him; and they say unto him, "Behold, your mother and your brethren without seek for you." And he answered them, and said, "Who is my mother and my brethren?" And looking round on them that sat round about him, he said, "Behold, my mother and my brethren! For whosoever shall do the will of God, the same is my brother, and sister, and mother."   Mark 3:31-35

Everything is indeed clean, but it is wrong for you to make others fall by what you eat; it is good not to eat meat or drink wine or do anything that makes your brother or sister stumble.
Romans 14:20-21

When they ask you about drinking and gambling, say:
there is some good in them but the bad far outweighs the good
Quran

Jesus was teaching in one of the synagogues on the Sabbath day. And behold, a woman that had a spirit of infirmity eighteen years; and she was bowed together, and could in no way lift herself up. And when Jesus saw her, he called her, and said to her, "Woman, you art loosed from your infirmity." And he laid his hands upon her: and immediately she was made straight, and glorified God. And the ruler of the synagogue, being moved with

indignation because Jesus had healed on the Sabbath, answered and said to the multitude, "There are six days in which men ought to work: in them therefore come and be healed, and not on the day of the Sabbath." But the Lord answered him, and said, "You hypocrites, do not each one of you on the Sabbath loose his ox or his ass from the stall, and lead him away to watering? And ought not this woman, being a daughter of Abraham, whom Satan had bound, lo, eighteen years, to have been loosed from this bond on the day of the Sabbath?" And as he said these things, all his adversaries were put to shame: and all the multitude rejoiced for all the glorious things that were done by him.
Luke 13:10-17

Since some have become so accustomed to idols until now, they still think of the food they eat as food offered to an idol; and their conscience, being weak, is defiled. Food will not bring us close to God. We are no worse off if we do not eat, and no better off if we do. But take care that this liberty of yours does not somehow become a stumbling block to the weak. For if others see you, who possess knowledge, eating in the temple of an idol, might they not, since their conscience is weak, be encouraged to the point of eating food sacrificed to idols? So by your knowledge whose weak believers for whom Christ died are destroyed. But when you thus sin against members of your family, and wound their conscience when it is weak, you sin against Christ. Therefore, if food is the cause of their falling, I will never eat meat, so that I may cause one of them to fall. 1st Corinthians 8:7-13

Regulation and Law

Wherefore, my brethren, you also were made dead to the law through the body of Christ; that you should be joined to another, [even] to him who was raised from the dead, that we might bring forth fruit unto God. While we were living in the flesh, our sinful passions, aroused by the law, were at work in our members to bear fruit for death. But now we are discharged from the law, dead to that which held us captive, so that we are slaves not under the old written code but in the new life of the Spirit. What then should we say? That the law is sin? By no means! Yet if it had not been for the law, I would not have known sin. I would not have known what it is to covet if the law had not said "You shall not covet." But sin, seizing an opportunity in the commandment, produced in me all kinds of covetousness. Apart from the law, sin lies dead. I was once alive apart from the law, but when the commandment came, sin revived and I died, and the very commandment that promised life proved death to me. For sin, seizing an opportunity in the commandment, deceived me and through it killed me. So the law is holy, and the commandment is holy and just and good. (...) For we know that the law is spiritual; but I am of the flesh, sold into slavery under sin. I do not understand my own actions. For I do not do what I want, But I do the very thing that I hate. But if what I would not, that I do, I consent unto the law that it is good. So now it is no more I that do it, but sin which dwells in me. For I know that in me, that is, in my flesh, dwells no good thing: for to will is present with me, but to do that which is good is not. For the good which I would I do not: but the evil which I would not, that I practice. But if what I would not, that I do, it is no more I that do it, but sin which dwells in me. I find then the law, that, to me who would do good, evil is present. For I delight in the law of God after the inward man: but I see a different law in my members, warring against the law of my mind, and bringing me into captivity under the law of sin which is in my members. Wretched man that I am! Who shall deliver me out of the body of this death? I thank God through Jesus Christ our Lord. So then I of myself with the mind, indeed, serve the law of God; but with the flesh the law of sin. Or are you ignorant, brethren (for I speak to men who know the law), that the law hath dominion over a man for so long time as he lives? For the woman that has a husband is bound by law to the husband while he lives; but if the husband dies, she is discharged from the law of the husband. There is therefore now no condemnation to them that are in Christ Jesus. For the law of the Spirit of life in Christ Jesus made me free from the law of sin and of death. For what the law could not do, in that it was weak through the flesh, God, sending his own Son in the likeness of sinful flesh and for sin, condemned sin in the flesh: that the ordinance of the law might be fulfilled in us, who walk not after the flesh, but after the Spirit. For they that are after the flesh mind the things of the flesh; but they that are after the Spirit the things of the Spirit. For the mind of the flesh is death; but the mind of the Spirit is life and peace: because the mind of the flesh is enmity against God; for it is not subject to the law of God, neither indeed can it be: and they that are in the flesh cannot please God. But you are not in the flesh but in the Spirit, if so be that the Spirit of God dwells in you. But if any man has not the Spirit of Christ, he is none of His. And if Christ is in you, the body is dead because of sin; but the spirit is life because of righteousness. But if the Spirit of him that raised up Jesus from the dead dwells in you, He that raised up Christ Jesus from the dead shall give life also to your mortal bodies through his Spirit that dwells in you.   So then, brethren, we are debtors, not to the flesh, to live after the flesh: for if you live after the flesh, you must die; but if by the Spirit you put to death the deeds of the body, you shall live. For as many as are led by the Spirit of God, these are sons of God. For you received not the spirit of bondage again unto fear; but the spirit of adoption, whereby we cry, Abba, Father. The Spirit himself bears witness with our spirit, that we are children of God: and if children, then heirs; heirs of God, and joint-heirs with Christ; if so be that we suffer with Him, that we may be also glorified with Him.

Romans 7:4- 8:17

The more taboos there are in the empire the poorer the people; the more sharpened tools the people have the more belligerent the state; the more skills the people have the further novelties multiply; the better known the laws and edicts the more thieves and robbers there are.   Tao Te Ching

If men had been forbidden to make porridge of camel's dung, they would have done it, saying that they would not have been forbidden to do it unless there had been some good in it.
            Hadith of the Prophet Muhammad

When one first goes to the Obaku temple in Kyoto he sees carved over the gate the words "The First Principle." The letters are unusually large, and those who appreciate calligraphy always admire them as being a masterpiece. They were drawn by Kosen two hundred years ago. When the master drew them he did so on paper, from which the workmen made the larger carving in wood. As Kosen sketched the letters a bold pupil was with him who had made several gallons of ink for the calligraphy and who never failed to criticize his master's work. "That is not good," he told Kosen after the first effort." "How is that one?" "Poor. Worse than before," pronounced the pupil. Kosen patiently wrote one sheet after another until eighty-four First Principles had accumulated, still without the approval of the pupil. Then, when the young man stepped outside for a few moments, Kosen thought: Now is my chance to escape his keen eye, and he wrote hurriedly, with a mind free of distraction: "The First Principle." "A masterpiece," pronounced the pupil.

Like a eunuch lusting for intimacy with a maiden is he who does right under compulsion.   Sirach *20:3*

When justice and benevolence are in the air, few people are really concerned with the good of others, but the majority are aware that this is a good thing, ripe for exploitation. They take advantage of the situation. For them, benevolence and justice are traps to catch birds. Thus benevolence and justice rapidly come to be associated with fraud and hypocrisy. Then everybody doubts. And this is when trouble really begins.   *Chuang Tzu*

He whose law is within himself walks in hiddenness. His acts are not influenced by approval or disapproval. He whose law is outside himself directs his will to what is beyond his control and seeks to extend his power over objects. He who walks in hiddenness has light to guide him in all his acts. He who seeks to extend his control is nothing but an operator. While he thinks he is surpassing others, others see him merely straining, stretching to stand on tiptoe. When he tries to extend his power over objects, those objects gain control of him. He who is controlled by objects loses possession of his inner self: if he no longer values himself, how can he value others. He is abandoned. He has nothing left! There is no deadlier weapon than the will! The sharpest sword is not equal to it! There is no robber so dangerous as Nature (Yang and Yin). Yet it is not nature that does the damage: it is man's own will.
Chuang Tzu

Horses have hooves so that their feet can grip on frost and snow, and hair so that they can withstand the wind and cold. They eat grass and drink water, they buck and gallop, for this is the innate nature of horses. Even if they had great towers and magnificent halls, they would not be interested in them. However, when Po Lo came on the scene, he said, "I know how to train horses."' He branded them, cut their hair and their hooves, put halters on their heads, bridled them, hobbled them and shut them up in stables. Out of ten horses at least two or three die. Then he makes them hungry and thirsty, gallops them, races them, parades them, runs them together. He keeps before them the fear of the bit and ropes, behind them the fear of the whip and crop. Now more than half the horses are dead. (...) In the time of perfect Virtue, people lived side by side with the birds and the beasts, sharing the world in common with all life. No one knew of distinctions such as nobles and the peasantry! Totally without wisdom but with virtue which does not disappear; totally without desire they are known as truly simple. If people are truly simple, they can follow their true nature. Then the sages come, going on about benevolence, straining for self-righteousness, and suddenly everyone begins to have doubts. They start to fuss over the music, cutting and trimming the rituals, and thus the whole world is disturbed. If the pure essence had not been so cut about, how could they have otherwise ended up with sacrificial bowls? If the raw jade was not broken apart, how could the symbols of power be made? If the Tao and Te- Way and Virtue- had not been ignored, how could benevolence and righteousness have been preferred? If innate nature had not been left behind, how could rituals and music have been invented? If the five colors had not been confused, how could patterns and designs have occurred? If the five notes had not been confused, how could they have been supplanted by the six tones? The abuse of the true elements to make artifacts was the crime of the craftsman. The abuse of the Tao and Te- Way and Virtue- to make benevolence and righteousness, this was the error of the sage. Horses, when they live wild, eat grass and drink water; when they are content, they entwine their necks and rub each other. When angry, they turn their backs on each other and kick out. This is what horses know. But if harnessed together and lined up under constraints, they know to look sideways and to arch their necks, to careen around and try to spit out the bit and rid themselves of the reins. The knowledge thus gained by the horse, and its wicked behavior, is in fact the fault of Po Lo.   *Chuang Tzu*

    If you want to be a great leader, you must learn to follow the Tao. Stop trying to control. Let go of fixed plans and concepts, and the world will govern itself. The more prohibitions you have, the less virtuous people will be. The more weapons you have, the less secure people will be. The more subsidies you have, the less self-reliant people will be. Therefore, the Master says: I let go of the law, and people became honest. I let go of economics, and people became prosperous. I let go of religion, and people become serene. I let go of all desire for the common good, and the good becomes common as grass. If a country is governed with tolerance, the people are comfortable and honest. If a country is governed with repression, the people are depressed and crafty. When the will to power is in charge, the higher the ideals, the lower the results. Try to make people happy and you lay the groundwork for misery. Try to make people moral and you lay the groundwork for vice. Thus the Master is content to serve as an example and not to impose her will. She is pointed, but doesn't pierce. Straightforward but supple. Radiant but easy on the eyes. For governing a country well, there is nothing better than moderation. The mark of a moderate man is freedom from his own ideas. Tolerant like the sky, all-pervading like sunlight, firm like a mountain, supple like a tree in the wind, he has no destination in view and makes use of anything life happens to bring his way. Nothing is impossible for him. Because he has let go, he can care for the people's welfare as a mother cares for her child. Governing a large country is like frying a small fish. You spoil it with too much poking. Center your country in the Tao and evil will have no power. Not that is isn't there, but you'll be able to step out of its way. Give evil nothing to oppose and it will disappear by itself.   Tao te Ching

When they lose their sense of awe, people turn to religion. When they no longer trust themselves, then they begin to depend on authority.   Tao te Ching

When taxes are too high, people go hungry. When the government is too intrusive, people lose their spirit. Act for the people's benefit. Trust them; leave them alone.   Tao te Ching

Men are born soft and supple; dead, they are stiff and hard. Plants are born tender and pliant; dead, they are brittle and dry. Thus whoever is stiff and inflexible is a disciple of death. Whoever is soft and yielding is a disciple of life. The hard and stiff will be broken. The soft and supple will prevail. (...) Nothing in the world is as soft and yielding as water. Yet for dissolving the hard and inflexible, nothing can surpass it. The soft overcomes the hard; the gentle

overcomes the rigid. Everyone knows this is true, but few can put it into practice. Therefore, the Master remains serene in the midst of sorrow. Evil cannot enter his heart. Because he has given up helping, he is people's greatest help. True sayings seem paradoxical.
Tao te Ching

Virtue continued to deteriorate and then Yao and Shen came to govern all below Heaven with the result that, ruling by decrees and grand plans, they polluted the purity of nature and destroyed simplicity. The Tao was abandoned and "good" substituted. Virtue was put at risk for the sake of opportunity. Then innate nature was abandoned and minds allowed to determine their own way. Heart linked with heart through knowledge, but were unable to give the world peace. Pomp and ceremony were added to this knowledge. This displaced simplicity and the heart was swamped, resulting in the people being confused and disobedient, with no way back to true innate nature nor to their origin.   *Chuang Tzu*

You shall therefore keep My statutes and My judgments, which if a man does, he shall live by them: I am the Lord.
Leviticus 18:5

Whoever has no rule over his own spirit is like a city broken down, without walls.   Proverbs 25:28

I know, and am persuaded in the Lord Jesus, that nothing is unclean of itself: save that to him who accounts anything to be unclean, to him it is unclean. For if because of meat your brother is grieved, you no longer walk in love. Destroy not with meat him for whom Christ died. Let not then your good be evil spoken of: for the kingdom of God is not eating and drinking, but righteousness and peace and joy in the Holy Spirit. For he that herein serves Christ is well-pleasing to God, and approved of men. So then let us follow after things which make for peace, and things whereby we may

edify one another. Overthrow not for meat's sake the work of God.
All things indeed are clean; howbeit it is evil for that man who eats
with offence. It is good not to eat flesh, nor to drink wine, nor [to
do anything] whereby your brother stumbles. The faith which you
have, have to yourself before God. Happy is he that judges not
himself in that which he approves. But he that doubts is condemned
if he eats, because [he eats] not of faith; and whatsoever is not of
faith is sin. Now we that are strong ought to bear the infirmities of
the weak, and not to please ourselves. Let each one of us please his
neighbor for that which is good, unto edifying.
Romans 14:14-15:2

Tell me, you that desire to be under the law, do you not hear
the law? For it is written, that Abraham had two sons, one by the
handmaid, and one by the freewoman. Howbeit the [son] by the
handmaid is born after the flesh; but the [son] by the freewoman
[is born] through promise. Which things contain an allegory: for
these [women] are two covenants; one from mount Sinai, bearing
children unto bondage, which is Hagar. Now this Hagar is mount
Sinai in Arabia and answered to the Jerusalem that now is: for she
is in bondage with her children. But the Jerusalem that is above is
free, which is our mother. For it is written, Rejoice, you barren;
Break forth and cry, you that travails not: For more are the children
of the desolate than of her that has the husband. Now we,
brethren, as Isaac was, are children of promise. But as then he that
was born after the flesh persecuted him [that was born] after the
Spirit, so also it is now. Howbeit what says the scripture? Cast out
the handmaid and her son: for the son of the handmaid shall not
inherit with the son of the freewoman. Wherefore, brethren, we are
not children of a handmaid, but of the freewoman. For freedom did
Christ set us free: stand fast therefore, and be not entangled again
in a yoke of bondage. Behold, I Paul say unto you, that, if you
receive circumcision, Christ will profit you nothing. Yea, I testify
again to every man that receives circumcision, that he is a debtor
to do the whole law. You are severed from Christ; you would be
justified by the law; you are fallen away from grace. For we
through the Spirit by faith wait for the hope of righteousness. For

in Christ Jesus neither circumcision avails anything, nor uncircumcision; but faith working through love. You were running well; who hindered you that you should not obey the truth? This persuasion [came] not of him that calls you. A little leaven leavens the whole lump. I have confidence toward you in the Lord, that you will be none otherwise minded: but he that troubles you shall bear his judgment, whosoever he be. But I, brethren, if I still preach circumcision, why am I still persecuted? Then has the stumbling-block of the cross been done away. I would that they that unsettle you would even go beyond circumcision. For you, brothers, were called for freedom; only [use] not your freedom for an occasion to the flesh, but through love be servants one to another. For the whole law is fulfilled in one word, [even] in this: You shall love your neighbor as yourself. But if you bite and devour one another, take heed that you be not consumed one of another. But I say, walk by the Spirit, and you shall not fulfill the lust of the flesh. For the flesh lusts against the Spirit, and the Spirit against the flesh; for these are contrary the one to the other; that you may not do the things that you would. But if you are led by the Spirit, you are not under the law. Now the works of the flesh are manifest, which are [these]: fornication, uncleanness, lasciviousness, idolatry, sorcery, enmities, strife, jealousies, wraths, factions, divisions, parties, envyings, drunkenness, revellings, and such like; of which I forewarn you, even as I did forewarn you, that they who practice such things shall not inherit the kingdom of God. But the fruit of the Spirit is love, joy, peace, longsuffering, kindness, goodness, faithfulness, meekness, self-control; against such there is no law. And they that are of Christ Jesus have crucified the flesh with the passions and the lusts thereof. If we live by the Spirit, by the Spirit let us also walk. Let us not become vainglorious, provoking one another, envying one another. (...) For neither is circumcision anything, nor uncircumcision, but a new creature.

      Galatians 4:21-5:26, 6:15

The World and its Alternative

Now as they went on their way, Jesus entered a certain village, where a woman named Martha welcomed him into her home. She had a sister named Mary, who sat at the Lord's feet and listened to what he was saying. But Martha was distracted by her many tasks; so she came to him and asked, "Lord, do you not care that my sister has left me to do all the work by myself? Tell her then to help me." But the Lord answered her, "Martha, Martha, you are worried and distracted by many things; there is need of only one thing. Mary has chosen the better part, which will not be taken away from her."   Luke 10:38-42

The Magic Horse- A king had two sons. The first helped the people by working for them in a manner they understood. The second was called "Lazy" because he was a dreamer, as far as anyone could see. The first son gained great honors in his land. The second obtained from a humble carpenter a wooden horse and sat astride it. But the horse was a magical one. It carried the rider, if he was sincere, to his heart's desire. Seeking his heart's desire, the young prince disappeared one day on the horse. He was absent a long time. After many adventures he returned with a beautiful princess from the Country of Light and his father was overjoyed at his safe return and listened to the story of the magic horse. The horse was made available to anyone who wanted it in that country. But many people preferred the obvious benefits which the actions of the first prince provided for them because to them the horse always looked like a plaything. They did not get beyond the outer appearance of the horse, which was not impressive. When the old king died, the prince who liked to play with toys became, by his wish, the king. But people in general despised him. They much preferred the excitement and interest of the discoveries and activities of the practical prince. Unless we listen to the "lazy" prince, whether he has a princess from the Country of Light with him or not, we shall not get beyond the outer appearance of the horse. Even if we like the horse, it is not it's outward shape which can help us travel to our destination.   Sufism

One of the dinner guests, on hearing this, said to him, "Blessed is anyone who will eat bread in the kingdom of God!" Then Jesus said to him, "Someone gave a great dinner and invited many. At the time for the dinner he sent his slaves to say to those who had been invited, "Come for everything is ready now." But they all alike began to make excuses. The first said to him, "I have bought a piece of land, and I must go out and see it; please give my regrets." Another said, "I have bought five yoke of oxen, and I am going to try them out; please accept my regrets." Another said, "I have just been married, and therefore I cannot come." So the slave returned and reported this to his master. Then the owner of the house became angry and said to his slave, "Go out at once into the streets and lanes of the town and bring in the poor, the crippled, the blind, and the lame." And the slave said, "Sir, what you have ordered has been done, and there is still room." Then the master said to the slave, "Go out into the roads and lanes, and compel people to come in, so that my house may be filled. For I tell you, none of those who were invited will taste my dinner."
                                                                Luke 14:15-24

"Me and Mine"- Some children were playing beside a river. They made sand castles and each child defended his castle claiming it as his own. When they were finished one child kicked over another child's castle and destroyed it. The owner of the castle flew into a rage and assaulted the child while calling on his comrades for help in punishing him. They beat him with sticks and stomped on him as he lay on the ground.... Then they went on playing with each child claiming his castle as his own saying, this is mine. But evening came and the children were called home. No one cared what became of his castle and each tore down his own with much delight.

"The Dance"- A disciple had asked permission to take part in the dance of the Sufis. The Sheikh said: 'Fast completely for three days then have a luscious meal prepared. If you then prefer the dance, you may take part in it.   *Al Ghazali*

And do not keep striving for what you are to eat and what you are to drink, and do not keep worrying. For it is the nations of the world that strive after all these things, and your Father knows that you need them. Instead, strive for his kingdom, and all these things will be given to you as well.   Luke 12:29-31

Take care! Be on your guard against all kinds of greed; for one's life does not consist of the abundance of possessions. Then he told them a parable: The land of a rich man produced abundantly. And he thought to himself, "What should I do, for I have no place to store my crops?" Then he said, "I will do this: I will pull down my barns and build larger ones, and there will I store all my grain and my goods. And I will say to my soul, Soul, you have ample goods laid up for many years; relax, eat drink, be merry." But God said to him, "You fool! This very night your life is being demanded of you. And the things you have prepared, whose will they be?" So it is with those who store up treasures for themselves but are not rich towards God.   Luke 12:15-21

No slave can serve two masters; for a slave will either hate the one and love the other, or be devoted to one and despise the other. You cannot serve God and wealth.
Luke 16:13

A certain ruler asked him, "Good Teacher, what must I do to inherit eternal life?" Jesus said to him, "Why do you call me good? No one is good but God alone. You know the commandments: You shall not commit adultery; You shall not murder; You shall not steal; You shall not bear false witness; Honor your father and mother." He replied, "I have kept all of these since my youth." When Jesus heard this, he said to him,

"There is one thing lacking. Sell all that you own and distribute the money to the poor, and you will have treasure in heaven; then come, follow me." But when he heard this, he became sad; for he was very rich. Jesus looked at him and said, "How hard it is for those who have wealth to enter into the kingdom of God! Indeed, it is easier for a camel to go through the eye of a needle than for someone who is rich to enter into the kingdom of God."
Luke 18:18-25

Do not be afraid, little flock, for it is your Father's good pleasure to give you the kingdom. Sell your possessions, and give alms. Make purses for yourselves that do not wear out, an unfailing treasure in heaven, where no thief comes near and nor moth destroys. For where your treasure is, there your heart is also.
Luke 12:32-34

Were I possessed of the least knowledge, I would, when walking on the great way, fear only paths that lead astray. The great way is easy, yet people prefer by-paths. The court is corrupt, the fields are overgrown with weeds, the granaries are empty; yet there are those dressed in fineries, with swords at their sides, filled with food and drink, and possessed of too much wealth. This is known as taking the lead in robbery. Far indeed is this from the Way.   Tao Te Ching

Maitreyi, said one day Yajnavalkya to his wife, "I am going to leave this present life, and retire to a life of meditation. Let me settle my possessions upon you and Katyayani." "If all the earth filled with riches beyond compare belonged to me, O my Lord," said Maitreyi, "should I thereby attain life eternal?" "Certainly not," said Yajnavalkya, "your life would only be as is the life of wealthy people. In wealth there is no hope of life eternal." Maitreyi said: "What should I then do with possessions that cannot give me life eternal? Give me instead your knowledge, O my Lord." On hearing this Yajnavalkya exclaimed: "Dear you are to me, beloved, and dear are the words you say. Come, sit down and I will teach; but hear my words with deep attention." [...] It is not for the love of the all that the all is dear; but for the love of the Soul in the all that the all is dear. [...] all will abandon the man who thinks that the all is apart from the Soul. Because religion, power, heavens, beings, gods and all rest on the Soul."   From the Brihadaranyaka Upanishad

He who has renounced the world for My sake will surely pray to Me; he must serve Me. Is there anything very remarkable about it? People will cry shame on him if he fails to do so. But he is blessed indeed who prays to Me in the midst of his worldly duties. He is trying to find Me, overcoming a great obstacle- pushing away, as it were, a huge block of stone weighing a ton. Such a man is a real hero. Live in the world like an ant. The world contains a mixture of truth and untruth, sugar and sand. Be an ant and take the sugar. Again, the world is a mixture of milk and water, the bliss of God-Consciousness and the pleasure of the sense enjoyment. Be a swan and drink the milk, leaving the water aside. Live in the world like a waterfowl. The water clings to the bird, but the bird shakes it off. Live in the world like a mudfish. The fish lives in the mud, but its skin is always bright and shiny. The world indeed is a mixture of truth and make-believe. Discard the make-believe and take the truth.
Ramakrishna

The Sufis do not abandon this world, nor do they hold that human appetites must be done away with. They only discipline those desires that are in discordance with the religious life and the dictates of sound reason. They don't throw away all things of this world, nor do they go after them with a vengeance. Rather, they know the true value and function of everything upon the earth. They save as much as is necessary. They eat as much as they need to stay healthy. They nourish their bodies and simultaneously set their hearts free. God becomes the focal point toward which their whole being leans. God becomes the object of their continual adoration and contemplation.   *al-Ghazzali*

The perfect mystic is neither an ecstatic devotee lost in contemplation of Oneness nor a saintly recluse shunning all commerce with mankind. The true saint goes in and out among the people, eats and sleeps with them, buys and sells in the market, marries and takes part in social intercourse, and never forgets God for a single moment.   *Abu Sa'id*

The world is a place of preparation where on is given many lessons and passes many tests. Choose less over more in it. Be satisfied with what you have, even if it is less than what others have. In fact, prefer to have less. This world is not bad- on the contrary, it is the field of the hereafter. What you plant here, you will reap there. This world is the way to eternal bliss and so is good- worthy to be cherished and to be praised. What is bad is what you do with the world when you become blind to truth and totally consumed by your desires, lust, and ambition for it. Our master the Prophet (peace and blessings be upon him), in whom wisdom was as clear as crystal, was asked, "What is worldliness?" He answered, "Everything that makes you heedless and causes you to forget your Lord." Therefore, the goods of this world are not harmful in themselves, but only when you let them render you forgetful, disobedient, and unaware of the Lord."   *Ibn Arabi*

When a heart finds repose with the beloved, how should it ever desire another? Did you ever see a moth flying to the sun, when all its hope lies in the candle flame? It is pointless to spread a hundred bunches of fragrant herbs before the nightingale, who only wishes for the rose's balmy breath. Once the water lily has been caressed by the warmth of the sun, will it ever show any interest in the moon? When a soul thirsts for a draught of clear water, it has no use for sugar.   *Jami*

Have you ever heard about the bird that lives in the south? The Phoenix that never grows old? This undying Phoenix rises out of the South Sea and flies to the Sea of the North, never alighting except on certain sacred trees. He will touch no food but the most exquisite rare fruits, drinks only from the clearest streams. Once an owl chewing a dead rat already half-decayed, saw the Phoenix fly over, looked up, and screeched with alarm, clutching the rat to himself in fear and dismay. Why are you so frantic clinging to your world and screeching at me in dismay?   *Chuang Tzu*

One day, Rabia asked, "Who shall lead us to our Beloved?" and her servant answered, "Our beloved is with us, but this world cuts us off from Him."   *Rabia*

And so, brethren, in this life we are pilgrims; we sigh in faith for our true country which we are unsure about. Why do we not know of what country we are? Because we have wandered so far away that we have forgotten it. But the Lord Christ, the king of that land, came down to us, and drove forgetfulness from our heart. God took to himself our flesh so that he might be our way back. We go forward through his Manhood so that we may be with him forever in his Godhead. Do not look for any path to him except himself; for if he had not vouchsafed to be the way, we could never have found the path. I do not tell you to look for the way- the way has come to you: arise and walk. You are not walking on the lake like Peter, but on another sea, for this world is a sea: trials its waves, temptations its storms, and men devouring each other as fishes do. Don't be afraid, step out stoutly lest you sink. Peter said, 'If it is you, bid me come to you on the water.' It was, and he heard his cry and raised him as he was sinking. Gaze in faith at this miracle, and do as Peter did. When the gale blows and the waves rise, and your weakness makes you fear you will be lost, cry out, 'Lord, I am sinking', and he who bade you walk will not let you perish.
St. Augustine

O you people! Eat of what is on earth, lawful and good; and do not follow the footsteps of the Evil One, for he is to you an avowed enemy.   Quran 2:168

Let not the Believers take for friends or helpers Unbelievers rather than Believers: if any do that, in nothing will there be help from Allah: except by way of precaution, that you may guard yourselves from them. But Allah cautions you to remember Himself; for the final goal is to Allah.   Quran 3:28

Were you to follow the common run of those on earth, they will lead you away from the Way of Allah.   Quran 6:116

That which is on earth We have made but as a glittering show for the earth, in order that We may test them- as to which of them is best in conduct. Verily that which is on the earth We shall make but as dust and dry soil without growth or herbage.
Quran 18: 7-8

Set forth to them the similitude of the life of this world: it is like the rain which We send down from the skies: the earth's vegetation absorbs it, but soon it becomes dry stubble, which the winds do scatter: it is only Allah Who prevails over all things. Wealth and sons are allurements of the life of this world: but the things that endure, Good Deeds, are best in the sight of your Lord, as rewards, and best as the foundation for hopes.   Quran 18: 45-46

Nor strain your eyes in longing for the things We have given for enjoyment to parties of them, the splendor of the life of this world, through which We test them: but the provision of your Lord is better and more enduring.   Quran 20:131

The material things which you are given are but the conveniences of this life and the glitter thereof; but that which is with Allah is better and more enduring: will you not then be wise?
Quran 28:60

Whatever you are given here is but a convenience of this life: but that which is with Allah is better and more lasting: it is for those who believe and put their trust in their Lord;
Quran 42:36

Were it not that all men might become of one evil way of life, We would provide, for everyone who blasphemies against Allah Most Gracious, silver roofs for their house, and silver stairways on which to go up, and silver doors to their homes, and thrones of silver on which they could recline, and also adornments of gold. But all this were nothing but conveniences of the present life: the Hereafter, in the sight of your Lord, is for the Righteous.   Quran 43:33-35

Look upon the world as you would look upon a bubble, look upon it thus as a mirage: the king of death does not see him who thus looks down upon the world. Come, look at this world, glittering like a royal chariot; the foolish are immersed in it, but the wise are not attached to it.   Dhammapada

Putting away the hankering after the world, he remains with a heart that hankers not, and purifies his mind of lusts. Putting away the corruption of the wish to injure, he remains with a heart free from ill-temper, and purifies his mind of malevolence. Putting away torpor of heart and mind, keeping his ideas alight, mindful and self-possessed, he purifies his mind of weakness and sloth. Putting away flurry and worry, he remains free from fretfulness, and with heart serene within, he purifies himself of irritability and vexation of spirit. Putting away wavering, he remains as one passed beyond perplexity; and no longer in suspense as to what is good, he purifies his mind of doubt.
Sammanaphala Sutta

That material shape, that feeling, perception, those impulses, that consciousness by which one, in defining the Tathagata, might define him- all have been got rid of by the Tathagata cut off at the

root, made like a palm-tree stump that can come to no further existence in the future. Freed from reckoning by material shape, feeling, perception, the impulses, consciousness, is the Tathagata; he is deep, immeasurable, unfathomable, as is the great ocean.
Samyutta-Nikaya

    Some children were playing beside a river. They made castles of sand, and each child defended his castle and said, 'This one is mine.' They kept their castles separate and would not allow any mistakes about which was whose. When the castles were all finished, one child kicked over someone else's castle and completely destroyed it. The owner of the castle flew into a rage, pulled the other child's hair, struck him with his fist and bawled out, 'He has spoiled my castle! Come along all of you and help me punish him as he deserves.' The others all came to his help. They beat the child ... Then they went on playing in their sand castles, each saying, 'This is mine; no one else may have it. Keep away! Don't touch my castle!' But evening came, it was getting dark and they all thought they ought to be going home. No one now cared what became of his castle. One child stamped on his, another pushed his over with both hands. Then they turned away and went back, each to his home. The leaders of this generation, that is to say most of them, throw away their lives in the pursuit of material gain. Isn't it pathetic! When the sage starts something, he will carefully have considered what he is doing and why he is doing it. Now this is like a man who takes the pearl of the Marquis of Sui and shoots a bird in the sky with it, high up in the air. People would obviously laugh at him. Why is this so? Because he has used something of great value to obtain something of little value. Now surely this life is even more valuable than the pearl of the Marquis of Sui!
Chuang Tzu

    How is there laughter, how is there joy, as this world is always burning? Why do you not seek a light, you who are shrouded in darkness?   Dhammapada

Thus shall you think of all this fleeting world: A star at dawn, a bubble in a stream; a flash of lightning in a summer cloud, a flickering lamp, a phantom, and a dream.
Diamond Sutra

Behold the universe in the glory of God: and all that lives and moves on earth. Leaving the transient, find joy in the Eternal: set not your heart on another's possession.
Isa Upanishad

There is the path of joy, and there is the path of pleasure. Both attract the soul. Who follows the first comes to good; who follows pleasure reaches not the End. The two paths in front of man. Pondering on them, the wise man chooses the path of joy; the fool takes the path of pleasure.   Katha Upanishad

The Creator made the senses outward-going: they go to the world of matter outside, not to the Spirit within. But a sage who sought immortality looked within himself and found his own Soul. The foolish run after outward pleasures and fall into the snares of vast-embracing death. But the wise have found immortality, and do not seek the Eternal in things that pass away.   Katha Upanishad

"All that has form is an illusory existence. When the illusory nature of form is perceived, the Tathagata is recognized. (...) Subhuti, what do you think? Does a srotapanna think, 'I have obtained the fruit of srotapanna?' Subhuti said, "No, World-Honored One, he does not. Why? Because while srotapanna means entering the stream, there is no entering here. A true srotapanna is one who does not enter sound, odor, flavor, touch, or any thought that arises. (...) All bodhisattvas should develop a pure, lucid mind that doesn't depend upon sight, sound, touch, flavor, smell, or any thought that arises in it. A bodhisattva should develop a mind that functions freely, without depending on anything whatsoever."
Diamond Sutra

It is the three gunas born of prakriti- sattva, rajas, and tamas- that bind the immortal Atman to the body. Sattva is pure, luminous light, and freedom from sorrow: it binds us with attachment to happiness and knowledge. Rajas is passion, arising from selfish desire and inordinate attachment. These keep man from seeing the Self through being attached to habitual action. Tamas is born of ignorance and deludes all creatures through heedlessness, indolence, and sleep. Sattva binds us to happiness; rajas binds us to action. Tamas, distorting our understanding, binds us to delusion.
Bhagavad Gita 14:5-9

I am easily attained by the person who always remembers me in the devotion of Yoga and who rests all their soul on me.
Bhagavad Gita 8:14

Then said Jesus unto his disciples, if any man would come after me, let him deny himself, and take up his cross, and follow me. For whosoever would save his life shall lose it: and whosoever shall lose his life for my sake shall find it. For what shall a man be profited, if he should gain the whole world, and forfeit his life? or what should a man give in exchange for his life? For the Son of man will come in the glory of his Father with his angels; and then shall he render unto every man according to his deeds. Verily I say unto you, there are some of them that stand here, who shall in no wise taste of death, till they see the Son of man coming in his kingdom.   Matthew 16:24-28

And there come his mother and his brethren; and, standing without, they sent unto him, calling him. And a multitude was sitting about him; and they say unto him, Behold, thy mother and thy brethren without seek for thee. And he answered them, and said, Who is my mother and my brethren? And looking round on them that sat round about him, he said, Behold, my mother and my brethren! For whosoever shall do the will of God, the same is my brother, and sister, and mother.   Mark 3:31-35

And he called unto him the multitude with his disciples, and said unto them, If any man would come after me, let him deny himself, and take up his cross, and follow me. For whosoever would save his life shall lose it; and whosoever shall lose his life for my sake and the gospel's shall save it. For what does it profit a man, to gain the whole world, and forfeit his life? For what should a man give in exchange for his life? For whosoever shall be ashamed of me and of my words in this adulterous and sinful generation, the Son of man also shall be ashamed of him, when he comes in the glory of his Father with the holy angels.   Mark 8:34-38

And as he was going forth into the way, there ran one to him, and kneeled to him, and asked him, Good Teacher, what shall I do that I may inherit eternal life? And Jesus said unto him, Why do you call me good? none is good save one, [even] God. You know the commandments, Do not kill, Do not commit adultery, Do not steal, Do not bear false witness, Do not defraud, Honor your father and mother. And he said unto him, Teacher, all these things have I observed from my youth. And Jesus looking upon him loved him, and said unto him, One thing you lack: go, sell whatsoever you have, and give to the poor, and you shall have treasure in heaven: and come, follow me. But his countenance fell at the saying, and he went away sorrowful: for he was one that had great possessions. And Jesus looked round about, and said unto his disciples, How hardly shall they that have riches enter into the kingdom of God! And the disciples were amazed at his words. But Jesus answered again, and said unto them, Children, how hard is it for them that trust in riches to enter into the kingdom of God! It is easier for a camel to go through a needle's eye, than for a rich man to enter into the kingdom of God. And they were astonished exceedingly, saying unto him, Then who can be saved?   Jesus looking upon them said, With men it is impossible, but not with God: for all things are possible with God.   Mark 10:17-27

And they come to Jerusalem: and he entered into the temple, and began to cast out them that sold and them that bought in the temple, and overthrew the tables of the money-changers, and the seats of them that sold the doves; and he would not suffer that any man should carry a vessel through the temple. And he taught, and said unto them, Is it not written, My house shall be called a house of prayer for all the nations? But you have made it a den of robbers.   Mark 11:15-17

And he led him up, and showed him all the kingdoms of the world in a moment of time. And the devil said unto him, To you I will give all this authority, and the glory of them: for it has been delivered unto me; and to whomsoever I will I give it. If you therefore will worship before me, it shall all be yours.
Luke 4:5-7

And he lifted up his eyes on his disciples, and said, Blessed are you, poor: for yours is the kingdom of God. Blessed are you that hunger now: for you shall be filled. Blessed are you that weep now: for you shall laugh. Blessed are you, when men shall hate you, and when they shall separate you from their company, and reproach you, and cast out your name as evil, for the Son of man's sake. Rejoice in that day, and leap for joy; for behold, your reward is great in heaven; for in the same manner did their fathers unto the prophets. But woe unto you that are rich! for you have received your consolation. Woe unto you, you that are full now! for you shall hunger. Woe unto you, you that laugh now! for you shall mourn and weep. Woe unto you, when all men shall speak well of you! for in the same manner did their fathers to the false prophets.
Luke 6:20-26

And being asked by the Pharisees, when the kingdom of God comes, he answered them and said, The kingdom of God comes not with observation: neither shall they say, Lo, here! or, There! for lo, the kingdom of God is within you. And he said unto the disciples, The days will come, when you shall desire to see one of the days of the Son of man, and shall not see it. And they shall say to you, Lo, there! Lo, here! go not away, nor follow after [them]: for as the lightning, when it lighteneth out of the one part under the heaven, shines unto the other part under heaven; so shall the Son of man be in his day. But first must he suffer many things and be rejected of this generation. And as it came to pass in the days of Noah, even so shall it be also in the days of the Son of man. They ate, they drank, they married, they were given in marriage, until the day that Noah entered into the ark, and the flood came, and destroyed them all. Likewise, even as it came to pass in the days of Lot; they ate, they drank, they bought, they sold, they planted, they built; but in the day that Lot went out from Sodom it rained fire and brimstone from heaven, and destroyed them all: after the same manner shall it be in the day that the Son of man is revealed. In that day, he that shall be on the housetop, and his goods in the house, let him not go down to take them away: and let him that is in the field likewise not return back. Remember Lot's wife. Whosoever shall seek to gain his life shall lose it: but whosoever shall lose his life shall preserve it. I say unto you, In that night there shall be two men on one bed; the one shall be taken, and the other shall be left. There shall be two women grinding together; the one shall be taken, and the other shall be left. There shall be two men in the field; the one shall be taken, and the other shall be left. And they answering say unto him, Where, Lord? And he said unto them, Where the body is, thither will the eagles also be gathered together.   Luke 18:18-25

Now there was a man of the Pharisees, named Nicodemus, a ruler of the Jews: the same came unto him by night, and said to him, Rabbi, we know that you are a teacher come from God; for no one can do these signs that you do, except God be with him. Jesus answered and said unto him, Verily, verily, I say unto you, Except one be born anew, he cannot see the kingdom of God. Nicodemus said to him, How can a man be born when he is old? can he enter a second time into his mother's womb, and be born? Jesus answered, Verily, verily, I say unto you, Except one be born of water and the

Spirit, he cannot enter into the kingdom of God! That which is born of the flesh is flesh; and that which is born of the Spirit is spirit. Marvel not that I said unto you, you must be born anew. The wind blows where it will, and you hear the voice thereof, but know not whence it comes, nor where it goes: so is every one that is born of the Spirit.   John 3:1-8

And Jesus answered them, saying, The hour is come, that the Son of man should be glorified. Verily, verily, I say unto you, Except a grain of wheat fall into the earth and die, it abides by itself alone; but if it die, it bears much fruit. He that loves his life loses it; and he that hates his life in this world shall keep it unto life eternal. If any man serve me, let him follow me; and where I am, there shall also my servant be: if any man serve me, him will the Father honor.
John 12:23-26

Jesus answered, My kingdom is not of this world: if my kingdom were of this world, then would my servants fight, that I should not be delivered to the Jews: but now is my kingdom not from here. Pilate therefore said unto him, Are you a king then? Jesus answered, You say that I am a king. To this end have I been born, and to this end am I come into the world, that I should bear witness unto the truth. Every one that is of the truth hears my voice.
John 18:36-37

For I reckon that the sufferings of this present time are not worthy to be compared with the glory which shall be revealed to us-ward. For the earnest expectation of the creation waits for the revealing of the sons of God. For the creation was subjected to vanity, not of its own will, but by reason of him who subjected it, in hope that the creation itself also shall be delivered from the bondage of corruption into the liberty of the glory of the children of God.
Romans 8:18-21

But now has Christ been raised from the dead, the first fruits of them that are asleep. For since by man came death, by man came also the resurrection of the dead. For as in Adam all die, so also in Christ shall all be made alive. But each in his own order: Christ the first fruits; then they that are Christ`s, at his coming. Then comes the end, when he shall deliver up the kingdom to God, even the Father; when he shall have abolished all rule and all authority and power. For he must reign, till he has put all his enemies under his feet. The last enemy that shall be abolished is death. For, He put all things in subjection under his feet. But when he said, All things are put in subjection, it is evident that he is excepted who did subject all things unto him. And when all things have been subjected unto him, then shall the Son also himself be subjected to him that did subject all things unto him, that God may be all in all. (...) So also is the resurrection of the dead. It is sown in corruption; it is raised in incorruption: it is sown in dishonor; it is raised in glory: it is sown in weakness; it is raised in power: it is sown a natural body; it is raised a spiritual body. If there is a natural body, there is also a spiritual body. So also it is written, The first man Adam became a living soul. The last Adam became a life-giving spirit. Howbeit that is not first which is spiritual, but that which is natural; then that which is spiritual. The first man is of the earth, earthly: the second man is of heaven. As is the earthly, such are they also that are earthly: and as is the heavenly, such are they also that are heavenly. And as we have borne the image of the earthly, we shall also bear the image of the heavenly. Now this I say, brethren, that flesh and blood cannot inherit the kingdom of God; neither does corruption inherit incorruption. Behold, I tell you a mystery: We all shall not sleep, but we shall all be changed, in a moment, in the twinkling of an eye, at the last trump: for the trumpet shall sound, and the dead shall be raised incorruptible, and we shall be changed. For this corruptible must put on incorruption, and this mortal must put on immortality. But when this corruptible shall have put on incorruption, and this mortal shall have put on immortality, then shall come to pass the saying that is written, Death is swallowed up in victory. O death, where is thy victory? O death, where is thy sting? The sting of death is sin; and the power of sin is the law: but thanks be to God, who gives us the victory through our Lord Jesus Christ. Wherefore, my beloved brethren, be steadfast, unmovable, always abounding in the work of the Lord, forasmuch as you know that your labor is not vain in the Lord.

1st Corinthians 15:20-28, 42-58

Love not the world, neither the things that are in the world. If any man loves the world, the love of the Father is not in him. For all that is in the world, the lust of the flesh and the lust of the eyes and the vain glory of life, is not of the Father, but is of the world. And the world passes away, and the lust thereof: but he that does the will of God abides forever. (...) We know that we are of God, and the whole world lies in the evil one.   1 John 2:15-17, 5:19

And you did he make alive, when you were dead through your trespasses and sins, wherein you once walked according to the course of this world, according to the prince of the powers of the air, of the spirit that now works in the sons of disobedience; among whom we also all once lived in the lust of our flesh, doing the desires of the flesh and of the mind, and were by nature children of wrath, even as the rest:-- but God, being rich in mercy, for his great love wherewith he loved us, even when we were dead through our trespasses, made us alive together with Christ (by grace have you been saved), and raised us up with him, and made us to sit with him in the heavenly places, in Christ Jesus: that in the ages to come he might show the exceeding riches of his grace in kindness toward us in Christ Jesus: for by grace have you been saved through faith; and that not of yourselves, it is the gift of God; not of works, that no man should glory. For we are his workmanship, created in Christ Jesus for good works, which God afore prepared that we should walk in them. Wherefore remember, that once you, the Gentiles in the flesh, who are called Uncircumcision by that which is called Circumcision, in the flesh, made by hands; that you were at that time separate from Christ, alienated from the commonwealth of Israel, and strangers from the covenants of the promise, having no hope and without God in the world. But now in Christ Jesus you that once were far off are made nigh in the blood of Christ. For he is our peace, who made both one, and brake down the middle wall of partition, having abolished in the flesh the enmity, the law of commandments in ordinances; that he might create in himself of the two one new man, making peace; and might reconcile them both in one body unto God through the cross, having slain the enmity thereby: and he came and preached peace to you that were far off, and peace to them that were nigh: for through him we both have our access in one Spirit unto the Father.   Ephesians 2:1-18

If you died with Christ from the rudiments of the world, why, as though living in the world, do you subject yourselves to ordinances, handle not, nor taste, nor touch (all which things are to perish with the using), after the precepts and doctrines of men? Which things have indeed a show of wisdom in will-worship, and humility, and severity to the body; but are not of any value against the indulgence of the flesh. If then you were raised together with Christ, seek the things that are above, where Christ is, seated on the right hand of God. Set your mind on the things that are above, not on the things that are upon the earth. For you died, and your life is hid with Christ in God. When Christ, our life, shall be manifested, then shall you also with him be manifested in glory. Put to death therefore your members which are upon the earth: fornication, uncleanness, passion, evil desire, and covetousness, which is idolatry; for which things` sake comes the wrath of God upon the sons of disobedience: wherein you also once walked, when you lived in these things; but now do you also put them all away: anger, wrath, malice, railing, shameful speaking out of your mouth: lie not one to another; seeing that you have put off the old man with his doings, and have put on the new man, that is being renewed unto knowledge after the image of him that created him: where there cannot be Greek and Jew, circumcision and uncircumcision, barbarian, Scythian, bondman, freeman; but Christ is all, and in all. Put on therefore, as God`s elect, holy and beloved, a heart of compassion, kindness, lowliness, meekness, longsuffering; forbearing one another, and forgiving each other, if any man has a complaint against any; even as the Lord forgave you, so also do you: and above all these things put on love, which is the bond of

perfectness. And let the peace of Christ rule in your hearts, to the which also you were called in one body; and be thankful. Let the word of Christ dwell in you richly; in all wisdom teaching and admonishing one another with psalms and hymns and spiritual songs, singing with grace in your hearts unto God. And whatsoever you do, in word or in deed, do all in the name of the Lord Jesus, giving thanks to God the Father through him.
Colossians 2:20- 3:17

You adulteresses, do you not know that the friendship of the world is enmity with God? Whosoever therefore would be a friend of the world makes himself an enemy of God. Or do you think that the scripture speaks in vain? Does the spirit which he made to dwell in us long unto envying? But he gives more grace. Wherefore the scripture says, God resists the proud, but gives grace to the humble. Be subject therefore unto God; but resist the devil, and he will flee from you. Draw nigh to God, and he will draw nigh to you. Cleanse your hands, you sinners; and purify your hearts, you double-minded. Be afflicted, and mourn, and weep: let your laughter be turned to mourning, and your joy to heaviness. Humble yourselves in the sight of the Lord, and he shall exalt you.   James 4:4-10

Bad company ruins good morals.   1 Corinthians 15:33

If while you are traveling you can't find someone your better or equal, then travel joyfully alone.   *Buddha*

Happy is the man who does not take the wicked for his guide, nor walk the road that sinners tread, nor take his seat among the scornful; the law of the Lord is his delight, the law his meditation night and day. He is like a tree planted beside a watercourse, which yields its fruit in season, and its leaf never withers... Wicked men are not like this, they are like chaff driven by the wind.   Psalms

This idea-of- "I", creates a world, which it believes exists outside itself, bestowing pleasure and pain. The Self is never

involved in this fantasy. One who knows this is free from pleasure and pain. [...] This world of friends and enemies and those who are neither, with its opposites of pleasure and pain, is truly a fantasy of the mind. It is born of ignorance and nothing else.
        Uddhava Gita *18:57,60*

  Who pities a snake charmer when he is bitten, or anyone who goes near a wild beast? So is it with the companion of the proud man, who is involved in his sins. (...) He who touches pitch blackens his hand; he who associates with an impious man learns his ways.
        Sirach *12:13-14, 13:1-2*

  A form seen in the distance becomes clearer the closer we get to it. If a mirage were water, why would it vanish when we draw near? The farther we are from the world, the more real it appears to us; the nearer we draw to it, the less visible it becomes, and, like a mirage, becomes signless. *Dalai Lama*

  Once upon a time, I, Chuang Tzu, dreamt that I was a butterfly, fluttering here and there; in all ways a butterfly. I was conscious only of following my fancies as a butterfly, and was unconscious of my individuality as a man. Suddenly, I awoke, and there I lay, myself again. Now I do not know whether I was then a man dreaming I was a butterfly, or whether I am now a butterfly, or whether I am now a butterfly dreaming I am a man.

  Remember your contemporaries who have passed away and were of your age. Remember the honors and fame they earned, the high posts they held, and the beautiful bodies they possessed. Today all of them are turned to dust. They have left orphans and widows behind them, their wealth is being wasted, and their houses turned into ruins. No sign of them is left today, and they lie in the dark holes underneath the earth. Picture their faces before your mind's eye and ponder. Do not fix hopes on your health, and do not laugh away life. Remember how they walked and now all their joints lie separated and the tongue with which they talked lightly is eaten away by the worms.   *al-Ghazzali*

Have We not made for him a pair of eyes? - and a tongue, and a pair of lips? - and shown him the two highways? But he has made no haste on the path that is steep. And what will explain to you the path that is steep? - It is freeing the bondman; or the giving of food in a day of privation to the orphan with claims of relationship, or to the indigent down in the dust. Then he will be of those who believe, and enjoin patience, constancy and self-restraint, and enjoin deeds of kindness and compassion. Such are the Companions of the Right Hand. But those who reject Our Signs, they are the unhappy Companions of the Left Hand.   On them will be Fire vaulted over all round.   Quran 90:8-20

The Tempter, Mara, Desire: Sin

The Lord looks down from heaven upon the children of men, to see if there are any who understand, who seek God. They have all turned aside, they have together become corrupt; there is none who does good, no, not one.   Psalms 14:2-3

O you children of Adam! Let not Satan seduce you, in the same manner as he got your parents out of the Garden, stripping them of their raiment, to expose their shame: for he and his tribe watch you from a position where you cannot see them: We made the Evil Ones friends only to those without Faith.   Quran 7:27

If a suggestion from Satan assails your mind, seek refuge with Allah; for He hears and knows all things. Those who fear Allah, when a thought of evil from Satan assaults them, bring Allah to remembrance then they see aright!   Quran 7: 200-201

And Satan will say when the matter is decided: "It was Allah Who gave you the promise of Truth: I too promised, but I failed in my promise to you. I had no authority over you except to call you, but you listened to me: then reproach not me, but reproach your own souls.   Quran 14:22

(Iblis said): "I am not one to prostrate myself to man, whom You created from sounding clay, from mud molded into shape." Allah said: "Then get out of here; for you are rejected, accursed. And the Curse shall be on you till the Day of Judgment." Iblis said: "O my Lord! Give me respite until the Day the dead are raised." Allah said: "Respite is granted to you till the Day of the Time Appointed." Iblis said: "O my Lord! because You have put me in the wrong, I will make wrong fair-seeming to them on the earth, and I will put them all in the wrong, - except Your servants among them, sincere and purified by Your grace." Allah said: "This Way of My sincere servants is indeed a Way that leads straight to Me. For over My servants no authority shall you have, except such as put themselves in the wrong and follow you." Quran 15:33-42

About the Evil One it is decreed that whoever turns to him for friendship, he will lead him astray, and he will guide him to the Penalty of the Fire. Quran 22:4

And say:"O my Lord! I seek refuge with You O my Lord! from the suggestions of the Evil Ones." Quran 23:97

O you who believe! Do not follow Satan's footsteps: if any will follow the footsteps of Satan, he will but command what is shameful and wrong: and were it not for the grace and mercy of Allah on you, not one of you would ever have been pure: but Allah purifies whom He pleases; and Allah is One who hears and knows all things. Quran 23:21

If anyone withdraws himself from remembrance of Allah Most Gracious, We appoint for him an evil one, to be an intimate companion to him. Such evil ones really hinder them from the Path, but they think they are being guided aright! At length, when such a one comes to Us, he says to his evil companion: "Would that between me and you were the distance of East and West!" Ah! Evil is the companion indeed! Quran 43:36-38

Say: I seek refuge with the Lord of the Dawn, from the mischief of created things; from the mischief of Darkness as it overspreads; from the mischief of those who practice secret arts: and from the mischief of the jealous one as he practices jealousy.
Quran 113

Say: I seek refuge with the Lord and Cherisher of Mankind, the King of Mankind, the God of Mankind, - from the mischief of the whisperer of evil, who withdraws after his whisper, - the same who whispers into the hearts of Mankind, - among Jinns and among Men.   Quran 114

If you do well, will you not be accepted? And if you do not do well, sin lies at the door. And its desire is for you, but you should rule over it. (...) I will never again curse the ground for man's sake, although the imagination of man's heart is evil from his youth.   Genesis 4:7, 21

You have tested my heart; you have visited me in the night; you have tried me and have found nothing; I have purposed that my mouth shall not transgress. Concerning the works of men, by the word of Your lips, I have kept away from the paths of the destroyer. Uphold my steps in Your paths, that my footsteps may not slip.
Psalms 17: 3-5

Who can understand his errors? Cleanse me from secret faults. Keep back Your servant also from presumptuous sins; let them not have dominion over me. Then I shall be blameless, and I shall be innocent of great transgression. Let the words of my mouth and the meditation of my heart be acceptable in Your sight, O Lord, my strength and my Redeemer.   Psalms 19:12-14

And he called them unto him, and said unto them in parables, How can Satan cast out Satan? And if a kingdom be divided against itself, that kingdom cannot stand. And if a house be divided against itself, that house will not be able to stand. And if Satan hath rise up against himself, and is divided, he cannot stand, but hath an end. But no one can enter into the house of the strong [man], and spoil his goods, except he first binds the strong [man]; and then he will spoil his house.
Mark 3:23-27

Let your "yes" be "yes" and your "no", "no".' For whatever is more than these is from the evil one.
Matthew 5:37

I returned, and saw under the sun, that the race is not to the swift, nor the battle to the strong, neither yet bread to the wise, nor yet riches to men of understanding, nor yet favor to men of skill; but time and chance happens to them all. For man also knows not his time: as the fishes that are taken in an evil net, and as the birds that are caught in the snare, even so are the sons of men snared in an evil time, when it falls suddenly upon them.
Ecclesiastes 9:11-12

But he, knowing their thoughts, said unto them, Every kingdom divided against itself is brought to desolation; and a house [divided] against a house falls. And if Satan also is divided against himself, how shall his kingdom stand? because you say that I cast out demons by Beelzebub. And if I by Beelzebub cast out demons, by whom do your sons cast them out? therefore shall they be your judges. But if I by the finger of God cast out demons, then is the kingdom of God come upon you. When the strong [man] fully armed guards his own court, his goods are in peace: but when a stronger than he shall come upon him, and overcome him, he takes from him his whole armor wherein he trusted, and divides his spoils. He that is not with me is against me; and he that gathers not with me scatters. The unclean spirit when he is gone out of the man, passes through water-less places, seeking rest, and finding none, he says, I will turn back unto my house whence I came out. And when he is come, he finds it swept and garnished. Then he goes, and takes seven other spirits more evil than himself; and they enter in and dwell there: and the last state of that man becomes worse than the first.   Luke 11:17-26

If a man therefore purge himself from these, he shall be a vessel unto honor, sanctified, meet for the master's use, prepared unto every good work. after righteousness, faith, love, pace, with them that call on the Lord out of a pure heart. But foolish and ignorant questionings refuse, knowing that they gender strife. And the Lord`s servant must not strive, but be gentle towards all, apt to teach, forbearing, in meekness correcting them that oppose themselves; if peradventure God may give them repentance unto the knowledge of the truth, and they may recover themselves out of the snare of the devil, having been taken captive by him unto his will.   2nd Timothy 2:22-26

>It is sin for him that knows to do good, and does it not.
>James 4:17

Arjuna asked, "What power is it, Krishna, that drives man to act sinfully against his true desire, even unwillingly, as if powerless over his own actions and compelled by force?" Krishna: "It is greedy desire and anger, born of passion, the great evil, the sum of destruction: this is the enemy of the soul. The perception of everything is clouded by desire: as fire by smoke, as a mirror by dust, as an unborn babe. Wisdom is clouded by desire, the ever-present enemy of the wise, desire in its innumerable forms, which like an eternal fire cannot find satisfaction. Kama hides in man's senses and mind and reason. Through these it blinds the soul, after having overclouded wisdom. Set your senses in harmony, and then slay sinful desire, the destroyer of vision and wisdom. They say that the power of the senses is great. But greater than the senses is the mind. Greater than the mind is Buddhi, reason; and greater than reason is He- the Spirit in man and in all. Know Him therefore who is above reason; and let his peace give you peace. Be a warrior and kill desire, the powerful enemy of the soul."
                               Bhagavad Gita 3:36-43

Without desire everything is sufficient. With seeking myriad things are impoverished. Plain vegetables can soothe hunger. A patched robe is enough to cover this bent old body. Alone I hike with a deer. Cheerfully I sing with village children. The stream under the cliffs cleanses my ears. The pine on the mountain top fits my heart.   *Ryokan*

Monks, what is the noble truth about the origin of suffering? Just this: craving, leading to rebirth, accompanied by pleasure and emotion, and finding satisfaction now here, now there, namely, the craving for sense-pleasure, the craving for new life and the craving for annihilation. Monks, what is the noble truth about the cessation of suffering? Just the complete indifference to and cessation of that very craving, the abandoning of it, the rejection of it, the freedom from it, the aversion toward it. Monks, what is the noble truth about the way that goes into the cessation of suffering?   Just this noble eightfold way, namely, right view, right purpose, right speech, right action, right livelihood, right effort, right mindfulness, and right concentration.   *Buddha*

If one loves someone because it gives them pleasure, one should not be regarded as loving that person at all.   The love is, in reality, though this is not perceived, directed towards the pleasure. The source of the pleasure is the secondary object of attention, and it is perceived only because the perception of the pleasure is not well enough developed for the real feeling to be identified and described.
El-Ghazali

One of Junaid's followers came to him with a purse containing five hundred gold pieces. "Have you any more money than this?" asked the Sufi. "Yes I have." "Do you desire more?" "Yes I do." "Then you must keep it, for you are in more need than I; for I have nothing and desire nothing. You have a great deal and still want more."'   *Attar of Nishapur-*

Shun fornication! Every sin that a person commits is outside the body; but the fornicator sins against the body itself. Or do you not know that your body is a temple of the Holy Spirit within you, which you have from God, and that you are not your own?   For you were bought with a price; therefore, glorify God in your body.
1 Corinthians 6:18-20

Do not boast that you have no pride because it is less visible than an ant's foot on a black stone in a dark night. And do not think that bringing it out from within is easy, for it is easier to extract a mountain from the earth with a needle.   *Hakim Jami*

Bishr son of Harith was asked why he did not teach. "I have stopped teaching because I find that I have a desire to teach. If this compulsion passes, I shall teach of my own free will."

Asceticism can be a weakness, the fulfillment of a desire, and due to lack of real fortitude.
Hasan of Basra

He who withdraws himself from actions, but ponders on their pleasure in his heart, he is under a delusion and is a false follower of the Path. The origin of suffering as a noble truth is this: It is the craving that produces renewal of being, accompanied by enjoyment and lust- in other words, craving for sensual desires, craving for being, craving for non-being. Cessation of suffering, as a noble truth, is this: It is remainder less, fading and ceasing... letting go and rejecting, of that same craving. The way leading to the cessation of suffering, as a noble truth is this: It is simply the eightfold path of right view, right intention, right speech, right action, right livelihood, right effort, right mindfulness, right concentration.   *Buddha*

Those who are immersed in craving run down the stream of desires as a spider runs down the web which he himself has spun; having cut this bond, the steadfast retire from the world, with no backward glance, leaving all sorrow behind.   *Buddha*

Greed for enlightenment and immortality is no different than greed for material wealth...   Hua Hu Ching 59

To stay up in the mountains is a fine thing, but the slightest attachment turns it into a market; the appreciation of old paintings is a refined hobby, but the slightest greed of possession turns one into a merchant; wine and poetry provide occasions of pleasure, but the slightest loss of freedom turns them into hell. Chinese proverb

Zen mind is not Zen mind. That is, if you are attached to Zen mind, then you have a problem, and your way is very narrow. Throwing away Zen mind is correct Zen mind. Only keep the question, "What is the best way of helping other people?"
Sueng Sahn

Your wealth and your children are but a temptation. God's reward is great. Therefore, fear God with all your hearts, and be attentive, obedient, and charitable. That will be best for you. Those that preserve themselves from their own greed will surely prosper. If the debtor is in straits, grant him a delay until he can discharge his debt; but if you waive the sum as alms it will be better for you, if you but knew it.   Quran

No man is a true believer unless he desires for his brother what he desires for himself.   Hadith of the Prophet Mohammad

Once, when I was grumbling over being obliged to eat meat and do no penance, I heard it said that sometimes there was more of self-love than desire of penance in such sorrow. *St. Teresa*

The true source of misery is the acquisition of anything that you hold dear. One who knows this and desires nothing will enjoy everlasting happiness. I once watched an osprey- carrying flesh in its beak, it was harassed by a bigger and more powerful osprey. Only after it had dropped the flesh was it again left in peace.
Uddhava Gita *4:1-2*

In the mind of a person under the influence of rajas, all manner of desires will arise. Each desire when focused on will in time become a burning passion. On the grip of these passions and devoid of all self-control the person will act in ways that inevitably lead to sorrow. Such a person stays focused on the quest for truth- rather than rushing into folly.   Uddhava Gita *8:10-12*

Theft, violence, lying and cheating, anger, quarrelsomeness, arrogance and pride, ostentation, enmity, distaste and rivalry, lust, intoxication and gambling- these fifteen human weaknesses are inherent in the pursuit of wealth (and possessions). Therefore, anyone seeking the well-being of the Self should avoid accumulation wealth.   Uddhava Gita *18:18-19*

There is not so much harm in the act of sinning as in the desire and thought of it: the act is but momentary and passing, whereas the desire is continuous. It is one thing when the body indulges in a pleasurable act for an hour and an entirely different thing when the mind and heart chew on it endlessly.
Bushanja

Now this, brethren is the Aryan Truth about the origin of suffering: it is that craving that leads downwards to birth, along with the lure and lust that lingers longingly now here, now there: namely the craving for sensation, the craving to be born again, the craving to have been done with rebirth. Such, brethren, is the Aryan Truth about the origin of suffering. And this, brethren, is the Aryan Truth about the ceasing of suffering: verily it is the utter passionless cessation of, the giving up, the forsaking, the release from, the absence of longing for, this craving.   Samyutta Nikaya

O you who believe! Fasting is prescribed to you as it was to those before you, that you may learn self-restraint.
Quran 2:183

Fear Allah, and know that Allah is with those who restrain themselves.   Quran 2:194

No soul shall have a load laid on it harder than it can bear.
Quran 2:233

Eat of the good things We have provided for your sustenance, but commit no excess therein, lest My Wrath should justly descend on you: and those on whom descends My Wrath, do perish indeed.
Quran 20:81

Do you see such a one who takes for his god his own passion or impulse? Could you be a disposer of affairs for him? Or do you think that most of them listen or understand?   Quran 25:43-44

But if they hearken not to you, know that they only follow their own lusts: and who is more astray than one who follows his own lusts, devoid of guidance from Allah? For Allah does not guide people given to wrong-doing.   Quran 28:50

He who lives looking for pleasures only, his senses uncontrolled, immoderate in his food, idle, and weak, Mara will certainly overthrow him, as the wind throws down a weak tree.
Dhammapada

As rain breaks through an ill-thatched house, passion will break through a vigilant mind.   Dhammapada

There is no satisfying lusts, even by a shower of gold pieces; he who knows that lusts have a short taste and cause pain, he is wise; even in heavenly pleasures he finds no satisfaction; the disciple who is fully awakened delights only in the destruction of all desires.
Dhammapada

Some people have wings but run after what they can see, what is far from truth. For the fire that leads them will give an illusion of truth, and will shine on then with transitory beauty. It will make them prisoners of the delights of darkness, and capture them in sweet-smelling pleasures. It will make them blind with unquenchable passion, it will inflame their souls, and be like a stake that is jammed into their hearts and can never be removed. Or like a bit in the mouth, it directs them as it wishes.   Book of Thomas 4:5-9

Woe to you who hope in the flesh, and in the prison that will perish! How long will you sleep? Or do you think that what you judge to be imperishable will not perish? You base your hope upon the world, and your god is this life. You are destroying your souls! (...) Your minds are deranged because of the smoldering fire within you, and you are delighted by the poisoning and beating by your enemies! Darkness has risen over you like the light, for you have exchanged your freedom for slavery.
Book of Thomas 7:2-4, 13-14

One who lives looking for pleasures only- uncontrolled sensually, immoderate in diet, idle, weak- this one Mara will surely overthrow, as the wind blows down a feeble tree. One who does not live looking for pleasures only- well controlled sensually, moderate in diet, diligent, and strong- this one Mara will surely not overthrow, any more than the wind blows down a mountain of stone.   Dhammapada

But the people whose whole watchfulness is always on guard against the evils of the body, who do not do what ought not to be done, and who consistently do what ought to be done- the harmful desires of such vigilant and wise people will come to an end.
Dhammapada

As a cut down tree grows up again so long as its main root is sound and firm, even so will pain return again and again if your proneness to thirst is not destroyed.   Dhammapada

When all desires that cling to the heart are surrendered, then a mortal becomes immortal, and even in this world he is one with Brahman. When all the ties that bind the heart are unloosened, then a mortal becomes immortal. This is the sacred teaching.
                                          Katha Upanishad

The senses harass the calmness of even the wisest men who strive for discernment and yoga. But the steadfast man thinks of me and commands his desire. His mind is stable because his desires are subdued, for if one's senses are under control, then one's mentality is settled naturally into the Self. Thinking about the pleasures of the senses breeds attraction: from attachment arises covetousness, the lust of possession, and this leads to a passion which will not fill our true desire; frustration leads to anger. Anger leads to confusion and confusion kills discrimination, reason and remembrance of what we have learned from past mistakes; discrimination gone, rational choice is rendered impossible; and when moral choice fails, man comes to utter ruin. But a person who moves in the world of the senses and yet keeps the senses in harmony, free from desire for pleasure and free from aversion, such a person finds tranquility. When calmness comes, sorrow goes; a person whose wisdom is tranquil is truly stable. The wavering person does not grow. Without growth there is no peace; without peace, there is no bliss. The mind is swayed by the senses; they destroy discrimination, as a storm drives boats off course and sinks them into the depths of the ocean. Only that man can be described as peaceful whose mind rests in the purity of the Atman.   Bhagavad Gita 2:60-68

He who abstains from actions, but thinks about their pleasures in his heart is a hypocrite and false follower of the Path in delusion who does not know the Way.   Bhagavad Gita 3:6

When the senses and mind contact objects, a person experiences cold and heat, pleasure and pain. These experiences are fleeting; they come and go and have no real reality. Bear them patiently, Arjuna. Those who are not distracted by these changes, who are steady in pleasure and pain, achieve serenity and are truly wise and fit for Eternity. Assert your strength and realize this! The impermanent has no reality; reality lies in the eternal. Those who have seen the boundary between these two have attained the end of all knowledge. Realize the Spirit which pervades the universe and is indestructibly interwoven in creation; no power can affect this unchanging, imperishable reality. The body is mortal, but he who dwells in the body is immortal and immeasurable.
Bhagavad Gita 2:14-18

The senses have been conditioned by attraction to the pleasant and aversion and disgust to the unpleasant. Do not be ruled by them; they are stumbling blocks in your path.
Bhagavad Gita 3:34

Pleasures conceived in the world of the senses have a beginning and an end and give birth to restlessness and misery, Arjuna. The wise do not look for fulfillment in them. But those who overcome the impulses of lust and anger which arise in the body are made whole and live in joy in the inner light of Brahman.   Bhagavad Gita 5:22-23

He who loves silver will not be satisfied with silver; nor he who loves abundance, with increase. This also is vanity.
Ecclesiastes 5:10

They will throw their silver into the streets, and their gold will be like refuse; their silver and their gold will not be able to deliver them in the day of the wrath of the Lord; they will not satisfy their souls, nor fill their stomachs, because it became their stumbling block of iniquity.   Ezekiel 7:19

You have heard that it was said to those of old, "You shall not commit adultery."' But I say to you that whoever looks at a woman with lust has already committed adultery with her in his heart.   Matthew 5:27-28

And one out of the multitude said unto him, Teacher, bid my brother divide the inheritance with me. But he said unto him, Man, who made me a judge or a divider over you? And he said unto them, Take heed, and keep yourselves from all covetousness: for a man's life consists not in the abundance of the things which he possesses. And he spoke a parable to them, saying, the ground of a certain rich man brought forth plentifully: and he reasoned within himself, saying, "What shall I do, because I have not where to put my fruits? And he said, This will I do: I will pull down my barns, and build greater; and there will I bestow all my grain and my goods. And I will say to my soul, Soul, thou hast much goods laid up for many years; take your ease, eat, drink, be merry. " But God said unto him, You foolish one, this night is your soul required of you; and the things which you have prepared, whose shall they be? So is he that lays up treasure for himself, and is not rich toward God
.Luke 12:13-21

Do not lay up for yourselves treasures on earth, where moth and rust destroy and where thieves break in and steal; but lay up for yourselves treasures in heaven, where neither moth nor rust destroys and where thieves do not break in and steal. For where your treasure is, there your heart will be also. (...) No one can serve two masters; for either he will hate the one and love the other, or else he will be loyal to the one and despise the other. You cannot serve God and mammon. Therefore, I say to you, do not worry about your life, what you will eat or what you will drink; nor about your body, what you will put on. Is not life more than food and the body more than clothing? Look at the birds of the air, for they neither sow nor reap nor gather into barns; yet your heavenly Father feeds them. Are you not of more value than they? Which of you could add one cubit to his stature by worrying? So why worry about clothing? Consider the lilies of the field, how they grow: they neither toil nor spin; and yet I say to you that even Solomon in all his glory was not arrayed like one of these. Now if God so clothes the grass of the field, which today is, and tomorrow is thrown into the oven, will He not much more clothe you, O you of little faith? Therefore, do not worry, saying, "What shall we eat?" or "what shall we drink?" or "what shall we wear?"'. For all these things the Gentiles seek. For your heavenly Father knows that you need all these things. But seek ye first the kingdom of God and His righteousness, and all these things shall be added to you. Therefore, do not worry about tomorrow, for tomorrow will worry about its own things. Sufficient for the day is its own trouble.   Matthew 6:19-34

He compares his body to a corpse and thinking that this body is the same as a corpse and a corpse the same as this body, he removes desire from his body.   Vijaya Sutta, Sutta Nipata

He who entangles himself with the passions while trying to overcome them is like a man who tries to put out a fire with straw.
St. Mark the Ascetic

Kill not your hearts with excess of eating and drinking. Torment not ourselves, lest God should punish you.
Hadith of the Prophet Mohammad

Sin itself drives us towards God, once we repent and have become aware of its burden, foul stink and lunacy. But if we refuse to repent sin does not drive us towards God. In itself it holds us fast with bonds that we cannot break, making the desires which drive us to our destruction all the more vehement and fierce.
St John of Karpathos

Do not let the Sun go down upon your anger: and do not make room for the devil' (Eph 4:26-27), by which Paul means: Do not make Christ, the Sun of righteousness, set in your heart by angering him through your assent to evil thoughts, thereby allowing the devil to find room in you because of Christ's departure. God has spoken of this Sun in the words of His prophet: 'But upon you that fear My name shall the Sun of righteousness arise with healing in His wings' (Mal 4:2). (...) The Gospel teaches us to cut off the roots of sin and not merely their fruits. When we have dug the roots of anger out of our heart, we will no longer act with hatred or envy. Whoever hates his brother is a murderer' (1 John 3:15).   *St. John Cassian*

He who is ignorant of the enemy's ambush is easily slain; and he who does not know the causes of the passions is soon brought low.   *St. Mark the Ascetic*

Reality of Deeds Done: Karma

Those who seek gain in Evil, and are girt round by their sins, they are Companions of the Fire: therein shall they abide (forever).
Quran 2:81

And be steadfast in prayer and regular in charity: and whatever good you send forth for your souls before you, you shall find it with Allah: for Allah sees well all that you do.
Quran 2:110

On the day when every soul shall be confronted with all of the good it has done, and all the evil it has done, it will wish there were a great distance between it and its evil. But Allah cautions you to remember Himself. And Allah is full of kindness to those who serve Him. Quran 3:30

Allah has heard the taunt of those who say: "Truly Allah is indigent and we are rich!"- We shall certainly record their word and (their act) of slaying the Prophets in defiance of right, and We shall say: "You taste the penalty of the Scorching Fire! This is because of the unrighteous deeds which your hands sent on before you: for Allah never harms those who serve Him.""
Quran 3:182

How then when they are seized by misfortune, because of the deeds which their hands sent forth? Then they come to you, swearing by Allah: We meant no more than good-will and conciliation!" Quran 4:62

If you could see when they are confronted with the Fire! They will say: "Would that we were but sent back! Then we would not reject the Signs of the Lord, but would be amongst those who believe!" Yes, in their own eyes will become manifest what they concealed before. But if they were returned, they would certainly relapse to the things they were forbidden, for they are indeed liars.   Quran 6:27-28

And say: "Work righteousness; soon will Allah observe your work, and His Messenger, and the Believers: soon will you be brought back to the Knower of what is hidden and what is open: then will He show you the truth of all that you did.""
Quran 9:105

On that Day Allah will pay them back all their just dues, and they will realize that Allah is the very Truth, that makes all things manifest.   Quran 23:25

But the Unbelievers- their deeds are like a mirage in sandy deserts, which the man parched with thirst mistakes for water; until when he comes up to it, he finds it to be nothing: but he finds Allah ever with him, and Allah will pay him his account: and Allah is swift in taking account.   Quran 24:39

Even if the wrongdoers had all that there is on earth and as much more, in vain would they offer it for ransom from the pain of the Penalty on the Day of Judgment: but something will confront them from Allah, which they could never have counted upon. For the evils of their deeds will confront them, and they will be completely encircled by that which they used to mock at!
Quran 39:47-48

He that works evil will not be requited but by the like thereof: and he that works a righteous deed- whether man or woman- and is a Believer- such will enter the Garden of Bliss: therein will they have abundance without measure.
Quran 40:40

Whatever misfortune happens to you, is because of the things your hands have wrought, and for many of them He grants forgiveness.   Quran 42:30

O you who believe! Fear Allah, and let every soul look to what provision he has sent forth for the morrow.   Quran 59:18

(On the heart of the transgressor) is the stain of the ill which they do! Verily, from the Light of their Lord, that Day, will they be veiled.   Quran 83:14-15

Fools of poor understanding have themselves for their greatest enemies, for they do evil deeds which bear bitter fruits. As long as the evil deed does not bear fruit, the fool thinks it is like honey; but when it ripens, then the fool suffers grief. An evil deed does not begin to smolder right away like newly drawn milk. Instead, smoldering like fire covered with ashes, if follows the fool.   Dhammapada

All we are is the result of what we have thought: it is founded on our thoughts, it is made up of our thoughts. If a man speaks or acts with an evil thought, pain follows him, as the wheel follows the foot of an ox that draws the carriage.   Dhammapada

The Master said, "In his errors a man is true to type. Observe the errors and you will know the man."
                                        Analects, Book 4:7

Every departure from the Tao contaminates one's spirit. Anger is a departure, resistance is a departure, self-absorption a departure. Over many lifetimes the burden of contaminations can become great. There is only one way to cleanse oneself of these contaminations, and that is to practice virtue. What is meant by this? To practice virtue is to selflessly offer assistance to others, giving without limitation one's time, abilities, and possessions in service, whenever and wherever needed, without prejudice concerning the identity of those in need. If your willingness to give blessings is limited, so also is your ability to receive them. This is the subtle operation of the Tao.   Hua Hu Ching 4

     A superior person cares for the well-being of all things. She does this by accepting responsibility for the energy she manifests, both actively and in the subtle realm.   Hua Hu Ching 37

     The natural laws of the universe are inviolable: energy condenses into substance. Food is eaten through the mouth and not the nose. A person who neglects to breathe will turn blue and die. Some things simply can't be dismissed. It is also a part of the cosmic law that what you say and do determines what happens in your life. The ordinary person thinks that this law is external to himself and he feels confined and controlled by it. So his desires trouble his mind, his mind troubles his spirit, and he lives in constant turmoil with himself and the world. His whole life is spent in struggling. The superior person recognizes that he and the subtle law are one. Therefore, he cultivates himself to accord with it, bringing moderation to his actions and clarity to his mind. Doing this, he finds himself at one with all that is divine and enlightened. His days are passed drinking in serenity and breathing out contentment. This is the profound, simple truth: you are the master of your life and death. What you do is what you are.
                              Hua Hu Ching 40

     The teacher cannot aid the student as long as the student's spirit is contaminated. The cleansing of the spiritual contamination is not the responsibility of the teacher, but of the student. It is accomplished by offering one's talent, resources, and life to the world.   Hua Hu Ching 73

     Fools with little understanding are their own greatest enemies for they do evil deeds which must bear bitter fruits.
                              Dhammapada

An evil deed does not begin to sour right away like newly drawn milk. Instead, smoldering like fire covered with ashes, it follows the fool.   Dhammapada

Mischief has appeared on land and sea because of the mead that the hands of men have earned, that Allah may give them a taste of some of their deeds: in order that they may turn back from Evil.
Quran 30:41

The border guard at Chang Wu said to Lao Tzu, "The ruler of a state must not be careless, nor should he be careless with the people. Previously when ploughing my fields, I was careless, and the result was a poor crop. When weeding, I was thoughtless, and the result was a diminished harvest. In recent years I changed my ways, I ploughed deep and was careful to bury the seed. My harvests are now plentiful and therefore I have all I need all year round." Chuang Tzu heard this and said, "People today, when looking after themselves and caring for their hearts, are very much like this border guard's description. They ignore Heaven, wander from their innate nature, dissolve their real being, extinguish their spirit and follow the common herd. So it is that someone who is careless with their innate nature causes evil and hatred to arise, affecting their innate nature like rank weeds and bushes. These weeds and bushes, when they first appear, seem helpful and supportive, but slowly they affect the innate nature. They become like a mass of suppurating sores which break out in scabs and ulcers, oozing puss from this disease. This is how it is."
Chuang Tzu

The Buddha replied, "Trust is the seed and composure the rain. Clarity is my plow and yoke, conscience my guide-pole and my mind is the harness. Wakefulness is my plow-blade and my goad. Well-guarded in action and in speech, and moderate in food, I use truth to weed and cultivate release. True effort is my oxen, drawing the plow steadily toward

Nirvana, freedom without regret. This is how I plow; it bears the deathless as its fruit. Whoever plows in this way, will become free of all sorrow and distress."   Samyutta Nikaya

The evil done by one's self, born of one's self, suckled by one's self, crushes the foolish including oneself, even as a diamond cuts a stone. Even as a creeping vine overcomes a tree, so the deeds of evildoers pull them down to a state their enemies would wish for them. (...) One whose evil deeds are covered by good deeds brightens up this world, like the moon when freed from the clouds.
Dhammapada

Only the actions done in God bind not the soul of man. There are demon-haunted worlds, regions of utter darkness. Whoever in life denies the Spirit falls into that darkness.   Isa Upanishad

According as a man acts and walks in the path of life, so he becomes. He that does good becomes good; he that does evil becomes evil. By pure actions he becomes pure; by evil actions he becomes evil. And they say in truth that a man is made of desire. As his desire is, so is his faith. As his faith is, so are his works. As his works are, so he becomes. It was said in this verse: a man comes with his actions to the end of his determination.
The Supreme Teaching

O son of noble family, at this time the great tornado of karma, terrifying, unbearable, whirling fiercely, will drive you from behind. Do not be afraid of it; it is your own confused projection. Dense darkness, terrifying and unbearable, will go before you, with terrible cries of "Strike!" and "Kill!" Do not be afraid of them. In the case of others who have done great evil, many flesh-eating demons will appear as a result of their karma, bearing various weapons, yelling war cries, shouting, Kill! Strike! and so on.
Tibetan Book of the Dead

What we are today comes from our thoughts of yesterday, and our present thoughts build our life of tomorrow: our life is the creation of our mind.   Dhammapada

Hold not a sin of little worth, thinking "this is little to me". The falling of drops of water will in time fill a water-jar. Even so the foolish man becomes full of evil, although he gathers it little by little. Hold not a deed of little worth, thinking "this is little to me". The falling drops of water will in time fill a water-jar. Even so the wise man becomes full of good, although he gathers it little by little.
     Dhammapada

When a fool does evil work, he forgets that he is lighting a fire wherein he must burn one day.   Dhammapada

He who overcomes the evil he has done with the good he afterwards does, he sheds a light over the world like that of the moon when free from clouds.   Dhammapada

The whole world is bound by action and all actions are traps except those done with purity of intention and freedom of attachment to results.   Bhagavad Gita 3:9

Offer all your works to God, throw off selfish bonds, and do your work in un-attachment: No sin can then stain thee, even as waters do not stain the leaf of the lotus.
     Bhagavad Gita 5:10

When work is done for a reward, the work brings pleasure, or pain, or both, in its time and it bears mixed fruit after death; but when a man does work in Eternity beyond the reach of karma, then Eternity is his reward. (...) When work is done as sacred work, unselfishly, with a peaceful mind, without lust or hate, with no desire for reward, then the work is pure.
     Bhagavad Gita 18:12,23

Remember now, whoever perished being innocent? Or where were the upright ever cut off? Even as I have seen, those who plow iniquity and sow trouble reap the same.   Job 4:7-8

Far be it from God to do wickedness, and from the Almighty to commit iniquity. For he repays man according to his work, and makes man to find a reward according to his way. Surely God will never do wickedly, nor will the Almighty pervert justice.
Job 34:10-12

Behold, the wicked brings forth iniquity; yes, he conceives trouble and brings forth falsehood. He made a pit and dug it out, and has fallen into the ditch which he made. His own trouble shall return upon his own head, and his violent dealing will come down on his own crown.   Psalms 7:14-16

The Lord rewarded me according to my righteousness: according to the cleanness of my hands he has recompensed me. For I have kept the ways of the Lord, and have not wickedly departed from my God. For all His judgments were before m, and I did not put away His statutes from me. I was also blameless before Him, and I kept myself from iniquity. Therefore, the Lord has recompensed me according to my righteousness, according to the cleanness of my hands in His sight. With the merciful You will show Yourself merciful; with a blameless man You will show Yourself blameless; with the pure You will show Yourself pure; and with the devious You will show Yourself shrewd. For You will save the humble people, but will bring down haughty looks. For You will light my lamp; the Lord my God will enlighten my darkness.
Psalms 18:20-27

Come, you children, listen to me; I will teach you the fear of the Lord. Who is the man who desires life, and loves many days, that he may see good? Keep your tongue from evil, and your lips from speaking deceit. Depart from evil and do good; seek peace and pursue it.   Psalms 34:11-14

How can a young man cleanse his way? By taking heed according to Your word. With my whole heart I have sought You; oh, let me not wander from Your commandments! Your word I have hidden in my heart, that I might not sin against You. Blessed are You, oh Lord.   Psalms 119:9-12

The integrity of the upright will guide them. (...) The righteousness of the blameless will direct his way aright.
Proverbs 11:3, 5

Commit your works to the Lord, and your thoughts will be established.   Proverbs 16:3

Whoever shuts his ears to the cry of the poor will also cry himself and not be heard.   Proverbs 21:13

Because the sentence against an evil work is not executed speedily, therefore the heart of the sons of men is fully set in them to do evil.   Ecclesiastes 8:11

Dead flies putrefy the perfumer's ointment, and cause it to give off a foul odor; so does a little folly to one respected for wisdom and honor.   Ecclesiastes 10:1

Rejoice, O young man, in your youth, and let your heart cheer you in the days of your youth; walk in the ways of your heart, and in the sight of your eyes; but know that for all these God will bring you into judgment. Therefore, remove sorrow from your heart, and put away evil from your flesh, for childhood and youth are vanity. (...) Fear God and keep His commandments, for this is man's all. For God will bring every work into judgment, including every secret thing, whether good or evil.   Ecclesiastes 11:9-10, 12:13-14

Wash yourselves, make yourselves clean; put away the evil of your doings from before My eyes. Cease to do evil, learn to do good; seek justice, rebuke the oppressor; defend the fatherless, plead for the widow. Come now and let us reason together. Though your sins are like scarlet, they shall be as white as snow; though they are red like crimson, they shall be as wool. If you are willing and obedient, you shall eat the good of the land; but if you refuse and rebel, you shall be devoured by the sword; for the mouth of the Lord has spoken.   Isaiah 1:16-20

Say to the righteous that it shall be well with them, for they shall eat the fruit of their doings. Woe to the wicked! It shall be ill with him, for the reward of his hands shall be given to him.
Isaiah 3:10-11

The earth mourns and fades away, the world languishes and fades away; the haughty people of the earth languish. The earth is also defiled under its inhabitants, because they have transgressed the laws, changed the ordinance, broken the everlasting covenant. Therefore, the curse has devoured the earth, and those who dwell in it are desolate. Therefore, the inhabitants of the earth are burned, and few men are left.   Isaiah 24:4-6

Behold, the Lord's hand is not shortened, that it cannot save; nor His ear heavy, that it cannot hear. But your iniquities have separated you from your God; and your sins have hidden His face from you.   Isaiah 59:1-2

You have polluted the land with your harlotries and your wickedness. Therefore, the showers have been withheld. (...) If you will return, O Israel, return to Me; and if you will put away your abominations from My sight, then you shall not be moved. And you shall swear, "The Lord lives", In truth, in judgment, and in righteousness; the nations shall bless themselves in Him, and in Him they shall glory. Break up your fallow ground, and do not sow among thorns. Circumcise yourselves to the Lord, and take away the foreskins of your hearts, you men of Judah and inhabitants of Jerusalem, lest my fury come forth like fire, and burn so that no one can quench it, because of the evil of your doings. (...) O Jerusalem, wash your heart from wickedness, that you may be saved. How long shall your evil thoughts lodge within you? (...) Your iniquities have turned these things away, and your sins have withheld good from you.   Jeremiah 3:2-3, 4:1-4,14, 5:25

In those days they shall say no more: "The fathers have eaten sour grapes, and the children's teeth are set on edge." But everyone shall die for his own iniquity; every man who eats the sour grapes, his teeth shall be set on edge.   Jeremiah 31:29-30

I will judge you according to your ways, and I will repay you for all your abominations.   Ezekiel 7:3

The word of the Lord came again to me, saying: "Son of man, when a land sins against Me by persistent unfaithfulness, I will stretch out My hand against it; I will cut off its supply of bread, send famine on it, and cut off man and beast from it."   Ezekiel 14:12

The word of the Lord came to me again, saying, What do you mean when you use this proverb concerning the land of Israel, saying: "The fathers have eaten sour grapes, and the children's teeth are set on edge? "As I live, says the Lord God, you shall no longer use this proverb in Israel. Behold, all souls are Mine; the soul of the father as well as the soul of the son is Mine; the soul who sins shall die. But if a man is just and does what is lawful and right; if he has not eaten on the mountains, nor lifted his eyes to the idols of the house of Israel, nor defiled his neighbor's wife, nor approached a woman during her impurity; if he has not oppressed anyone, but has given his bread to the hungry and covered the naked with clothing; if he has not exacted usury nor taken increase, but has withdrawn his hand from iniquity and executed true judgment between man and man; if he has walked in My statutes and kept My judgments faithfully- He is just; he shall surely live! Says the Lord God. (...) The soul who sins shall die. The son shall not bear the guilt of the father, nor the father bear the guilt of the son. The righteousness of the righteous shall be upon himself, and the wickedness of the wicked shall be upon himself. (...) Therefore I will judge you, O house of Israel, every one according to his ways, says the Lord God. Repent, and turn from all your transgressions, so that iniquity will not be your ruin. Cast away from you all the transgressions which you have committed, and get yourselves a new heart and a new spirit. For why should you die, O house of Israel? For I have no pleasure in the death of one who dies, says the Lord God. Therefore, turn and live!   Ezekiel 18:1-9,20,30-32

    Sow for yourselves righteousness; reap in mercy; break up your fallow ground, for it is time to seek the Lord, till He comes and rains righteousness on you. You have plowed wickedness; you have reaped iniquity. You have eaten the fruit of your lies, because you trusted in your own way.   Hosea 10:12-13

    As you have done it, it shall be done to you; your reprisal shall return upon your own head.   Obadiah 1:15

    Every tree which does not bear good fruit is cut down and thrown into the fire. I indeed baptize you with water unto repentance, but He who is coming after me is mightier than I, whose sandals I am not worthy to carry. He will baptize you with the Holy Spirit and fire. His winnowing fan is in His hand, and He will thoroughly clean out His threshing floor; and gather His wheat into the barn; but He will burn up the chaff with unquenchable fire. (...) For there is no good tree that brings forth corrupt fruit; nor again a corrupt tree that brings forth good fruit. For each tree is known by its own fruit. For of thorns men do not gather figs, nor of a bramble bush gather they grapes. The good man out of the good treasure of his heart brings forth that which is good; and the evil [man] out of the evil [treasure] brings forth that which is evil: for out of the abundance of the heart his mouth speaks.
                            Matthew 3:10-12, Luke 6:43-45

    Beware of false prophets, who come to you in sheep's clothing, for inwardly they are ravenous wolves. You will know them by their fruits. Do men gather grapes from thorn bushes or figs from thistles? Even so, every good tree bears good fruit, but a bad

tree bears bad fruit. A good tree cannot bear bad fruit, nor can a bad tree bear good fruit. Every tree that does not bear good fruit is cut down and thrown into the fire. Therefore, by their fruits you will know them. (...) Either make the tree good and its fruit good, or else make the tree bad and its fruit bad; for a tree is known by its fruit. Brood of vipers! How can you, being evil, speak good things? For out of the abundance of the heart the mouth speaks. A good man out of the good treasure of his heart brings forth good things, and an evil man out of the evil treasure brings forth evil things. But I say to you that for every idle word men may speak, they will give account of it in the day of judgment. For by your words you will be justified, and by your words you will be condemned.
Matthew 7:15-20, 12:33-37

A brahmin seeking the Buddha said: "O recluse, I plough and sow, and having plowed and sown, I eat. You also, recluse, should plough and sow; and having plowed and sown, you should eat." "I too, brahmin, plough and sow; and having plowed and sown, I eat." "You claim to be a farmer, yet we do not see your ploughing." "Confidence is the seed; self-control the rein; wisdom my yoke and plough; modesty is my pole; mind is my rope; mindfulness is my ploughshare and goad. Bodily action is well-guarded, speech is well-guarded, moderate in food, I make the truth the destroyer of weeds and calm my release. Exertion is my yoked oxen which carries me towards Nirvana. It goes onward without stopping; having gone there one has no regrets. In this way the ploughing is done; it bears the fruit of immortality.
Kasibharadvaja Sutta, Sutta Nipata

Whoever is angry, harbors ill-will, is evil-minded and envious; whose views are delusive, who is deceitful, he is known to be an outcast. Whoever destroys life, whether bird or animal, insect or fish, has no compassion for life (...) Whoever commits perjury either for his own benefit or others (...). Whoever having committed an offense wishes to conceal it from other and is a hypocrite (...). Whoever exalts himself and despises others, smug in his self-conceit (...) Whoever is a provoker of quarrels or is avaricious, has

malicious desires, is envious, shameless, and has no qualms in committing evil (...). One does not become an outcast by birth, one does not become a brahmin by birth. It is by deed that one becomes an outcast, it is by deed that one becomes a brahmin.
         Vasala Sutta, Sutta Nipata

You are spreading pollution when you act like this. It is an insult to men who do good, and it is a polluted action in itself. If you accumulate actions like this, you will fall into the pool of misery states. Why is this? It is because the things that men do just do not disappear into the past. They will come back to us; they will return to their maker. Kokalika Sutta, Sutta Nipata

Here on earth he who gives, spoiling his gift for the sake of heaven or on account of fear, for fame, or for comfort, reaps spoiled fruit. Whoever gives something for the good of others, with heart full of sympathy, not heeding his own good, reaps unspoiled fruit. (...) Every fruit corresponds to the deeds. Pancagatidipani

And as they were eating, Jesus took bread, and blessed, and brake it; and he gave to the disciples, and said, Take, eat; this is my body. And he took a cup, and gave thanks, and gave to them, saying, Drink you all of it; for this is my blood of the covenant, which is poured out for many unto remission of sins. But I say unto you, I shall not drink henceforth of this fruit of the vine, until that day when I drink it new with you in my Father's kingdom.
         Matthew 26:26-29

Iniquities prevail against me: As for our transgressions, You will forgive them. Psalm 65:3

Who knows the spirit of man, whether it goes upward, and the spirit of the beast, whether it goes downward to the earth? Wherefore I saw that there is nothing better, than that a man should rejoice in his works; for that is his portion: for who shall bring him [back] to see what shall be after him? (...) Rejoice, O young man, in your youth, and let your heart cheer you in the days of your youth,

and walk in the ways of your heart, and in the sight of your eyes; but
know that for all these things God will bring you into judgment.
Therefore, remove sorrow from your heart, and put away evil from
your flesh; for youth and the dawn of life are vanity. (...) Remember
also your Creator in the days of youth, before the evil days come, and
the years draw nigh, when you will say, I have no pleasure in them;
before the sun, and the light, and the moon, and the stars, are
darkened, and the clouds return after the rain; in the day when the
keepers of the house shall tremble, and the strong men shall bow
themselves, and the grinders cease because they are few, and those
that look out of the windows shall be darkened, and the doors shall
be shut in the street; when the sound of the grinding is low, and one
shall rise up at the voice of a bird, and all the daughters of music
shall be brought low; yea, they shall be afraid of [that which is] high,
and terrors [shall be] in the way; and the almond-tree shall blossom,
and the grasshopper shall be a burden, and desire shall fail; because
man goes to his everlasting home, and the mourners go about the
streets: before the silver cord is loosed, or the golden bowl is broken,
or the pitcher is broken at the fountain, or the wheel broken at the
cistern, and the dust returns to the earth as it was, and the spirit
returns unto God who gave it. Vanity of vanities, says the Preacher;
all is vanity. And further, because the Preacher was wise, he still
taught the people knowledge; yea, he pondered, and sought out, [and]
set in order many proverbs. The Preacher sought to find out
acceptable words, and that which was written uprightly, [even] words
of truth. The words of the wise are as goads; and as nails well
fastened are [the words of] the masters of assemblies, [which] are
given from one shepherd. And furthermore, my son, be admonished:
of making many books there is no end; and much study is a
weariness of the flesh. [This is] the end of the matter; all has been
heard: fear God, and keep his commandments; for this is the whole
[duty] of man. For God will bring every work into judgment, with
every hidden thing, whether it be good, or whether it be evil.
Ecclesiastes 3:21-22, 11:9-10, 12:1-14

And he came into all the region round about the Jordan,
preaching the baptism of repentance unto remission of sins; as it is
written in the book of the words of Isaiah the prophet, The voice
of one crying in the wilderness, Make ready the way of the Lord,
Make his paths straight. Every valley shall be filled, And every
mountain and hill shall be brought low; And the crooked shall
become straight, And the rough ways smooth; And all flesh shall
see the salvation of God. He said therefore to the multitudes that
went out to be baptized of him, You offspring of vipers, who

warned you to flee from the wrath to come? Bring forth therefore fruits worthy of repentance, and begin not to say within yourselves, We have Abraham for our father: for I say to you, that God is able of these stones to raise up children unto Abraham. And even now the axe also lies at the root of the trees: every tree therefore that brings not forth good fruit is hewn down, and cast into the fire. And the multitudes asked him, saying, What then must we do? And he answered and said unto them, He that has two coats, let him impart to him that has none; and he that has food, let him do likewise. And there came also publicans to be baptized, and they said unto him, Teacher, what must we do? And he said unto them, Extort no more than that which is appointed you. And soldiers also asked him, saying, And we, what must we do? And he said unto them, Extort from no man by violence, neither accuse [any one] wrongfully; and be content with your wages. And as the people were in expectation, and all men reasoned in their hearts concerning John, whether he were the Christ; John answered, saying unto them all, I indeed baptize you with water; but there comes he that is mightier than I, the latchet of whose shoes I am not worthy to unloose: he shall baptize you in the Holy Spirit and [in] fire: whose fan is in his hand, thoroughly to cleanse his threshing-floor, and to gather the wheat into his garner; but the chaff he will burn up with unquenchable fire.

Luke 3:3-17

And seeing their faith, he said, Man, your sins are forgiven you. And the scribes and the Pharisees began to reason, saying, Who is this that speaks blasphemies? Who can forgive sins, but God alone? But Jesus perceiving their reasonings, answered and said unto them, Why reason you in your hearts? Which is easier, to say, Your sins are forgiven you; or to say, Arise and walk? But that you may know that the Son of man has authority on earth to forgive sins (he said unto him that was palsied), I say unto you, Arise, and take up your couch, and go to your house.

Luke 5:20-24

For we are God's fellow-workers: you are God's husbandry, God's building. According to the grace of God which was given unto me, as a wise master builder. I laid a foundation; and another builds thereon. But let each man take heed how he builds thereon. For other foundation can no man lay than that which is laid, which is Jesus Christ. But if any man builds on the foundation gold, silver, costly stones, wood, hay, stubble; each man's work shall be made manifest: for the day shall declare it, because it is revealed in fire; and the fire itself shall prove each man's work of what sort it is. If any man's work shall abide which he built thereon, he shall receive a reward. If any man's work shall be burned, he shall suffer loss: but he himself shall be saved; yet so as through fire. Know you not that you are a temple of God, and [that] the Spirit of God dwells in you? If any man destroys the temple of God, him shall God destroy; for the temple of God is holy, and such are you. Let no man deceive himself. If any man thinks that he is wise among you in this world, let him become a fool, that he may become wise. For the wisdom of this world is foolishness with God. For it is written, He that takes the wise in their craftiness: and again, The Lord knows the reasonings of the wise that they are vain. Wherefore let no one glory in men. For all things are yours; whether Paul, or Apollos, or Cephas, or the world, or life, or death, or things present, or things to come; all are yours; and you are Christ's; and Christ is God's.
1 Corinthians 3:9-23

Who has believed our report? And to whom has the arm of the Lord been revealed? For He shall grow up before Him as a tender plant, and as a root out of dry ground. He has no form or comeliness; and when we see Him, there is no beauty that we should desire Him. He is despised and rejected by men. A Man of sorrows and acquainted with grief. And we hid, as it were, our faces from Him; he was despised, and we did not esteem Him. Surely He has born our griefs and carried our sorrows; yet we esteemed Him stricken, smitten by God, and afflicted. But He was wounded for our transgressions, he was bruised for our iniquities; the chastisement of our peace was upon Him, and by His stripes we are healed. All we like sheep have gone astray: we have turned, every one, to his own

way; and the Lord has laid on Him the iniquity of us all. He was oppressed and He was afflicted. Yet He opened not His mouth; He was led as a lamb to the slaughter, and as a sheep before its shearers is silent, so He opened not His mouth. He was taken from prison and from judgment, and who will declare His generation? For He was cut off from the land of the living: for the transgressions of My people He was stricken. And they made His grave with the wicked- but with the rich at His death, because He had done no violence, nor was there any deceit in His mouth. Yet it pleased the Lord to bruise Him; He has put Him in grief. When You make His soul an offering for sin, He shall see His seed, He shall prolong His days, and the pleasure of the Lord shall prosper in His hand. He shall see the labor of His soul, and be satisfied. By His knowledge My righteous Servant shall justify many, for He shall bear their iniquities. Therefore, I will divide Him a portion with the great, and He shall divide the spoil with the strong, because He poured out His soul unto death, and He was numbered with the transgressors, and He bore the sin of many, and made intercession for the transgressors.
                                                                    Isaiah 53

For I received of the Lord that which also I delivered unto you, that the Lord Jesus in the night in which he was betrayed took bread; and when he had given thanks, he brake it, and said, This is my body, which is for you: this do in remembrance of me. In like manner also the cup, after supper, saying, This cup is the new covenant in my blood: this do, as often as you drink, in remembrance of me.   1st Corinthians 11:23-25

Wherefore also we make it our aim, whether at home or absent, to be well-pleasing unto him. For we must all be made manifest before the judgment-seat of Christ; that each one may receive the things [done] in the body, according to what he has done, whether [it be] good or bad. Knowing therefore the fear of the Lord, we persuade men, but we are made manifest unto God; and I hope that we are made manifest also in your consciences. (...) For the love of Christ constrains us; because we thus judge, that one died for all, therefore all died; and he died for all, that they that live should no longer live unto themselves, but unto him who for their sakes died and rose again. Wherefore we henceforth know no man after the flesh: even though we have known Christ after the flesh, yet now we know [him so] no more. Wherefore if any man is in Christ, [he is] a new creature: the old things are passed away; behold, they are become new. But all things are of God, who reconciled us to himself through Christ, and gave unto us the ministry of reconciliation; to wit, that God was in Christ reconciling the world unto himself, not reckoning unto them their trespasses, and having committed unto us the word of reconciliation. We are ambassadors therefore on behalf of Christ, as though God were entreating by us: we beseech [you] on behalf of Christ, be reconciled to God. Him who knew no sin he made [to be] sin on our behalf; that we might become the righteousness of God in him.   2nd Corinthians 5:9-11, 14-21

And this I pray, that your love may abound yet more and more in knowledge and all discernment; so that you may approve the things that are excellent; that you may be sincere and void of offence unto the day of Christ; being filled with the fruits of righteousness, which are through Jesus Christ, unto the glory and praise of God.Philippians 1:9-11

When our learning exceeds our deeds we are like trees whose branches are many but whose roots are few: the wind comes and uproots them... But when our deeds exceed our learning we are like trees whose branches are few but whose roots are many, so that even if all the winds of the world were to come and blow against them, they would be unable to move them.
                                        Talmud

A man came to the shopkeeper to buy a measure of wine. The shopkeeper said to him: Bring me your vessel. But the man opened his bag.... Said the shopkeeper to him: How can you buy wine ... if you have no vessel at hand? Similarly: God says to the wicked: You have no good deeds with you- how then do you wish to learn Torah?   Talmud

All that we are is a result of what we have thought: it is founded on our thoughts; it is made up of our thoughts. If a man speaks or acts with an evil thought, pain follows him, as the wheel follows the foot of the ox that draws the wagon. All that we are is a result of what we have thought: it is founded on our thoughts; it is made up of our thoughts. If a man speaks or acts with a pure thought, happiness follows him, like a shadow that never leaves him. Mindfulness is the way to the deathless, inattentiveness the way to death. Those who are diligently attentive do not die, those who are thoughtless are as if dead already. As a fletcher makes straight his arrow, a wise man makes straight his trembling and unsteady mind, which is difficult to guard, difficult to hold back. It is good to tame the mind, which is difficult to hold in and flighty, rushing; a tamed mind brings happiness.   *Buddha*

Everything has mind in the lead, has mind in the forefront, is made by mind. If one speaks or acts with a corrupt mind, misery will follow, as the wheel of a cart follows the foot of the ox. Everything has mind in the lead, mind in the forefront. If one speaks or acts with a pure mind, happiness will follow, like a shadow that never leaves. "He reviled me; he injured me; he defeated me; he deprived me." In those who harbor such grudges, hatred never ceases. "He reviled me; he injured me; he defeated me; he deprived me." In those who do not harbor such thoughts, hatred eventually ceases. Hatreds do not cease in this world by hating, but by not hating; this is an eternal truth.   Dhammapada

Man is made by his belief. As he believes it, so he is.
                              Dhammapada

It is mind which gives things their quality, their foundation and their being. Whoever speaks or acts with impure mind, him sorrow follows, as the wheel follows the steps of the ox that draws the cart.   Dhammapada

Why have you said, "I have sinned so much, and God in His mercy has not punished my sins"? How many times do I smite you, and you know not! You are bound in my chains from head to foot. On your heart is rust on rust collected so that you are blind to divine mysteries. When a man is stubborn and follows evil practices, he casts dust in the eyes of his discernment. Old shame for sin and calling on God quit him; dust five layers deep settles on his mirror, rust spots begin to gnaw his iron, the color of his jewel grows less and less.   *Jalal-uddin Rumi*

Of forgiveness be not overconfident, adding sin upon sin. Say not: "Great is his mercy; my many sins he will forgive." For mercy and anger alike are with him; upon the wicked alights his wrath. Delay not your conversion to the Lord, put it not off from day to day. Sirach *5:5-8*

Pride, Hypocrisy, and Vanity: Attachment

The Sufi Abu Hashim said: "It is easier to uproot a mountain with a needle than to expel base pride from the heart. Never preen yourself that you are prideless: for pride is more invisible than an ant's footprint on a black stone in the dark of night.

On the Day of Judgment the Lord shall ask the learned men, "What did you do with the knowledge and the learning I conferred on you?" They will reply, "We spent it in Your way." The Lord shall say, "You are liars." And the angels shall also repeat the same charge. The Lord shall further say, "You spent it in earning applause, in passing for learned men and seeking praise of the people." The Lord shall ask the rich men, "I gave you wealth. What did you do with it?" They will say, "We gifted the riches in Your way." Then the Lord and the angels will say, "You are liars, you spent it so that people may call you very charitable." Then the Lord shall summon those who gave away their lives in the Holy Wars. They will be asked, "How did you spend your life I gave you?" They will reply, "We sacrificed it in Your Path." The Lord and the angels will call them liars and say, "You gave away your lives that people might call you brave and style you martyrs."
El Ghazzali

The lower self likes praise. It continually enjoins a person to put on pretensions, so that people will compliment it. Indeed, there are many worshipers and ascetics who are thus controlled by the lower self. [...] One of the latent vices and secret maladies of the lower self is its love of praise. Whoever imbibes a draught of it will try and move the seven heavens and seven sublunar realms for the flutter of an eyelash.   *Qushayri*

The first duty is to behave with purity of intention. It should never be forgotten that every deed and every action is judged according to the intention behind it. Therefore, whatever the lover does, whatever action the lover performs, must be done for the sake of God. Actions performed with complete sincerity and for God's sake are accepted and approved. But deeds that are done to be seen others and to win their praise and love may be adulterated with hypocrisy. *Sheikh Muzaffer*

To be a sage one must disregard fame, one must refrain from haughtiness, pride and hypocrisy and not let others know of one's good deeds. One must not misuse the light of the lamp lit in honor of the one Reality.   Uddhava Gita *6:40*

One of the prominent Sufis of Central Asia was examining candidates who wanted to become his disciples. "Anyone," he said, "who wants entertainment, not learning, who wishes to argue, not study, who is impatient, who wants to take rather than give- should raise his hand." Nobody moved. "Very good" said the teacher, "now you will come and see some of my pupils, who have been with me for three years." He led them into the meditation-hall, where a row of people were sitting. Addressing them, he said: "Let those who wish to be entertained, not to learn, who are impatient and want to argue, the takers and not givers- let them stand up." The whole row of disciples got to their feet. The sage addressed the first group. "In your own eyes, you are better people now than you would be in three years time if you stayed here. Your present vanity helps you even to feel worthy. So reflect well, as you return to your homes, before coming here again at some future time if you wish, whether you want to feel better than you are or worse than the world thinks you to be."   *A Veiled Gazelle,*- Idries Shah

A nun who was searching for enlightenment made a statue of Buddha and covered it with gold leaf. Wherever she went she carried this golden Buddha with her. Years passed and, still carrying her Buddha, the nun went to live in a small temple in a country where there were many Buddhas, each one with its own particular shrine. The nun wished to burn incense before her golden Buddha. Not liking the idea of the perfume straying to the others, she devised a tunnel through which the smoke would ascend only to her statue. This blackened the nose of the golden Buddha, making it especially ugly.

O you who believe! Why do you say that which you do not? Grievously odious is it in the sight of Allah that you say that which you do not.   Quran 61:2-3

The pride of your heart has deceived you.   Obadiah 1:3

But what think you? A man had two sons; and he came to the first, and said, "Son, go work to-day in the vineyard." And he answered and said, "I will not": but afterward he repented himself, and went. And he came to the second, and said likewise. And he answered and said, "I [go], sir": and went not. Which of the two did the will of his father? They say, The first. Jesus said unto them, "Verily I say unto you, that the publicans and the harlots go into the kingdom of God before you. For John came unto you in the way of righteousness, and you believed him not; but the publicans and the harlots believed him: and you, when you saw it, did not even repent yourselves afterward, that you might believe him."
                                            Matthew 21:28-32

Then spoke Jesus to the multitudes and to his disciples, saying, The scribes and the Pharisees sit on Moses seat: all things therefore whatsoever they bid you, [these] do and observe: but do not after their works; for they say, and do not. Yea, they bind heavy burdens and grievous to be borne, and lay them on men's shoulders; but they themselves will not move them with their finger. But all their works they do to be seen of men: for they make broad their phylacteries, and enlarge the borders [of their garments], and love the chief place at feasts, and the chief seats in the synagogues, and the salutations in the marketplaces, and to be called of men, Rabbi. (...) Woe unto you, scribes and Pharisees, hypocrites! for you cleanse the outside of the cup and of the platter, but within are full from extortion and excess. You blind Pharisee, cleanse first the inside of the cup and of the platter, that the outside thereof may become clean also. Woe unto you, scribes and Pharisees, hypocrites! for you are like unto whited sepulchers, which outwardly appear beautiful, but inwardly are full of dead men's bones, and of all uncleanness. Even so you also outwardly appear righteous unto men, but inwardly you are full of hypocrisy and iniquity. Matthew 23:1-7, 25-28

And he spoke also this parable unto certain who trusted in themselves that they were righteous, and set all others at naught: Two men went up into the temple to pray; the one a Pharisee, and the other a publican. The Pharisee stood and prayed thus with himself, God, I thank thee, that I am not as the rest of men, extortioners, unjust, adulterers, or even as this publican. I fast twice in the week; I give tithes of all that I get. But the publican, standing afar off, would not lift up so much as his eyes unto heaven, but smote his breast, saying, God, be thou merciful to me a sinner. I say unto you, This man went down to his house justified rather than the other: for every one that exalteth himself shall be humbled; but he that humbles himself shall be exalted.   Luke 18:9-14

The vice of self-esteem, however, is difficult to fight against, because it has many forms and appears in all our activities- in our way of speaking, in what we say and in our silences, at work, in vigils and fasts, in prayer and reading, in stillness and long-suffering. Through all these it seeks to strike down the soldier of Christ. When it cannot seduce a man with extravagant clothes, it tries to tempt him with shabby ones. When it cannot flatter him with honor, it inflates him with enduring dishonor. When it cannot persuade him to feel proud because of his display of eloquence, it entices him through silence into thinking he has achieved stillness. When it cannot puff him up with the thought of his luxurious table, it lures him into fasting for the sake of praise. In short, every task, every activity, gives this malicious demon a chance for battle.

St. John Cassian

Self-justification is worse than the original offense.
Sheikh Ziaudin

The Master said, The gentleman is ashamed when the words he utters outstrips his deeds.   Analects, Book 14:27

Tzu-kung asked, "Is there a single word which can be a guide to conduct throughout one's life?" The Master said, "It is perhaps the word shu. Do not impose on others what you yourself do not desire." Analects, Book 15:24   *shu-* using oneself as a measure in gauging the wishes of others

Like a beautiful flower without scent are the fait but fruitless words of the one who speaks of virtue but does not act accordingly.
Dhammapada

Narrated Abi Waih: "Hudhaifa bin Al-Yaman said, 'The hypocrites of today are worse than those of the lifetime of the Prophet, because in those days they used to do evil deeds secretly but today they do such deeds openly.'"
Hadith of the Prophet Mohammad

Punishment and Tribulation

Mischief has appeared on land and sea because of the meed that the hands of men have earned, that Allah may give them a taste of some of their deeds: in order that they may turn back from Evil.   Quran 30:41

Do men think that they will be left alone on saying, "We believe", and that they will not be tested? We tested those before them, and Allah will certainly know those who are true from those who are false.   Quran 29:2-3

You should know in your heart that as a man chastens his son, so the Lord your God chastens you.   Deuteronomy 8:5

Behold, happy is the man whom God corrects; therefore, do not despise the chastening of the Almighty, for he bruises, but He binds up; he wounds but His hands make whole.   Job 5:17-18

He does not withdraw His eyes from the righteous; but they are on the throne with kings, for He has seated them forever, and they are exalted. And if they are bound in fetters, held in the cords of affliction, then He tells them their work and their transgressions- that they have acted defiantly. He also opens their ear to instruction, and commands that they turn from iniquity. If they obey and serve Him, they shall spend their days in prosperity, and their years in pleasures. But if they do not obey, they shall perish by the sword, and they shall die without knowledge. But the hypocrites in heart store up wrath; they do not cry for help when he binds them. They die in youth, and their life ends among the perverted persons. He delivers the poor in their affliction, and opens their ears in oppression. (...) Who teaches like Him?   Job 36:7-15, 22

For You, O God, have tested us; You have refined us as silver is refined. You brought us into the net; you laid affliction on our backs. You have caused men to ride over our heads; we went through the fire and through water; but You brought us out to rich fulfillment.   Psalms 67:10-12

Search me, O God, and know my heart; try me, and know my anxieties; and see if there is any wicked way in me, and lead me in the way everlasting.   Psalm 139:23-24

My son, do not despise the chastening of the Lord, nor detest His correction; for whom the Lord loves He corrects, just as a father the son in whom he delights. (...) Harsh discipline is for him who forsakes the way, and he who hates correction will die. (...) The ear that hears the rebuke of the life will abide among the wise. He who disdains instruction despises his own soul, but he who heeds rebuke gets understanding. The fear of the Lord is the instruction of wisdom, and before honor is humility.
Proverbs 3:11-12, 15:10, 31-33

He who is often rebuked, and hardens his neck, will suddenly be destroyed, and that without remedy.
Proverbs 29:1

The brood of evildoers shall never be named. Prepare slaughter for his children because of the iniquity of their fathers, lest they rise up and possess the land, and fill the face of the world with cities.   Isaiah 14:21

Your own wickedness will rebuke you. Know therefore and see that it is an evil and bitter thing that you have forsaken the Lord your God, and the fear of Me is not in you, says the Lord God of hosts.   Jeremiah 2:19

That slave who knew what his master wanted, but did not prepare himself or do what was wanted, will receive a severe beating. But the one who did not know and did what deserved a

beating will receive a light beating. From everyone to whom much has been given, much will be required; and from the one to whom much has been entrusted, even more will be demanded.
                             Luke 12: 47-48

For three transgressions of Israel, and for four, I will not turn away its punishment, because they sell the righteous for silver, and the poor for a pair of sandals. They trample on the dust of the earth which is on the head of the poor, and pervert the way of the humble.
                             Amos 2:6-7

My child, when you come to serve the Lord, prepare yourself for testing. Set your heart right and be steadfast and do not be impetuous in time of calamity. Accept whatever befalls you, and in times of humiliation be patient. For gold is tested in the fire, and those found acceptable, in the furnace of humiliation. Sirach 2:1-2

How can you criticize your brother's faults if your words create a rift between the two of you? You must realize that alienation of the heart only results from mentioning a fault already known to your brother. To draw his attention to what he is unaware of is compassion itself. Someone who draws your attention to an unpleasant habit, or a negative feature of your character, so that you can cleanse yourself of it is like one who warns you of a snake or scorpion under your robe- he has shown concern lest you perish. If you disapprove of that, how great is your folly.   *al-Ghazzali*

Why is it that in spite of your attraction to give yourself entirely to God, and your pious reading, you seem to remain always at the entrance of the interior life without the power of entering? I will tell you the reason, my dear sister, for I see it very distinctly; it is because you have misused this attraction by inordinate desires, by over-eagerness, and a natural activity, thus displeasing God, and stifling the gentle action of grace. Also, because in your conduct there has been a secret and imperceptible presumption which has

made you rely on your own industry and your own efforts. Without noticing it you have acted as if you aspired to do all the work by your own industry, and even to do more than God desired. You who would have taken yourself to task for any worldly ambition, have, without scruple, allowed yourself to be carried away by a still more subtle ambition, and by a desire for a high position in the spiritual life. But, be comforted; thanks to the merciful sternness of God's dealings with you, so far nothing is lost; on the contrary, you have gained greatly. God punishes you for these imperfections like a good father, with tenderness; and enables you to find a remedy for the evil in the chastisement he awards you.
John-Pierre de Caussade

For every one shall be salted with fire. Salt is good: but if the salt has lost its saltiness, wherewith will ye season it? Have salt in yourselves, and be at peace one with another.
Mark 9:49-50

And he said unto them, Go into all the world, and preach the gospel to the whole creation. He that believes and is baptized shall be saved; but he that disbelieves shall be condemned.
Mark 16:15

He spoke also this parable; A certain man had a fig tree planted in his vineyard; and he came and sought fruit thereon, and found none. Then said he to the dresser of his vineyard, Behold, these three years I come seeking fruit on this fig tree, and find none: cut it down; why encumbers it the ground? And he answering said to him, Lord, let it alone this year also, till I shall dig about it, and dung it: And if it bears fruit, well: and if not, then after that you shall cut it down.   Mark 16:15-1

He said therefore, A certain nobleman went into a far country, to receive for himself a kingdom, and to return. And he called ten servants of his, and gave them ten pounds, and said unto them, Trade [herewith] till I come. But his citizens hated him, and sent a message after him, saying, We will not that this man reign over us. And it came to pass, when he was come back again, having received the kingdom, that he commanded these servants, unto whom he had given the money, to be called to him, that he might know what they had gained by trading. And the first came before him, saying, Lord, your pound has made ten pounds more. And he said unto him, Well done, good servant: because you were found faithful in a very little, authority over ten cities. And the second came, saying, Your pound, Lord, has made five pounds. And he said unto him also, Be also over five cities. And another came, saying, Lord, behold, [here is] your pound, which I kept laid up in a napkin: for I feared you, because you are an austere man: you take up that which you laid not down, and reap that which you did not sow. He said unto him, Out of your own mouth will I judge you, you wicked servant. You knew that I am an austere man, taking up that which I laid not down, and reaping that which I did not sow; then why did you not put my money into the bank, and I at my coming I could have received with it interest? And he said unto them that stood by, Take away from him the pound, and give it unto him that has the ten pounds. And they said unto him, Lord, he has ten pounds. I say unto you, that unto every one that has shall be given; but from him that has not, even that which he has shall be taken away from him. But these mine enemies, that would not that I should reign over them, bring hither, and slay them before me.

Luke 19:12-27

And when he drew near, he saw the city and wept over it, saying, If you had known in this day, even thou, the things which belong unto peace! but now they are hid from your eyes. For the days shall come upon you, when your enemies shall cast up a bank about you, and compass you round, and keep you in on every side, and shall dash you to the ground, and your children within you; and they shall not leave in you one stone upon another; because you knew not the time of your visitation.   Luke 19:41-44

    And he began to speak unto the people this parable: A man planted a vineyard, and let it out to husbandmen, and went into another country for a long time. And at the season he sent unto the husbandmen a servant, that they should give him of the fruit of the vineyard: but the husbandmen beat him, and sent him away empty. And he sent yet another servant: and him also they beat, and handled him shamefully, and sent him away empty. And he sent yet a third: and him also they wounded, and cast him forth. And the lord of the vineyard said, What shall I do? I will send my beloved son; it may be they will reverence him. But when the husbandmen saw him, they reasoned one with another, saying, This is the heir; let us kill him, that the inheritance may be ours. And they cast him forth out of the vineyard, and killed him. What therefore will the lord of the vineyard do unto them? He will come and destroy these husbandmen, and will give the vineyard unto others. And when they heard it, they said, God forbid.
Luke 20:9-16

    And he said, Take heed that you be not led astray: for many shall come in my name, saying, I am [he]; and, The time is at hand: go not after them. And when you shall hear of wars and tumults, be not terrified: for these things must needs come to pass first; but the end is not immediately. Then said he unto them, Nation shall rise against nation, and kingdom against kingdom; and there shall be great earthquakes, and in diverse places famines and pestilences; and there shall be terrors and great signs from heaven. But before all these things, they shall lay their hands on you, and shall persecute you, delivering you up to the synagogues and prisons, bringing you before kings and governors for my name's sake. It shall turn out unto you for a testimony. Settle it therefore in your hearts, not to meditate beforehand how to answer: for I will give you a mouth and wisdom, which all your adversaries shall not be able to withstand or to gainsay. But you shall be delivered up even by parents, and brethren, and kinsfolk, and friends; and [some] of you shall they cause to be put to death. And you shall be hated of all men for my name's sake. And not a hair of your head shall perish. In your patience you shall win your souls. But when you see Jerusalem compassed with armies, then know that her desolation is at hand. Then let them that are in Judaea flee unto the mountains; and let them that are in the midst of her depart out; and let not them that are in the country enter therein. For these are days of vengeance, that all things which are written may be fulfilled. Woe unto them that are with child and to them that give suck in those days! for there shall be great distress upon the land, and wrath unto this people. And they shall fall by the edge of the sword, and shall be led captive into all the nations: and Jerusalem shall be trodden down of the Gentiles, until the times of the Gentiles be fulfilled. And there shall be signs in sun and moon and stars; and upon the earth distress of nations, in perplexity for the roaring of the sea and the billows; men fainting for fear, and for expectation of the things which are coming on the world: for the powers of the heavens shall be shaken. And then shall they see the Son of man coming in a cloud with power and great glory. But when these things begin to come to pass, look up, and lift up your heads; because your redemption draws near. And he spoke to them a parable: Behold the fig tree, and all the trees: when they now shoot forth, you see it and know of your own selves that the summer is now nigh. Even so also, when you see these things coming to pass, know that the kingdom of God is near. Verily I say unto you, This generation shall not pass away, till all things be accomplished. Heaven and earth shall pass away: but my words shall not pass away. But take heed to yourselves, lest haply your hearts be overcharged with surfeiting, and drunkenness, and cares of this life, and that day come on you suddenly as a snare: for [so] shall it come upon all them that dwell on the face of all the earth. But watch at every season, making supplication, that you may prevail to escape all these things that shall come to pass, and to stand before the Son of man.

Luke 21:8-36

All have sinned, and fall short of the glory of God.
Romans 3:23

To you that are afflicted rest with us, at the revelation of the Lord Jesus from heaven with the angels of his power in flaming fire, rendering vengeance to them that know not God, and to them that obey not the gospel of our Lord Jesus: who shall suffer punishment, [even] eternal destruction from the face of the Lord and from the glory of his might, when he shall come to be glorified in his saints, and to be marveled at in all them that believed (because our testimony unto you was believed) in that day. To which end we also pray always for you, that our God may count you worthy of your calling, and fulfill every desire of goodness and [every] work of faith, with power; that the name of our Lord Jesus may be glorified in you, and you in him, according to the grace of our God and the Lord Jesus Christ. Now we beseech you, brethren, touching the coming of our Lord Jesus Christ, and our gathering together unto him; to the end that you be not quickly shaken from your mind, nor yet be troubled, either by spirit, or by word, or by epistle as from us, as that the day of the Lord is just at hand; let no man beguile you in any wise: for [it will not be,] except the falling away come first, and the man of sin be revealed, the son of perdition, he that opposes and exalts himself against all that is called God or that is worshipped; so that he sits in the temple of God, setting himself forth as God.   2nd Thessalonians

Being therefore justified by faith, we have peace with God through our Lord Jesus Christ; through whom also we have had our access by faith into this grace wherein we stand; and we rejoice in hope of the glory of God. And not only so, but we also rejoice in our tribulations: knowing that tribulation brings forth steadfastness; and steadfastness, approvedness; and approvedness, hope: and hope putteth not to shame; because the love of God has been shed abroad in our hearts through the Holy Spirit which was given unto us.   Romans 5:1-5

All chastening seems for the present to be not joyous but grievous; yet afterward it yields peaceable fruit unto them that have been exercised thereby, [even the fruit] of righteousness.

Hebrews 12:11

James, a servant of God and of the Lord Jesus Christ, to the twelve tribes which are of the Dispersion, greetings. Count it all joy, my brethren, when you fall into manifold temptations; Knowing that the proving of your faith brings forth patience. And let patience have [its] perfect work, that you may be perfect and entire, lacking in nothing. But if any of you lack wisdom, let him ask of God, who gives to all liberally and upbraids not; and it shall be given him. But let him ask in faith, nothing doubting: for he that doubts is like the surge of the sea driven by the wind and tossed. For let not that man think that he shall receive anything of the Lord; a double minded man, unstable in all his ways. But let the brother of low degree glory in his high estate: and the rich, in that he is made low: because as the flower of the grass he shall pass away. For the sun arises with the scorching wind, and withers the grass: and the flower thereof falls, and the grace of the fashion of it perishes: so also shall the rich man fade away in his goings. Blessed is the man that endures temptation; for when he has been approved, he shall receive the crown of life, which [the Lord] promised to them that love him. Let no man say when he is tempted, I am tempted of God; for God cannot be tempted with evil, and he himself tempts no man: but each man is tempted, when he is drawn away by his own lust, and enticed. Then the lust, when it has conceived, bears sin: and the sin, when it is full grown, brings forth death.

James 1:2-15

Duty

    Who among you would say to your slave who has just come in from plowing or tending sheep in the field, "Come here at once and take your place at the table?" Would you not rather say to him, "Prepare supper for me, put on your apron and serve me while I eat and drink; later you may eat and drink?" Do you thank the slave for doing what was commanded? So you also, when you have done all that you were ordered to do, say, "We are worthless slaves; we have done only what we ought to have done!""
Luke 17:7-10

    ..."no human being will be justified in his sight by deeds prescribed by the law, for through the law comes the knowledge of sin. Romans 3:20

    Then what becomes of boasting? It is excluded. By what law? By that of works? No, but by the law of faith. For we hold that a person is justified by faith apart from works prescribed by the law.
Romans 3:27-28

    What do you have that you did not receive? And if you received it, why do you boast as if it were not a gift?
1 Corinthians 4:7

    ...present you bodies as living sacrifices, holy and acceptable to God, which is your spiritual worship. Do not be conformed to this world, but be transformed by the renewing of your minds, so that you may discern what is the will of God- what is good and acceptable and perfect. Romans 12:1-2

    So, whether you eat or drink, or whatever you do, do everything for the glory of God.
1 Corinthians 10:31

If you want to be a true doer of divine works, your first aim must be to be totally free from all desire and self-regarding ego. All your life must be an offering and a sacrifice to the Supreme; your only object in action shall be to serve, to receive, to fulfill, to become a manifesting instrument of the Divine Shakti in her works. You must grow in the divine consciousness till there is no difference between your will and hers, no motive except her impulsion in you, no action that is not her conscious action in you and through you. Until you are capable of this complete dynamic identification, you have to regard yourself as a soul and body created for her service, one who does all for her sake. Even if the idea of the separate worker is strong in you and you feel that it is you who do the act, yet it must be done for her. All stress of egoistic choice, all hankering after personal profit, all stipulation of self-regarding desire must be extirpated from the nature. There must be no demand for fruit and no seeking for reward; the only fruit for you is the pleasure of the Divine Mother and the fulfillment of her work, your only reward a constant progression in divine consciousness and calm and strength and bliss. The joy of service and the joy of inner growth through works is the sufficient recompense of the selfless worker.
Aurobindo

O my Lord, if I worship you from fear of hell, burn me in hell. If I worship you from hope of Paradise, bar me from its gates. But if I worship you for yourself alone, grant me then the beauty of your face. *Rabia*

Bayazid said, "Paradise is of no worth to those who love." Rabia had a related saying: "First the neighbor, then the house." That is, the neighbor, or God, is more important than the house, or Paradise. *Attar*

In cell and cloister, in monastery and synagogue: some fear hell and others dream of Paradise. But no man who really knows the secrets of his God has planted seeks like this within his own heart. *Omar Khayyam*

I will not serve God like a laborer, in expectation of my wages.   *Rabia*

Service is the performing of duty without either reluctance or delight. The dutiful is neither an exploited slave nor one who seeks reward. People will get out of the performing of duty what they can get out of it. If they put aside immediate enjoyment of duty and also immediate reluctance to duty, they are in a position to benefit from the other content in service. This it is which refines their perceptions.   *Pahlawan-i-Zaif*

In action I am free, because I am free from desire for the results of actions. The man who can see this truth, in his work and life he remains free and pure.   Bhagavad Gita 4:14

A sacrifice is pure when it is an offering of adoration in harmony with the holy law, with no expectation of a reward, and with the heart saying "it is my duty."
Bhagavad Gita 17:11

He who does holy work, Arjuna, because it ought to be done, and surrenders selfishness and thought of reward, his work is pure, and is peace. This man sees and has no doubts: he surrenders, he is pure and has peace. Work, pleasant or painful, is for him joy. For there is no man on earth who can fully renounce living work, but he who renounces the reward of his work is in truth a man of renunciation. When work is done for a reward, the work brings pleasure or pain, or both, in its time; but when a man does work in Eternity beyond the hold of karma, then Eternity is his reward.
Bhagavad Gita 18:9-12

Follow your duty, Arjuna, as your nature dictates it. All work fetters, as all fire gives smoke. Only selfless duty saves. Detachment, discipline, desirelessness, renunciation- these bring the true perfection of freedom leading to the highest state of knowledge occurring when a person attains Brahman.
Bhagavad Gita 18:48

Charity

Who is generous? - he whose good works are never done with any gain in view. Whatever is done for praise, or recompense, deem it, not generosity, but so much trade. Someone asked a generous man: When you give to the poor, when you are lavish with your gifts to beggars, don't you sense any vanity in your heart of hearts? Away with you! he retorted. My rule is to apply myself to giving like the strainer in the hand of the cook: everything the cook pours in passes through the strainer; but the strainer does not thereby lay any claim to the merit of giving. Expect no reward for an act of charity. Expecting something in return leads to a scheming mind. So an ancient once said; Throw away false spirituality like an old pair of shoes." *Kyong Ho*

Kind words and covering of faults are better than charity followed by injury. Quran 2:263

Some people want to see God with their eyes as they see a cow, and to love Him as they love their cow- for the milk and cheese and profit it brings them. This is how it is with people who love God for the sake of outward wealth or inward comfort. They do not rightly love God, when they love Him for their own advantage. Indeed, I tell you the truth, any object you have in your mind, however good, will be a barrier between you and the inmost Truth. *Eckhart*

Whatever alms you give shall rebound to your own advantage, provided that you give them for the love of God.
Quran

In everything do to others as you would have them do to you; for this is the law and the prophets. Matthew 7:12

Whoever has two coats must share with anyone who has none; and whoever has food must do likewise. Luke 3:11

Christ has no body now on earth but yours, no hands but yours, no feet but yours, yours are the eyes through which is to look out Christ's compassion to the world. Yours are the feet with which he is to go about doing good; yours are the hands with which he is to bless men now.   *Teresa of Avila*

We all long for heaven where God is, but we have it in our power to be in heaven with Him at this very moment. But being happy with Him now means: loving as he loves, helping as he helps, giving as he gives, serving as he serves, rescuing as he rescues, being with Him twenty-four hours, touching Him in his distressing disguise.   *Mother Teresa*

Only a thief would enjoy things given to them and not show thanks for them in sacrifice and self-less action which is the purest worship.   Bhagavad Gita 3:12

A kind word with forgiveness is better than charity followed by an insult.   Quran

What actions are most excellent? To gladden the heart of a human being, to feed the hungry, to help the afflicted, to lighten the sorrow of the sorrowful, and to remove the wrongs of the injured.   Hadith of the Prophet Mohammad

Feed the hungry and visit the sick, and free the captive, if he be unjustly confined. Assist any person oppressed, whether Muslim or non-Muslim.
    Hadith of the Prophet Mohammad

All of those who are in the condition of unhappiness in the world are that way because of desiring their own release. All of those who are in a condition of happiness in the world are that way from seeking the release of others. Whatever calamities there are, and whatever sorrows and fears come to the world, they are a result of attachment to self. Why is that attachment mine? Not having extinguished self, one is not able to extinguish sorrow; just as one who has not extinguished a fire is not able to extinguish burning. It follows that for the sake of tranquilizing my own sorrow, and for the tranquilizing of the other's sorrow, I give myself to others and accept others like myself. *Shantideva*

That person is not a perfect Muslim who eats his fill and leaves his neighbors hungry.
Hadith of the Prophet Mohammad

The best of all alms is that which the right hand gives and the left hand knows not of.
Hadith of the Prophet Mohammad

If you straighten out some trouble between two individuals, that is an alms. If you help a lame man with his beast, mounting him thereon, or hoisting up on to it his baggage, that is an alms. A good word is an alms. In every step you take while walking to prayers there is an alms. Your smiling in your brother's face, is charity, and your exhorting mankind to virtuous deeds, is charity; and your prohibiting the forbidden, is charity; and your showing men the road, in the land in which they lose it, is charity; and your assisting the blind, is charity.   Hadith of the Prophet Mohammad

Fear God, in treating dumb animals and ride them when they are fit to be ridden and get off them when they are tired.
Hadith of the Prophet Mohammad

An adulteress passed by a dog at a well; and the dog was holding out his tongue from thirst, which was near killing him, and the woman drew off her boot, and tied it to the end of her garment, and drew water for the dog, and gave him to drink; and she was forgiven for that act.
Hadith of the Prophet Mohammad

"Are there rewards for doing good to quadrupeds, and giving them water to drink?" Mohammad said, "Verily there are heavenly rewards for any act of kindness to a live animal.""

(...) many people not only lose the benefit, but are even the worse for all their mortifications. It is because they mistake the whole nature and worth of them. They practice them for their own sakes, as things good in themselves; they think them to be real parts of holiness, and so rest in them and look no further, but grow full of self-esteem and self-admiration for their own progress in them. This makes them self-sufficient, morose, severe judges of all those that fall short in their mortifications. And thus their own self-denials do only that for them which indulgences do for other people; they withstand and hinder the operation of God upon their souls, and instead of being really self-denials, they strengthen and keep up the kingdom of self.
William Law

When a man practices charity in order to be reborn in heaven, or for fame, or reward, or from fear, such charity can obtain no pure effect.
Sutra on the Distinction and Protection of the Dharma

St. Francois de Sales used to say, "I hear of nothing but perfection on every side, so far as talk goes; but I see very few people who really practice it. Everybody has his own notion of perfection. One man thinks that it lies in the cut of his clothes, another in fasting, a third in almsgiving, or in frequenting the Sacraments, in meditation, in some special gift of contemplation, or in extraordinary gifts or graces- but they confuse the means, or the results, with the end and cause." For my part, the only perfection I know of is a hearty love of God, and to love one's neighbor as oneself. Charity is the only virtue which rightly unites us to God and man. Such union is our final aim and end, and all the rest is mere delusion." *Jean Pierre Camus*

The bread of charity is life itself for the needy; he who withholds is a man of blood.   Sirach *34: 21*

I am not pleased by an offering- no matter how grand- that is

made by one who lacks devotion. But I am delighted when someone filled with devotion offers even the smallest thing. Imagine then, how I receive gifts of fragrant oils, incense, flowers and food that are offered with love.
Uddhava Gita *22:18*

Obligatory charity for the sake of God is due from every single part of your body, even from every root of your hair. In fact, charity is due for every instant of your life. Charity of the eye means looking with consideration and averting your gaze from desires and things similar to them. Charity of the ear means listening to the best of sounds, such as wisdom, the Koran, and the benefits of faith contained in warnings and good counsel, and by avoiding lies, slander, and similar things. Charity of tongue means to give good advice, to awaken those who are heedless, and to give abundant glorification and remembrance and other, similar things. Charity of hand means spending money on others, to be generous with God's blessing to you, to use your hand to write down knowledge and information by means of which others will benefit in obedience to God, and to restrain your hand from evil. Charity of the foot means to hasten to carry one's duty to God by visiting virtuous people, attending assemblies of remembrance, putting things right between people, maintaining ties of kinship, engaging in jihad (inner struggle), and doing things that will make your heart sound and your faith correct. *al-Sadiq*

Whatever of good you give benefits your own souls, and you shall only do so seeking the Face of Allah. Quran 2:272

In sharing one's property with one's companion there are three degrees. The lowest degree is where you place your companion on the same footing as your slave or your servant, attending to his or her need from your surplus. If some need befalls him when you have more than you require, you give spontaneously, not obliging him to ask. To oblige your companion to ask is the ultimate shortcoming in fulfilling one's duty. At the second degree you place your companion on the same footing as yourself. You are content to have him or her as partner in your property and to treat him or her like yourself, to the point of sharing it equally. At the third degree, the highest of all, you prefer your companion to yourself and set his or her need before your own.   *al-Ghazzali*

They ask you how much to give in charity; say: "What is beyond your needs."   Quran 2:21

Be steadfast in prayer and regular in charity: and whatever good you send forth for your \souls before you, you shall find it with Allah: for Allah sees all that you do.   Quran 2:110

Kind words and the covering of faults are better than charity followed by injury. Allah is Free of all wants, and He is most Forbearing. O you who believe! Cancel not your charity by reminders of your generosity or by injury, - like those who spend their substances to be seen of men, but believe neither in Allah nor in the Last Day. They are in Parable like a hard, barren rock, on which is a little soil: on it falls heavy rain, which leaves it just a bare stone. They will be able to do nothing with anything they have earned. And Allah does not guide those who reject Faith. And the likeness of those who spend their substance seeking to please Allah and to strengthen their souls, is as a garden, high and fertile: heavy rain falls on it but it makes it yield a double increase of harvest, and if it does not receive heavy rain, light moisture suffices it. Allah sees well whatever you do.   Quran 2:263-265

When I see the poor dervish unfed, my own food is pain and poison to me.   *Saadi of Shiraz*

Charity is pure and Sattvic when done for the sake of love, expecting nothing in return, and given at the right time to the right person. Rajasic charity is impure, reluctant giving that expects a return and looks for a reward. Tamasik charity is a gift of darkness given to the wrong person at the wrong time, without concern and with proud contempt.   Bhagavad Gita 17:20-22

For the poor will never cease from the land: therefore, I command you, saying, 'You shall open your hand wide to your brother, to your poor and needy, in your land.'
                              Deuteronomy 15:11

He looked up and saw rich people putting their gifts into the treasury; he also saw a poor widow put in two small copper coins. He said, "Truly I tell you, this poor widow has put in more than all of them; for all of them have contributed out of their abundance but she out of her poverty has put in all she had to live on."
                              Luke 21;1-4

Love, Kindness and Compassion

And no one has ascended into heaven, but he that descended out of heaven, [even] the Son of man, who is in heaven. And as Moses lifted up the serpent in the wilderness, even so must the Son of man be lifted up; that whosoever believes may in him have eternal life. For God so loved the world, that he gave his only begotten Son, that whosoever believes in him should not perish, but have eternal life. For God sent not the Son into the world to judge the world; but that the world should be saved through him. He that believes in him is not judged: he that believes not has been judged already, because he has not believed on the name of the only begotten Son of God. And this is the judgment, that the light is come into the world, and men loved the darkness rather than the light; for their works were evil. For every one that does evil hates the light, and comes not to the light, because his works should be reproved. But he that doeth the truth comes to the light, that his works may be made manifest, that they have been wrought in God.
John 3:13-21

If I speak in the tongues of mortals and of angels, but do not have love, I am a noisy gong or a clanging cymbal. And if I have prophetic powers, and understand all mysteries and all knowledge, and if I have all faith so as to move mountains, but do not have love, I am nothing. If I give away all my possessions, and if I hand over my body so that I may boast, but do not have love, I gain nothing. Love is patient; love is kind; love is not envious or boastful or arrogant or rude. It does not insist on its own way; it is not irritable or resentful; it does not rejoice in wrongdoing, but rejoices in the truth. It bears all things, believes all things, hopes all things, endures all things. Love never ends. But as for prophecies, they will come to an end; as for tongues, they will cease; as for knowledge, it will come to an end. For we know only in part, and we prophesy only in part; but when the complete comes, the partial will come to an end. When I was a child, I spoke like a child, I thought like a child, I reasoned like a child; when I became an adult,

I put an end to childish ways. For now, we see in a mirror, dimly, but then we will see face to face. Now I know only in part; then I will know fully, even as I have been fully known. And now faith, hope, and love abide, these three; and the greatest of these is love.
         1st Corinthians 13:1-13

  Better indeed is knowledge than mechanical practice. Better than knowledge is meditation. Better still is surrender in love, because there follows immediate peace. The one that I love is incapable of ill will, and returns love for hatred. Living beyond the reach of I and mine and of pleasure and pain, full of mercy, contented, self-controlled, firm in faith, with all their heart and all their mind given to me- with such people I am in love. Not agitating the world or by it agitated, they stand above the sway of elation, competition, and fear, accepting life good and bad as it comes. They are pure, efficient, detached, ready to meet every demand I make on them as a humble instrument of my work.
      Bhagavad Gita

  Be aware of me always, adore me, make every act an offering to me, and you shall come to me; this I promise, for you are dear to me. Leave all other support, and look to me for protection. I shall purify you from the sins of the past. Do not grieve.
         Bhagavad Gita

  Give me your mind and your heart and worship me always with your actions, offerings and adoration; and thus with your soul in harmony, and making me your goal supreme, you will in truth come to be united with me. Bhagavad Gita 9:34

  You shall love the Lord your God with all your heart, and with all you soul and with all your mind- This is the greatest and first commandment. And the second is like it: You shall love you neighbor as yourself. On these two commandments hang all of the law and the prophets." Matthew 22:37-40

Those who have all the powers of their soul in harmony, and the same loving mind for all; who find joy in the good of all beings- they come into my very self.   Bhagavad Gita 12:4

Only by love and single-minded devotion can men see me, and know me, and come to me. He who works for me, who loves me and sets me as his ideal, whose End Supreme I am, free from attachments to all things, and with love for all creation, he in truth enters into my peace.   Bhagavad Gita 11:54-55

I give you a new commandment, that you love one another. Just as I have loved you, you also should love one another. By this everyone will know that you are my disciples, if you have love for one another.   *Jesus*

Abuse nobody, and if a man abuses you, and lays open a vice which he knows about in you; then do not disclose one which you know of in him.   Hadith of the Prophet Mohammad

He that loves not does not know God, for God is love.
1 John:4

By love may He be gotten and holden, but by thoughts never.
The Cloud of Unknowing

Love breathes the spirit of God; its words and works are the inspiration of God. Love speaks not of itself, but of the Word, the eternal Word of God speaks in it. All that love speaks, that God speaks, because love is God. Love is heaven revealed in the soul; it is light and truth; it is infallible; it has no errors, for all errors are the want of love. Love has no more of pride than light has of darkness; it stands and bears all its fruits from a depth and root of humility.
William Law

Love seeks no cause beyond itself and no fruit; it is its own fruit, its own enjoyment. I love because I love; I love in order that I may love... Of all the motions and affections of the soul, love is the only one by means of which the creature, though not on equal terms, is able to treat with the Creator and to give back something resembling what has been given to it... When God loves, he only desires to be loved, knowing that love will render all those who love Him happy.   *St. Bernard*

Let everyone understand that real love of God does not consist in tear-shedding, nor in that sweetness and tenderness for which we usually long, just because they console us, but in serving God in justice, fortitude of soul and humility.
St. Teresa

By love I do not mean any natural tenderness, which is more or less in people according to their constitution; but I mean a larger principle of the soul, founded in reason and piety, which makes us tender, kind and gentle to all our fellow creatures as creatures of God, and for his sake.   *William Law*

One man may declare that he cannot fast; but can he declare that he cannot love God? Another may affirm that he cannot preserve virginity or sell all his goods in order to give the price to the poor; but can he tell me that he cannot love his enemies? All that is necessary is to look into one's own heart; for what God asks of us is not found at a great distance.   *St. Jerome*

You may try a hundred things, but love alone will release you from yourself. So never flee from love- not even from love in an earthly disguise- for it is a preparation for the supreme Truth. How will you ever read the Koran without first learning the alphabet?   *Jami*

Love is to see what is good and beautiful in everything. It is to learn from everything, to see the gifts of God and the generosity of God in everything. It is to be thankful for all of God's bounties. This is the first step on the road to the love of God. This is just a seed of love. In time, the seed will grow and become a tree and bear fruit. Then, whoever tastes of that fruit will know what real love is. It will be difficult for those who have tasted to tell of it to those who have not.   *Sheikh Muzaffer*

Love makes us speak; love makes us moan; love makes us die; love brings us to life; love makes us drunk and bewildered; it sometimes makes one a king. Love and the lover have no rigid doctrine. Whichever direction the lover takes, he turns towards his beloved. Wherever he may be, he is with his beloved. Wherever he goes, he goes with his beloved. He cannot do anything, cannot survive for even one minute, without his beloved. He constantly recalls his beloved, as his beloved remembers him. Lover and beloved, rememberer and remembered, are ever in each other's company, always together.   *Sheikh Muzaffer*

A person often remembers the object of his love.   One who is a lover of God also remembers Him, always and everywhere. On the bough of the beloved's rosebush, love's nightingale sings its love incessantly.   *Sheikh Muzaffer*

Listen friends, love is like the sun. The heart without love is nothing but a piece of stone.   *Kabakli*

God is love, yea, all love; and so all love that nothing but love can come from him; and the Christian religion is nothing else but an open full manifestation of his universal love towards all mankind. As the light of the sun has only one common nature towards all objects that can receive it, so God has only one common nature of goodness towards all created nature, breaking forth in infinite flames of love upon every part of creation and calling everything to the highest happiness it is capable of. God so loved man, when his fall was foreseen, that he choose him to salvation in Christ Jesus before the foundation of the world. When man was actually fallen, God was so without all wrath towards him that he sent his only begotten Son into the world to redeem him. Therefore, God has no nature towards man but love, and all that he does to man is love.
     William Law

Love is the chief among the passions of the soul; it draws all things to itself and makes us like the one we love. Take care not to admit any evil love lest you become evil yourself.
Francis de Sales

As the bee draws honey from all plants and makes use of them only for that end, so the soul most easily draws the sweetness of love from all that happens to it. It makes all things subservient to the end of loving God, whether they are bitter or sweet. In all its occupations its joy is the love of God.
St. John of the Cross

True love accepts with perfect resignation, yes, even with joy, whatever comes to it from the hand of the Beloved, for perfect love casts out fear.   *St. John of the Cross*

The little white dove has returned to the ark with the bough. And now the turtle-dove its desired mate on the green banks has found. The Bridegroom calls the soul the turtledove because when it is seeking after the Beloved it is like the turtle-dove when it cannot find its desired mate. It is said that when it cannot find its mate it will not sit on any green bough, or drink cool refreshing water, nor rest in the shade, nor mingle with its companions. But when it finds its mate it does all these things. Such too must be the soul if it is to attain union with the Bridegroom. The soul's love and anxiety must be such that it cannot rest on the green boughs of any joy, nor drink the waters of the world's honor and glory, nor shelter in the shade of created help and protection. It must mourn its loneliness until it finds the Bridegroom to its heart's content.   *St. John of the Cross*

Hatred does not cease by hatred at any time; hatred ceases by love- this is an eternal law.   Dhammapada

And in the same way, O monks, as at the end of the rainy season, the sun, rising into the clear and cloudless sky, banishes all the dark spaces and glows and shines and blazes forth: in the same way again, as at night's end the morning star glows and shines and blazes forth: so, O monks, none of the means employed to acquire religious merit has a sixteenth part of the value of loving-kindness. Loving-kindness, which is freedom of heart, absorbs them: it glows, it shines, it blazes forth.   Itivuttaka Sutta

Humility

Blessed are you who are poor, for yours is the kingdom of God. Blessed are you who are hungry now, for you will be filled. Blessed are those who weep now, for you will laugh. Blessed are you when people hate you, and when they exclude you, revile you and defame you on account of the Son of Man. Rejoice in that day and leap for joy, for surely your reward is great in heaven; for that is what their ancestors did to the prophets. But woe to you who are rich. For you have received your consolation. Woe to you that are full now, for you will be hungry. Woe to you who are laughing now, for you will mourn and weep. Woe to you when all speak well of you, for that is what their ancestors did to the false prophets.
                              Luke 6:20-26

Forever free of desire, it can be called small; yet, as it lays no claim to being master when the myriad creatures turn to it, it can be called great. It is because it never attempts itself to be great that it succeeds in becoming great.   Tao Te Ching

A man is supple and weak when living, but hard and stiff when dead. Grass and trees are pliant and fragile when living, but dried and shriveled when dead. Thus the hard and the strong are the comrades of death; the supple and the weak are the comrades of life. Therefore, a weapon that is strong will not vanquish; a tree that is strong will suffer the axe. The strong and big takes the lower position, the supple and weak takes the higher position.
                              Tao Te Ching

In the world there is nothing more submissive and weak than water. Yet for attacking that which is hard and strong nothing can surpass it. This is because there is nothing that can take its place. That the weak overcomes the strong, and the submissive overcomes the hard, everyone in the world knows yet no one can put this knowledge into practice.   Tao Te Ching

Truly I tell you, unless you change and become like children, you will never enter the kingdom of heaven. Whoever becomes humble like this child is the greatest in the kingdom of heaven. Whoever welcomes such child in my name welcomes me. Matthew 18:3-5

The greatest among you will be your servant. All who exalt themselves will be humbled, and all who humble themselves will be exalted." (...) But Jesus called them unto him, and said, You know that the rulers of the Gentiles lord it over them, and their great ones exercise authority over them. Not so shall it be among you: but whosoever would become great among you shall be your minister; and whosoever would be first among you shall be your servant: even as the Son of man came not to be ministered unto, but to minister, and to give his life a ransom for many.
Matthew 23:11-12, 20:25-28

The reason why the River and the Sea are able to be king of the hundred valleys is that they excel in taking the lower position. Hence they are able to be king of the hundred valleys. Therefore, desiring to rule over the people, one must in one's words humble oneself before them; and, desiring to lead the people, one must, in one's person follow behind them. Therefore, the sage takes his place over the people yet is no burden; takes his place ahead of the people yet causes no obstruction. That is why the empire supports him joyfully and never tires of doing so. It is because he does not contend that no one in the empire is in a position to contend with him.   Tao Te Ching

The earth is very thick. Lowly, below all else, it bears everything and nurtures all beings. It can bear even the weight of the great mountains, and it can endure even the erosive force of great waters. It tolerates being pierced by plants and trees, and it submits to the tread of birds and beasts. What I realize as I observe this is the Tao of emulating heaven and earth. If people can be open-minded and magnanimous, be receptive to all, take pity on the old and the poor, assist those in peril and rescue those in trouble, give of themselves without seeking reward, never bear grudges, look upon others and self impartially, and realize all as one, then people can be companions of heaven. If people can be flexible and yielding, humble, with self-control, entirely free of agitation, cleared of all volatility, not angered by criticism, ignoring insult, docilely accepting all hardships, illnesses, and natural disasters, utterly without anxiety or resentment when faced with danger or adversity, then people can be companions of earth. With the of nobility heaven and the humility of earth, one joins in with the attributes of heaven and earth and extends to eternity with them.   *Liu I Ming*

He who stands on tiptoes doesn't stand firm. He who rushes ahead doesn't go far. He who tries to shine dims his own light. He who defines himself can't really know who he is. He who has power over others can't empower himself. He who clings to his work will create nothing that endures.   Tao Te Ching

Why was man created on the sixth day? So that should he become overbearing he can be told: The gnat was created before you were.   Talmud

His disciples said, "When will you become revealed to us and when shall we see you?" Jesus said, "When you disrobe without being ashamed and take up your garments and place them under your feet like little children and tread on them, then [will you see] the son of the living one, and then you will not be afraid.""
                              Gospel of Thomas

Do not treat men with scorn, nor walk proudly on the earth: Allah does not love the arrogant and the vainglorious. Rather let your gait be modest and your voice low: the harshest of voices is the braying of an ass.   Quran 31:18-19

A man must become truly poor and as free from his own creaturely will as he was when he was born. And I tell you, by the eternal truth, that so long as you desire to fulfill the will of God and have any hankering after eternity and God, for just so long you are not truly poor. He alone as spiritual poverty who wills nothing, knows nothing, desires nothing.   *Eckhart*

I have but one word to say to you concerning love for your neighbor, namely that nothing save humility can mold you to it; nothing but the consciousness of your own weakness can make you indulgent and pitiful to that of others. You will answer, I quite understand that humility should produce forbearance towards others, but how am I first to acquire humility? Two things combined will bring that about; you must never separate them. The first is contemplation of the deep gulf, whence God's all-powerful hand has drawn you out, and over which he ever holds you, so to say, suspended. The second is the presence of that all-penetrating God. It is only in beholding and loving God that we can learn forgetfulness of self, measure duly the nothingness which has dazzled us, and accustom ourselves thankfully to decrease beneath that great Majesty which absorbs all things. Love God and you will be humble; love God and you will throw off the love of self; love God and you will love all that He gives you to love for love of Him.
Fenelon

More and more, humble your pride; what awaits man is worms.   Sirach *7:17*

Odious to the Lord and to men is arrogance, and the sin of oppression they both hate. Dominion is transferred from one people to another because of the violence of the arrogant. Why are dust and ashes proud? Even during life man's body decays. ... The beginning of pride is man's stubbornness, in withdrawing his heart from his Maker; for pride is the reservoir of sin, a source which runs over with vice.   Sirach *10:7-13*

You will not be a mystic until you are like the earth- both the righteous and the sinner tread upon it- and until you are like the clouds- they shade all things- and until you are like the rain- it waters all things, whether it loves them or not.   *Bayazid Bistami*

I saw my lower self in the form of a rat. I asked, "Who are you?" It replied, "I am the destruction of the heedless, for I incite them to wickedness. I am the salvation of the friends-of-God, for if it were not for me, they would be proud of their purity and their actions. When they see me in themselves, all their pride disappears."   *Hujwiri*

One day a man came to the teacher Bayazid and said, "I have fasted and prayed for thirty years and have found none of the spiritual joy of which you speak." "If you had fasted for three hundred years, you would never find it," answered the sage. "How is that?" asked the man. "Your selfishness is acting as a veil between you and God.". "Tell me the cure." "It is a cure that you cannot carry out," said Bayazid. Those around him pressed him to reveal it. After a time, he spoke: "Go into the nearest barbershop and have your head shaved; strip yourself of your clothes except for a loincloth. Take a nosebag full of walnuts, hang it around your neck. Go into the market and cry out- Anybody who gives me a slap on the neck shall have a walnut. Then proceed to the law courts and do the same thing." "I can't do that," said the man. "Suggest some other remedy." "This is the indispensable preliminary to a cure," answered Bayazid. "But as I told you, you are incurable."   *al-Ghazzali*

Blessed is the man who knows his own weakness, because awareness of this becomes for him the foundation and beginning of all that is good and beautiful. For when someone realizes and perceives that he is truly and indeed weak, then he draws in his soul from the diffuseness which dissipates knowledge, and he becomes all the more watchful of his soul. But no one can perceive his own weakness unless he has been remiss a little, has neglected some small thing, has been surrounded by trials, either in the matter of things which cause the body suffering, or in that of ways in which the soul is subject to the passions. Only then, by comparing his own weakness, will he realize how great is the assistance which comes from God. When someone is aware that he is in need of divine help, he makes many prayers. And once he has made much supplication,

his heart is humbled, for there is no one who is in need and asks who is not humbled. A broken and humbled heart, God will not despise. As long as the heart is not humbled it cannot cease from wandering; for humility concentrates the heart.
Isaac of Syria

Give up yourselves to the meek and humble spirit of the holy Jesus, the overcomer of all fire and pride and wrath. This is the only way, the one truth and the one life. There is no other door into the sheepfold of God. Everything else is the working of the devil in the fallen nature of man. Humility must sow the seed, or there can be no reaping in heaven. Look not at pride only as an unbecoming temper; nor at humility only as a descent virtue; for the one is death and the other is life; the one is hell and the other is heaven. So much as you have of pride, so much you have of the fallen angel within you; so much as you have of true humility, so much you have of the Lamb of God within you. Learn of me for I am meek and lowly of heart. If this lesson is unlearned, we must be said to have left our Master, as those disciples did who went back and walked no more with him.   *William Law*

Seek Allah's help with patient perseverance and prayer: it is indeed hard, except to those who bring a lowly spirit.
Quran 2:45

Before you We sent Messengers to many nations, and We afflicted the nations with suffering and adversity, that they might learn humility.   Quran 6:42

Nor say of anything "I shall do so and so tomorrow"- without adding, "So please Allah!" And call your Lord to mind when you forget and say, "I hope that my Lord will guide me ever closer even than this to the right road.""   Quran 18: 23-24

And your Lord says: Call on Me; I will answer your Prayer: but those who are too arrogant to serve Me will surely find themselves in Hell- in humiliation.   Quran 40:60

Some cultivate themselves in part to serve others, in part to serve their own pride. They will understand, at best, half of the truth. But those who improve themselves for the sake of the world- to these, the whole truth of the universe will be revealed. So seek this whole truth, practice it in your daily life, and humbly share it with others. You will enter the realm of the divine.
        Hua Hu Ching 16

Foolish people follow after vanity. Wise people guard vigilance as their greatest treasure.
        Dhammapada

He will teach the gentle His ways. Psalm 25:9

Now the man Moses was very meek, above all the men that were upon the face of the earth. Numbers 12:3

Learn from Me, for I am gentle and humble in heart: and you will find rest for your souls. Matthew 11:29

Do not let the kingdom of heaven become a desert within you. Do not be proud because of the light that brings enlightenment. Rather, act toward yourselves as I also acted toward you: I put myself under a curse for you, that you might be saved.
        Secret Book of James 8:14-15

Can you coax your mind from its wandering and keep to the original oneness? Can you let your body become supple as a newborn child's? Can you cleanse your inner vision until you see nothing but the light? Can you love people and lead them without imposing your will? Can you deal with the most vital matters by letting events take their course? Can you step back from your own mind and thus understand all things? Giving birth and nourishing, having without possessing, acting with no expectations, leading and not trying to control: this is the supreme virtue. Tao te Ching 10

The Master sees things as they are without trying to control them. She lets them go their own way, and resides at the center of the circle.   Tao te Ching 29

Humility means trusting the Tao, thus never needing to be defensive. A great nation is like a great man: when he makes a mistake, he realizes it. Having realized it, he admits it. Having admitted it, he corrects it. He considers those who point out his faults as his most benevolent teachers. He thinks of his enemy as the shadow that he himself casts.   Tao te Ching 61

The Master is above the people and no one feels oppressed. She goes ahead of the people and no one feels manipulated. The whole world is grateful to her. Because she competes with no one, no one can compete with her.   Tao te Ching 66

The Lord also will be a refuge for the oppressed, a refuge in times of trouble. And those who know Your name will put their trust in You; for You, Lord, have not forsaken those who seek You. (...) He does not forget the cry of the humble.
Psalms 9:9-10,12

The Lord is near those who have a broken heart, and saves those who have a contrite spirit.   Psalms 34:18

Everyone proud in heart is an abomination to the Lord. (...) Pride goes before destruction, and a haughty spirit before a fall. Better to be of a humble spirit with the lowly than to divide the spoil with the proud.   Proverbs 16:5. 18-19

Blessed are the poor in spirit, for theirs is the kingdom of heaven. Blessed are those who mourn, for they shall be comforted. Blessed are the meek, for they shall inherit the earth. Blessed are those who hunger and thirst for righteousness, for they shall be filled. Blessed are the merciful, for they shall obtain mercy. Blessed are the pure in heart, for they shall see God.   Matthew 5:3-10

The greater you are the more you must humble yourself; so you will find favor in the sight of the Lord. For great is the might of the Lord; but by the humble He is glorified. Their conceit has led many astray, and wrong opinion has impaired their judgment.
Sirach 3:18-19

And he sat down, and called the twelve; and he said unto them, If any man would be first, he shall be last of all, and servant of all. And he took a little child, and set him in the midst of them: and taking him in his arms, he said unto them, Whosoever shall receive one of such little children in my name, receives me: and whosoever receives me, receives not me, but Him that sent me. (...) But when Jesus saw it, he was moved with indignation, and said unto them, Suffer the little children to come unto me; forbid them not: for to such belongs the kingdom of God. Verily I say unto you, Whosoever shall not receive the kingdom of God as a little child, he shall in no wise enter therein. (...) And Jesus called them to him, and said unto them, You know that they who are accounted to rule over the Gentiles lord it over them; and their great ones exercise authority over them. But it is not so among you: but whosoever would become great among you, shall be your minister; and whosoever would be first among you, shall be servant of all. For the Son of man also came not to be ministered unto, but to minister, and to give his life a ransom for many.   Mark 9:35-37, 10:14-15, 42-45

What advantage then has the Jew? or what is the profit of circumcision? Much every way: first of all, that they were entrusted with the oracles of God. For what if some were without faith? shall their want of faith make of none effect the faithfulness of God? God forbid: yea, let God be found true, but every man a liar; as it is written, That you might be justified in thy words, And might prevail when you come into judgment. But if our righteousness commends the righteousness of God, what shall we say? Is God unrighteous who visits with wrath? (I speak after the manner of men.) God forbid: for then how shall God judge the world? But if the truth of God through my lie abounded unto his glory, why am I also still judged as a sinner? and why not (as we are slanderously reported, and as some affirm that we say), Let us do evil, that good may come? whose condemnation is just. What then? are we better than they? No, in no wise: for we before laid to the charge both of Jews and Greeks, that they are all under sin; as it is written, There is none

righteous, no, not one; There is none that understands, There is none that seeks after God; They have all turned aside, they are together become unprofitable; There is none that does good, no, not, so much as one: Their throat is an open sepulcher; With their tongues they have used deceit: The poison of asps is under their lips: Whose mouth is full of cursing and bitterness: Their feet are swift to shed blood; Destruction and misery are in their ways; And the way of peace have they not known: There is no fear of God before their eyes. Now we know that what things so ever the law says, it speaks to them that are under the law; that every mouth may be stopped, and all the world may be brought under the judgment of God: because by the works of the law shall no flesh be justified in his sight; for through the law [comes] the knowledge of sin. But now apart from the law a righteousness of God has been manifested, being witnessed by the law and the prophets, being witnessed by the law and the prophets; even the righteousness of God through faith in Jesus Christ unto all them that believe; for there is no distinction; for all have sinned, and fall short of the glory of God; being justified freely by his grace through the redemption that is in Christ Jesus: whom God set forth [to be] a propitiation, through faith, in his blood, to show his righteousness because of the passing over of the sins done afore time, in the forbearance of God; for the showing, [I say], of his righteousness at this present season: that he might himself be just, and the justifier of him that has faith in Jesus.
                                                            Romans 3:1-26

    Have this mind in you, which was also in Christ Jesus: who, existing in the form of God, counted not the being on an equality with God a thing to be grasped, but emptied himself, taking the form of a servant, being made in the likeness of men; and being found in fashion as a man, he humbled himself, becoming obedient [even] unto death, yea, the death of the cross. Wherefore also God highly exalted him, and gave unto him the name which is above every name; that in the name of Jesus every knee should bow, of [things] in heaven and [things] on earth and [things] under the earth, and that every tongue should confess that Jesus Christ is Lord, to the glory of God the Father. So then, my beloved, even as you have

always obeyed, not as in my presence only, but now much more in my absence, work out your own salvation with fear and trembling; for it is God who works in you both to will and to work, for his good pleasure. Do all things without murmuring and questioning: that you may become blameless and harmless, children of God without blemish in the midst of a crooked and perverse generation, among whom you are seen as lights in the world, holding forth the Word of life; that I may have whereof to glory in the day of Christ, that I did not run in vain neither labor in vain.
Philippians 2:5-16

What do you have which you did not receive? Now if you received it, why do you boast, as if you had not received it?
1st Corinthians 4:7

For Christ sent me not to baptize, but to preach the gospel: not in wisdom of words, lest the cross of Christ should be made void. For the word of the cross is to them that perish foolishness; but unto us who are saved it is the power of God. For it is written, I will destroy the wisdom of the wise, And the discernment of the discerning will I bring to naught. Where is the wise? where is the scribe? where is the disputer of this world? Has not God made foolish the wisdom of the world? For seeing that in the wisdom of God the world through its wisdom knew not God, it was God's good pleasure through the foolishness of the preaching to save them that believe. Seeing that Jews ask for signs, and Greeks seek after wisdom: but we preach Christ crucified, unto Jews a stumbling block, and unto Gentiles foolishness; but unto them that are called, both Jews and Greeks, Christ the power of God, and the wisdom of God. Because the foolishness of God is wiser than men; and the weakness of God is stronger than men. For behold your calling, brothers, that not many wise after the flesh, not many mighty, not many noble, [are called]: but God chose the foolish things of the world, that he might put to shame them that are wise; and God chose the weak things of the world, that he might put to shame the things that are strong; and the base things of the world, and the things that are despised, did God choose, and the things that are not, that he might bring to naught the things that are: that no flesh should glory before God. But of him are you in Christ Jesus, who was made unto us wisdom from God, and righteousness and sanctification, and redemption: that, according as it is written, He that glories, let him glory in the Lord.   1st Corinthians 1:17-31

Every good gift is from above.   James 1:17

Faith and Action

The right relation between prayer and conduct is not that conduct is supremely important and prayer may help it, but that prayer is extremely important and conduct tests it.
Archbishop Temple

Work is for the purification of the mind, not for the perception of Reality. The realization of Truth is brought about by discrimination, and not in the least by ten million acts.
Shankara

If you have faith the size of a mustard seed, you will say to this mountain, 'Move from here to there,' and it will move: and nothing will be impossible for you.   Matthew *17:20-21*

So I tell you, whatever you ask for in prayer, believe that you have received it, and it will be yours.   Mark *11:24*

Piety, truthfulness and compassion combined with learning and austerity will not purify a mind devoid of devotion.
Uddhava Gita *9:22*

Faith is the knowledge of the heart, the words of the tongue, and the actions of the body.   *Hadith of the Prophet Muhammad*

I do not worry about the things that you do not know, but I am cautious in appraising how you apply what you do know.
Hadith of the Prophet Muhammad

No one of you truly believe until you wish for your brother that which you wish for yourself.
Hadith of the Prophet Muhammad

To completely trust in God is to be like a child who knows deeply that even if he does not call for the mother, the mother is totally aware of his condition and is looking after him.   *al-Ghazzali*

He heals out nature from within, kinder to us than we are to ourselves. His kindness makes the worthless worthy; and in return he is content with his servant's gratitude and patience. You have broken faith, yet still he keeps his faith with you: he is truer to you than you are to yourself.   *Sana'i*

The Religion before Allah is Islam (submission to His Will): nor did the People of the Book dissent there from except through envy of each other, after knowledge had come to them. But if any deny the Signs of Allah, Allah is swift in calling to account. So if they dispute with you, say: I have submitted my whole self to Allah and so have those who follow me. And say to the People of the Book and to those who are unlearned: Do you also submit yourselves? If they do, they are in right guidance, but if they turn back, your duty is to convey the Message; and in Allah's sight are all His servants.   Quran 3:19-20

Someone asked the master Ali Ramitani, "What is faith?" He replied, "Uprooting and binding. - uprooting one's heart from the world, to bind it to God. This matter is like a pile of trash under the eaves of someone's house; from morning to night rain beats on it wind blows on it, but nobody pays attention to it. They do not realize there is an inexhaustible treasure trove within it; if they could avail themselves of it, they could take from it and put it to use for a hundred aeons and a thousand lifetimes without exhausting it. You should know that this treasury doesn't come from outside; it all emerges from your faith. If you can have complete faith in it, you certainly won't be cheated. If you do not have complete faith, you will never realize it even in countless aeons. So I ask you to have faith in this way, so you can avoid being destitute beggars. But tell me, where is this treasury right now? If you don't go into the tiger's den, how can you catch a tiger cub?   *Kao-feng*

My Promise is not within the reach of evil-doers.
Quran 2:124

Whoever submits his whole self to Allah, and is a doer of good, has grasped indeed the most trustworthy handhold; and with Allah rests the End and Decision of all affairs.
Quran 31:22

Those who aspire to the Land of Happiness must abide in the group of perfect faith. None are to be found there who long for wrong or unsettled faith. *Shinran Shonen*

In the quest of Ojo, need it be that any fall? Sincerity of heart is lacking, that is all. *Honen*

True understanding in a person has two attributes: awareness and action. Together they form a natural tai chi.
Hua Hu Ching 53

The man who arises in faith, whoever remembers his high purpose, whose work is pure, and who carefully considers his work, who in self-possession lives the life of perfection, and who ever, forever, is watchful, that man shall arise in glory. By arising in faith and watchfulness, by self-possession and self-harmony, the wise man makes an island for his soul which many waters cannot overflow. Dhammapada

Discipline and discrimination show the face of Brahma. It is the product of action done in knowledge. Know this, and be free. Bhagavad Gita 4:32

Abraham believed in the Lord, and He accounted it to him for righteousness. Genesis 15:6

Blessed are those who put their trust in Him. (...) But You, O Lord are a shield for me, my glory and the One who lifts up my head.

I cried to the Lord with my voice, and he heard me from His holy hill. Selah. I lay down and slept; I awoke, for the Lord sustained me, I will not be afraid of ten thousands of people who have set themselves against me all around. (...) My defense is of God who saves the upright in heart.   Psalms 2:12, 3:3-6, 6:10

    Make Your face shine upon Your servant: save me for Your mercies sake. (...) Oh, love the Lord, all you His saints! For the Lord preserves the faithful, and full repays the proud person. Be of good courage, and He shall strengthen your heart, all you who hope in the Lord. (...) Many sorrows shall be to the wicked; but he who trusts in the Lord, mercy shall surround him. Be glad in the Lord and rejoice, you righteous: and shout for joy, all you upright in heart! (...) Behold, the eye of the Lord is on those who fear Him, on those who fear Him, on those who hope in His mercy, to deliver their soul from death, and to keep them alive in famine. Our soul waits for the Lord; He is our help and our shield. For our heart shall rejoice in Him, because we have trusted in His holy name. Let your mercy, O Lord, be upon us, just as we hope in You.
        Psalms 31:16, 23-24, 32:10-11, 33:18-22

    Trust in the Lord, and do good; dwell in the land, and feed on His faithfulness. Delight yourself also in the Lord, and He shall give you the desires of your heart. Commit your way to the Lord, trust also in Him, and He shall bring it to pass. He shall bring forth your righteousness as the light, and your justice as the noonday. Rest in the Lord, and wait patiently for Him; (...) But the salvation of the righteous is from the Lord; He is their strength in the time of trouble. And the Lord shall help them and deliver them; he shall deliver them from the wicked, and save them, because they trust in Him.
        Psalms 37:3-7, 39-40

    Those who trust in the Lord are like Mount Zion, which cannot be moved, but abides forever.   Psalms 125:1

How precious is Your loving-kindness, O God! Therefore, the children of men put their trust under the shadow of Your wings. They are abundantly satisfied with the fullness of Your house, and You give them drink from the river of Your pleasures. For with You is the fountain of life; in Your light we see light.   Psalms 36:7-9

Trust in Him at all times, you people; pour out your heart before Him; God is a refuge for us. Selah.   Psalms 62:8

Out of the depths I have cried to You, O Lord; Lord, hear my voice! Let Your ears be attentive to the voice of my supplications. If You, Lord, should mark iniquities, O Lord, who could stand? But these is forgiveness with You, that You may be feared. I wait for the Lord, my soul waits, and in His word I do hope. My soul waits for the Lord more than those who watch for the morning- yes, more than those who watch for the morning. O Israel, hope in the Lord; for with the Lord there is abundant redemption. And He shall redeem Israel from all his iniquities.   Psalm 130

Behold the proud, his soul is not upright in him; but the just shall live by his faith.   Habakkuk 2:4

Practice and understanding which are both complete are like the two wheels of a cart. Benefitting oneself and benefitting others are like the two wings of a bird. (...) One who wishes to become a field of merit for others while breaking the precepts is like a bird with broken wings who tries to fly into the sky with a tortoise on its back. A person who is not liberated from his own transgressions cannot redeem the transgressions of others.
Pancagatidipani

Whoever is faithful in a very little is faithful also in much; and whoever is dishonest in a very little is dishonest also in much.
Luke 16:10.

Look around you at people who have virtues. You will find that many people have not been ennobled by their practices, though they have that repute. The practice of virtues is in itself next to nothing. A thread is not made into a jewel because it passes through the holes in a series of pearls. I was unable to learn, let alone teach, until I realized that a desolate place is not made fertile merely by the presence of a treasure beneath the ground. *Hamid Qalindoz*

I am the goal and the means, the prosperity and the freedom from all sorrows...   Uddhava Gita 14:2

Believers, be ever mindful of God...Surely in remembrance of God are all hearts comforted. Remember Me, then, and I will remember you.   Quran

Now in the morning as he returned to the city, he hungered. And seeing a fig tree by the way side, he came to it, and found nothing thereon, but leaves only; and he said unto it, Let there be no fruit from thee henceforward forever. And immediately the fig tree withered away. And when the disciples saw it, they marveled, saying, How did the fig tree immediately wither away? And Jesus answered and said unto them, Verily I say unto you, If you have faith, and doubt not, you shall not only do what is done to the fig tree, but even if you shall say unto this mountain, Be thou taken up and cast into the sea, it shall be done. And all things, whatsoever you shall ask in prayer, believing, you shall receive.   Matthew 21:18-22

And he said unto her, Daughter, your faith has made you whole; go in peace.   Mark 5:34

And Jesus said unto him, Go your way; your faith has made you whole. And straightway he received his sight, and followed him in the way.   Mark 10:52

And Jesus answering said unto them, Have faith in God. Verily I say unto you, Whosoever shall say unto this mountain, Be thou taken up and cast into the sea; and shall not doubt in his heart, but shall believe that what he said comes to pass; he shall have it.

Therefore, I say unto you, All things whatsoever you pray and ask for, believe that you receive them, and you shall have them.
Mark 11:22-24

What shall we say then? That the Gentiles, who followed not after righteousness, attained to righteousness, even the righteousness which is of faith: but Israel, following after a law of righteousness, did not arrive at [that] law. Wherefore? Because [they sought it] not by faith, but as it were by works. They stumbled at the stone of stumbling; even as it is written, Behold, I lay in Zion a stone of stumbling and a rock of offence: And he that believeth on him shall not be put to shame.   Romans 9:30-33

We being Jews by nature, and not sinners of the Gentiles, yet knowing that a man is not justified by the works of the law but through faith in Jesus Christ, even we believed on Christ Jesus, that we might be justified by faith in Christ, and not by the works of the law: because by the works of the law shall no flesh be justified. (...) For I through the law died unto the law, that I might live unto God. I have been crucified with Christ; and it is no longer I that live, but Christ living in me: and that [life] which I now live in the flesh I live in faith, [the faith] which is in the Son of God, who loved me, and gave himself up for me. I do not make void the grace of God: for if righteousness is through the law, then Christ died for naught. (...) Even as Abraham believed God, and it was reckoned unto him for righteousness. Know therefore that they that are of faith, the same are sons of Abraham. And the scripture, foreseeing that God would justify the Gentiles by faith, preached the gospel beforehand unto Abraham, [saying,] In thee shall all the nations be blessed. So then they that are of faith are blessed with the faithful Abraham. For as many as are of the works of the law are under a curse: for it is written, Cursed is everyone who continues not in all things that are written in the book of the law, to do them. Now that no man is justified by the law before God, is evident: for, The righteous shall live by faith; and the law is not of faith; but, He that does them shall live in them. (...) the law is become our tutor [to bring us] unto

Christ, that we might be justified by faith. But now faith that is come, we are no longer under a tutor. For you are all sons of God, through faith, in Christ Jesus. For as many of you as were baptized into Christ did put on Christ. There can be neither Jew nor Greek, there can be neither bond nor free, there can be no male and female; for you all are one [man] in Christ Jesus. And if you are Christ`s, then are you Abraham`s seed, heirs according to promise. But I say that so long as the heir is a child, he differs nothing from a bondservant though he is lord of all; but is under guardians and stewards until the day appointed of the father. So we also, when we were children, were held in bondage under the rudiments of the world: but when the fullness of the time came, God sent forth his Son, born of a woman, born under the law, that he might redeem them that were under the law, that we might receive the adoption of sons. And because you are sons, God sent forth the Spirit of his Son into our hearts, crying, Abba, Father. So that you are no longer a bondservant, but a son; and if a son, then an heir through God. Howbeit at that time, not knowing God, you were in bondage to them that by nature are no gods: but now that you have come to know God, or rather to be known by God, how do you turn back again to the weak and beggarly rudiments, do you desire to be in bondage over again?
        Galatians 2:15- 4:8

       For this cause I bow my knees unto the Father, from whom every family in heaven and on earth is named, that he would grant you, according to the riches of his glory, that you may be strengthened with power through his Spirit in the inward man; that Christ may dwell in your hearts through faith; to the end that you, being rooted and grounded in love, may be strong to apprehend with all the saints what is the breadth and length and height and depth, and to know the love of Christ which passes knowledge, that you may be filled with all the fullness of God.
        Ephesians 3:14-19

Grace to you and peace from God the Father, and our Lord Jesus Christ, who gave himself for our sins, that he might deliver us out of this present evil world, according to the will of our God and Father: to whom [be] the glory forever and ever. Amen.
Galatians 1:3-5

Servants, be obedient unto them that according to the flesh are your masters, with fear and trembling, in singleness of your heart, as unto Christ; not in the way of eye-service, as men-pleasers; but as servants of Christ, doing the will of God from the heart; with good will doing service, as unto the Lord, and not unto men: knowing that whatsoever good thing each one does, the same shall he receive again from the Lord, whether [he be] bond or free. Ephesians 6:5-8

Now faith is assurance of [things] hoped for, a conviction of things not seen. For therein the elders had witness borne to them. By faith we understand that the worlds have been framed by the word of God, so that what is seen has not been made out of things which appear. By faith Abel offered unto God a more excellent sacrifice than Cain, through which he had witness borne to him that he was righteous, God bearing witness in respect of his gifts: and through it he being dead yet speaks. By faith Enoch was translated that he should not see death; and he was not found, because God translated him: for he has had witness borne to him that before his translation he had been well-pleasing unto God: And without faith it is impossible to be well-pleasing [unto him]; for he that comes to God must believe that he is, and [that] He rewards them that seek after Him.   Hebrews 11:1-6

So speak you, and so do, as men that are to be judged by a law of liberty. For judgment [is] without mercy to him that has showed no mercy: mercy glories against judgment. What does it profit, my brethren, if a man say he has faith, but have not works? can that faith save him? If a brother or sister be naked and in lack of daily food, and one of you say unto them, Go in peace, be warmed and filled; and yet you give them not the things needful to the body; what does it profit? Even so faith, if it have not works, is dead in itself. Yea, a man will say, You have faith, and I have works: show me your faith apart from your works, and I by my works will show you my faith. You believe that God is one; you do well: the demons also believe, and shudder. But will you know, O vain man, that faith apart from works is barren? Was not Abraham our father justified by works, in that he offered up Isaac his son upon the altar? You see that faith wrought with his works, and by works was faith made perfect; and the scripture was fulfilled which says, And Abraham believed God, and it was reckoned unto him for righteousness; and he was called the friend of God. You see that by works a man is justified, and not only by faith.   James 2:12-24

Who is wise and understanding among you? let him show by his good life his works in meekness of wisdom. But if you have bitter jealousy and faction in your heart, glory not and lie not against the truth. This wisdom is not [a wisdom] that comes down from above, but is earthly, sensual, devilish. For where jealousy and faction are, there is confusion and every vile deed. But the wisdom that is from above is first pure, then peaceable, gentle, easy to be entreated, full of mercy and good fruits, without variance, without hypocrisy. And the fruit of righteousness is sown in peace for them that make peace.   James 3:13-18

He who loves Me will keep My commandments, and he will be loved by My Father, and I will love him, and will manifest Myself to him.   John 14:21

Non-judgment

"Do not judge, and you will not be judged; do not condemn, and you will not be condemned. Forgive, and you will be forgiven; give, and it will be given to you. A good measure, pressed down, shaken together, running over, will be put into your lap; for the measure you give will be the measure you get back." And he spoke also a parable unto them, "Can the blind guide the blind? shall they not both fall into a pit? The disciple is not above his teacher: but everyone when he is perfected shall be as his teacher. And why behold the speck that is in your brother's eye, but consider not the beam that is in your own eye? Or how can you say to your brother, Brother, let me cast out the mote that is in your eye, when you yourself don't behold the beam that is in your own eye? You hypocrite, cast out first the beam of your own eye, and then you shall see clearly to cast out the mote that is in your brother's eye."
Luke 6:37-42

When Bankei held his seclusion-weeks of meditation, pupils from many parts of Japan came to attend. During one of these gatherings a pupil was caught stealing. The matter was reported to Bankei with the request that he expel the student. Bankei ignored the case. Later the pupil was caught in a similar act, and again Bankei disregarded the matter. This angered the other pupils, who drew up a petition asking that the student be expelled, stating that they would leave otherwise. When Bankei had read the petition he called everyone before him. "You are wise brothers," he told them. "You know that is right and what is not right. You may go somewhere else to study if you wish, but this poor brother does not even know right from wrong. Who will teach him if I do not? I am going to keep him here even if all the rest of you leave." A torrent of tears cleansed the face of the brother who had stolen. All desire to steal had vanished.

Therefore, you have no excuse, whoever you are, when you judge others; for in passing judgment on another you condemn yourself, because you, the judge, are doing the very same things.
$$\text{Romans 2:1}$$

Then Peter came and said to him, "Lord if another member of the church sins against me, how often should I forgive? As many as seven times?" Jesus said to him, "Not seven times, but, I tell you seventy-seven times."   Matthew 18:21-22

If the mind is happy, not only the body but the whole world will be happy. So one must find out how to become happy oneself. Wanting to reform the world without discovering one's true self is like trying to cover the whole world with leather to avoid the pain of walking on stones and thorns. It is much simpler to wear shoes.   *Ramana Maharshi*

She said moreover, that is one would attain to purity of mind it was necessary to abstain altogether from any judgment on one's neighbor and from all empty talk about his conduct. In creatures one should always seek only for the will of God. With great force she said: For no reason whatever should one judge the actions of creatures or their motives. Even when we see that it is an actual sin, we ought not to pass judgment on it, but have holy and sincere compassion and offer it up to God with humble and devout prayer.
From the Testament of St. Catherine of Siena

Forgive your neighbor's injustice; then when you pray, your own sins will be forgiven. Should a man nourish anger against his fellows and expect healing from the Lord? Should a man refuse mercy to his fellows, yet seek pardon for his own sins?
Sirach *28:2-4*

Judging another to be good or bad is evil. To cease making judgments between good and bad, that is true goodness.
Uddhava Gita *14:45*

Understanding the essential oneness of Purusha and Prakriti helps you avoid making judgments about the nature and actions of others. To praise or criticize is to make a commitment to that which is unreal. This can only lead to a vision that is always limited to a duality. When an individual is dreaming or sleeping deeply he or she loses awareness of the external world. If you see only the world of multiplicities and do not extend your vision to the One, you will be like the dreamer and the sleeper and continue to encounter the illusion of death. In a duality that does not really exist what is real and what is unreal? What is good and what is bad? Yet making such judgments and speaking about them gives them a reality in one's mind. Reflections, echoes and mirages- even though one knows they are unreal will cause a reaction. Thus the body continues to inspire a fear of death as long as one continues to identify with it. [...] All exist within the Self alone and only appear as separate on account of maya. One who knows this and for whom this knowledge has become reality neither judges nor criticizes. Such a person moves about in this world like the sun which shines on all alike.
Uddhava Gita *23:7-8*

One day the prophet Abraham invited a person to dinner, but when he learned that he was an infidel he canceled the invitation and turned him out. Immediately the Divine Voice reprimanded him, saying, "You did not give him food for a day even because he belonged to a different religion, yet for the last several years I am feeding him in spite of his heresy. Had you fed him for one night, you would not have become poor on that account." *al-Ghazzali*

We did not create the heavens and the earth except for just means. And the Hour is surely coming when this will be manifest. So overlook any human faults with gracious forgiveness.
Quran 15:85

Let not a wise person note the perversities of others, nor what they have done or left undone.   Dhammapada

If you close your mind in judgments and traffic with desires, your heart will be troubled. If you keep your mind from judging and aren't led by the senses, your heart will find peace.
Tao te Ching 52

Even as a lotus may grow from roadside garbage and spread joy to many traveling souls with its scent, so a true follower of the Buddha shines light to multitudes of blind mortals.   Dhammapada

The results of karma cannot be known by thought and so should not be speculated about. Thus thinking, one would come to distraction and distress. Therefore, Ananda, do not be the judge of people; do not make assumptions about others. A person is destroyed by holding judgments about others.   Anguttura Nikaya

Do not rejoice over me, my enemy; when I fall, I will arise; when I sit in darkness, the Lord will be a light to me. I will bear the indignation of the Lord, because I have sinned against Him, until He pleads my case and executes justice for me. He will bring me forth to the light; I will see His righteousness.   Micah 7:8-9

If you forgive men their trespasses, your heavenly Father will also forgive you. But if you do not forgive men their trespasses, neither will your Father forgive your trespasses. (...) Judge not, that you be not judged. For with what judgment you judge, you will be judged; and with the measure you use, it will be measured back to you. And why do you look at the speck in your brother's eye, but do not consider the plank in your own eye? Or how can you say to your brother, "Let me remove the speck from your eye"; and look, a plank is in your own eye? Hypocrite! First remove the plank from your own eye, and then you will see clearly to remove the speck from your brother's eye.   Matthew 6:14, 7:1-5

Passion and hatred spring from egoism. So do discontentment, attachment and terror. Speculative thoughts also spring there from and harass the mind like bugs do a crow. They spring from desire, are in one's self like the shoots which spring from the branches of a banyan tree. They are attached to sense desires like a maluva creeper which overgrows the jungle.
　　　　　　　　　　　Suciloma Sutta, Sutta Nipata

Forms, sounds, tastes, odors and contacts completely intoxicate people...The monk having thus obtained his meal and returned alone, should sit in solitude; reflecting within himself, he should be self-composed, avoiding distractions... Therefore, in being detached from these things, the monk must be like a drop of water on a lotus leaf.　　Dhammika Sutta, Sutta Nipata

Forms, both high and low come across, like tongues of flame from a log. Develop the mind of equilibrium. You will always be getting praise and blame, but do not let either affect the poise of the mind; follow the calmness, the absence of pride. When a person is desire less, when a monk has extinguished the river of becomings, when he has given up all activities of duty and obligation- he "ought to" and "ought not to"- then the fever is passed. Be razor sharp. Let go of the chained minds, the states involving attachment. Do not spend much time thinking about irrelevancies. No defilements, no ties, no dependency; only dedication to the practices of a pure life.　　Nalaka Sutta, Sutta Nipata

It is perception, consciousness, that is the source of all the basic obstacles.
　　　　　　　　Kalahavivada Sutta, Sutta Nipata

And whensoever you stand praying, forgive, if you have aught against any one; that your Father also who is in heaven may forgive you your trespasses. But if you do not forgive, neither will your Father who is in heaven forgive your trespasses.
　　　　　　　　　　　　Mark 11:25-26

And he said unto his disciples, It is impossible but that occasions of stumbling should come; but woe unto him, through whom they come! It were well for him if a millstone were hanged about his neck, and he were thrown into the sea, rather than that he should cause one of these little ones to stumble. Take heed to yourselves: if your brother sin, rebuke him; and if he repents, forgive him. And if he sins against you seven times in the day, and seven times turn again to you, saying, I repent; you shall forgive him.
Luke 17:1-4

And Jesus said unto them, The sons of this world marry, and are given in marriage: but they that are accounted worthy to attain to that world, and the resurrection from the dead, neither marry, nor are given in marriage: for neither can they die any more: for they are equal unto the angels; and are sons of God, being sons of the resurrection. But that the dead are raised, even Moses showed, in [the place concerning] the Bush, when he called the Lord the God of Abraham, and the God of Isaac, and the God of Jacob. Now he is not the God of the dead, but of the living: for all live unto him.
Luke 20:34-38

But Jesus went unto the mount of Olives. And early in the morning he came again into the temple, and all the people came unto him; and he sat down, and taught them. And the scribes and the Pharisees bring a woman taken in adultery; and having set her in the midst, they say unto him, Teacher, this woman has been taken in adultery, in the very act. Now in the law Moses commanded us to stone such: what do you say we should do with her? And this they said, trying him, that they might have [whereof] to accuse him. But Jesus stooped down, and with his finger wrote on the ground. But when they continued asking him, he lifted up himself, and said unto them, He that is without sin among you, let him first cast a stone at her. And again he stooped down, and with his finger wrote on the ground. And they, when they heard it, went out one by one, beginning from the eldest, [even] unto the last: and Jesus was left alone, and the woman, where she was, in the midst. And Jesus lifted up himself, and said unto her, Woman, where are they? did no man condemn you? And she said, No man, Lord. And Jesus said, Neither do I condemn you: go your way; from henceforth sin no more. Again therefore Jesus spoke unto them, saying, I am the light of the world: he that follows me shall not walk in the darkness, but shall have the light of life.   John 8:1-12

   Wherefore judge nothing before the time, until the Lord come, who will both bring to light the hidden things of darkness, and make manifest the counsels of the hearts; and then shall each man have his praise from God. (...) For who among men knows the things of a man, save the spirit of the man, which is in him? even so the things of God none knows, save the Spirit of God. But we received, not the spirit of the world, but the spirit which is from God; that we might know the things that were freely given to us of God.
            1st Corinthians 4:5, 2:11-12

   A builder was commissioned by a good man to construct and prepare a house which was to be given to the needy. The builder started work; but soon he found himself surrounded by people. Some of them wanted to learn how to build houses. Of these, only a few had the necessary ability. Some of the people remonstrated with the builder, saying: "You select only the people whom you like." Others reviled him, saying: "You are building this house for yourself." The builder said to them: "I cannot teach everyone. And I am building this house for some needy person." They replied: "You have provided the excuse after the accusation, and merely in order to answer it." He said: "But what if it is the truth? Is it still to be called a lie?" They told him: "This is sheer sophistry; we will not listen." The builder carried on with his work. Some of his assistants became so attached to the house that, for their own good, he sent them away. The detractors cried: "Now he begins to show his true colors. See what he has done to his only real friends: cast them out!" One of the builder's friends explained: "He has done this for a sufficient reason. It is for the good of the others." "Then why does he not speak for himself, explaining it in detail to us all?" they cried. The builder, sacrificing time which was needed in the making of the building, went to them himself, and said: "I am here to tell you what I have done and why." They immediately shouted: "See, having found that his hireling cannot convince us, he has come in person, trying to deceive us! Do not listen to him." The builder went back to his work, while the others called after him: "See how he slinks away... he cannot confuse us, for we are clear-thinking people." One of the people, who was more fair-minded than the rest, said to them: "Could we not come to some accommodation in this matter; perhaps the builder is really trying to do something good. On the other hand, if he is not, we can perhaps determine the situation on the basis of facts, not opinions." A few of the people agreed, though the majority dissented. This majority were divided among those who thought that the fair-minded man was in the builder's pay and those who thought that he was weak of intellect. The few now approached the builder saying: "Show us an authorization from your charitable employer, so that we may be convinced." But when the authorization arrived, it was found that none of them could read. "Bring me a man who can read, and I shall be delighted, so that we can have an end to this," said the builder. Some of these went away in disgust, saying: "We asked for proof, and all he does is mutter about reading and writing." Others searched and returned with sharp-witted and crafty illiterates who claimed that they could read. All of these, assuming that nobody in the world could read, asked the builder for large sums of money in exchange for attesting the truth of his authorization. He refused to conspire with them. Literate people, you see, are very scarce in that country. Those who can read and write are not trusted by the populace, or else have other things to do. The facts of the situation are these. People interpret them as they desire.   *Mudir Ali Sabri*

To become a saint of God, you must covet nothing in this world or the next and you must give yourself entirely to God and turn your face to Him. To desire this world is turning away from God for the sake of what is transitory. To covet the next world means turning away from God for the sake of what is everlasting.
Ibrahim Adham

The works of God are all of them good; every need when it comes he fills. No cause then to say: This is not as good as that; for each shows its worth at the proper time.   Sirach *39:33-34*

Mercy

"You have heart it said, "An eye for an eye and a tooth for a tooth." But I say to you, Do not resist an evil doer. But if anyone strikes you on the right cheek, turn the other also; and if anyone wants to sue you and take your coat, give your cloak as well; and if anyone forces you to go one mile, go also the second mile. Give to everyone that begs from you, and do not refuse anyone who wants to borrow from you. You have heard it said, "You shall love neighbor and hate your enemy." But I say to you, Love your enemies and pray for those who persecute you, so that you may be children of you Father in heaven; for he makes his sun rise on the evil and the good, and sends rain on the righteous and on the unrighteous. For if you love only those who love you, what reward do you have? Do not even the tax collectors do the same? And if you greet only your brothers and sisters, what more are you doing than others? Do not even the Gentiles do the same? Be perfect, therefore, as your heavenly Father is perfect." Matthew 5:38-48

Do that which consists in taking no action; pursue that which is not meddlesome; savor that which has no flavor. Make the small big and the few many; do good to him who has done you an injury.
Tao Te Ching

"He abused me, he beat me, he defeated me, he robbed me, - in those who harbor such thoughts hatred will never cease. He abused me, he beat me, he defeated me. - in those who do not keep such thoughts hatred will cease. Hatred does not cease by returning hatred: hatred ceases by love alone: this is an ancient law.
Buddha

Just then a lawyer stood up to test Jesus. "Teacher" he said, "what must one due to inherit eternal life?" He said to him, "What is written in the law? What do you read there?" He answered, "You shall love the Lord your God with all your heart, and with all your soul, and with all your strength, and with all your mind; and you neighbor as yourself." And he said to him, "You have given the right answer; do this, and you will live." But wanting to justify himself, he asked Jesus, "And who is my neighbor?" Jesus replied, "A man was going from Jerusalem to Jericho, and fell into the hands of robbers who stripped him, beat him, and went away, leaving him half dead. Now by chance a priest was going down that road; and when he saw him, he passed by on the other side. So likewise a Levite, when he came to the place and saw him, passed by on the other side. But a Samaritan while traveling came near him; and when he saw him, he was moved with pity. He went to him and bandaged his wounds, having poured oil and wine on them. Then he put him on his own animal, brought him to an inn, and took care of him. The next day he took out two denarii, gave them to the innkeeper, and said, "Take care of him; and when I come back, I will repay you whatever more you spend." Which of these three, do you think, was a neighbor to the man who fell into the hands of the robbers?" He said, "The one who showed him mercy", Jesus said to him, "Go and do likewise."'"   Luke 10:29-37

Verily my mercy takes precedence over my wrath.   Quran

If the unbeliever knew the extent of the Lord's mercy, even he would not despair of Paradise.   Quran

(Abraham) said: And who despairs of the mercy of his Lord, but such as go astray.   Quran 15:56

Say: O My servants who have transgressed against their souls! Do not despair of the Mercy of Allah: for Allah forgives all sins: for He is Oft-Forgiving, Most Merciful. You turn to your Lord in repentance and bow to His Will, before the Penalty comes on you: after that you shall not be helped.   Quran 39:53-54

Return, O Lord, deliver me! Oh, save me for Your mercies sake!   Psalms 6:4

Gracious is the Lord, and righteous; yes, our God is merciful. The Lord preserves the simple; I was brought low, and He saved me. Return to your rest, O my soul, for the Lord has dealt bountifully with you.   Psalms 116:5-7

The Lord is gracious and full of compassion, slow to anger and great in mercy. The Lord is good to all, and His tender mercies are over all His works.   Psalm 145:8-9

He who covers his sins will not prosper, but whoever confesses and forsakes them will have mercy. Happy is the man who is always reverent, but he who hardens his heart will fall into calamity.   Proverbs 28:13-14

Praise the Lord of hosts, for the Lord is good, for His mercy endures forever.   Jeremiah 33:11

I cried out to the Lord because of my affliction, and He answered me. Out of the belly of Sheoul I cried, and You have heard my voice. For You cast me into the deep, into the heart of the seas, and the floods surrounded me; all Your billows and Your waves passed over me. Then I said, "I have been cast out of Your sight; yet I will look again toward Your holy temple." The waters surrounded me, even to my soul. The deep closed around me; weeds were wrapped around my head. I went down to the moorings of the mountains; the earth with its bars closed behind me forever; yet You have brought up my life from the pit, O Lord, my God. When my soul fainted within me, I remembered the Lord; and my prayer went up to You into Your holy temple. Those who regard worthless idols forsake their own Mercy. But I will sacrifice to You with the voice of thanksgiving; I will pay what I have vowed. Salvation is of the Lord.   Jonah 2:1-9

A certain lender had two debtors: the one owed five hundred shillings, and the other fifty. When they had not [wherewith] to pay, he forgave them both. Which of them therefore will love him most? Simon answered and said, He, I suppose, to whom he forgave the most. And he said to him, You have rightly judged. And turning to the woman, he said unto Simon, Do you see this woman? I entered into your house, you gave me no water for my feet: but she has wetted my feet with her tears, and wiped them with her hair. You gave me no kiss: but she, since the time I came in, has not ceased to kiss my feet. My head with oil you did not anoint: but she has anointed my feet with ointment. Wherefore I say to you, Her sins, which are many, are forgiven; for she loved much: but to whom little is forgiven, [the same] loves little. And he said unto her, Your sins are forgiven. And they that sat at meat with him began to say within themselves, Who is this that even forgives sins? And he said unto the woman, Your faith has saved you; go in peace.   Luke 7:41-50

Execute true justice, show mercy and compassion everyone to his brother. Do not oppress the widow or the fatherless, the alien or the poor. Let none of you plan evil in his heart against his brother.
Zechariah 7:9-10

And as they were eating, he took bread, and when he had blessed, he brake it, and gave to them, and said, Take ye: this is my body. And he took a cup, and when he had given thanks, he gave to them: and they all drank of it. And he said unto them, This is my blood of the covenant, which is poured out for many.
Mark 14:22-24

And he received a cup, and when he had given thanks, he said, Take this, and divide it among yourselves: for I say unto you, I shall not drink from henceforth of the fruit of the vine, until the kingdom of God shall come. And he took bread, and when he had given thanks, he brake it, and gave to them, saying, This is my body which is given for you: this do in remembrance of me. And the cup in like manner after supper, saying, This cup is the new covenant in my blood, [even] that which is poured out for you.
Luke 22:17-20

Thus it is written, that the Christ should suffer, and rise again from the dead the third day; and that repentance and remission of sins should be preached in his name unto all the nations, beginning from Jerusalem. You are witnesses of these things. And behold, I send forth the promise of my Father upon you: but tarry ye in the city, until ye be clothed with power from on high.   Luke 24:46-49

He is the stone which was set at naught of you the builders, which was made the head of the corner. And in none other is there salvation: for neither is there any other name under heaven, that is given among men, wherein we must be saved. (...) Be it known unto you therefore, brethren, that through this man is proclaimed unto you remission of sins: and by him every one that believes is justified from all things, from which you could not be justified by the law of Moses. (...) And when there had been much questioning, Peter rose up, and said unto them, Brethren, you know that a good while ago God made choice among you, that by my mouth the Gentiles should hear the word of the gospel, and believe. And God, who knows the heart, bare them witness, giving them the Holy Spirit, even as he did unto us; and he made no distinction between us and them, cleansing their hearts by faith. Now therefore why do you make trial of God, that you should put a yoke upon the neck of the disciples which neither our fathers nor we were able to bear? But we believe that we shall be saved through the grace of the Lord Jesus, in like manner as they.   Acts 4:11-12, 13:38-39, 15:7-11

And he has said unto me, My grace is sufficient for you: for [my] power is made perfect in weakness. Most gladly therefore will I rather glory in my weaknesses, that the power of Christ may rest upon me.   2 Corinthians 12:9

For it became him, for whom are all things, and through whom are all things, in bringing many sons unto glory, to make the author of their salvation perfect through sufferings. For both he that sanctifies and they that are sanctified are all of one: for which cause he is not ashamed to call them brethren, saying, I will declare your name unto my brethren, In the midst of the congregation will I sing your praise. And again, I will put my trust in him. And again, Behold, I and the children whom God has given me. Since then the children are sharers in flesh and blood, he also himself in like manner partook of the same; that through death he might bring to naught him that had the power of death, that is, the devil; and might deliver all them who through fear of death were all their lifetime subject to bondage. For verily not to angels does he give help, but he gives help to the seed of Abraham. Wherefore it behooved him in all things to be made like unto his brethren, that he might become a merciful and faithful high priest in things pertaining to God, to make propitiation for the sins of the people. For in that he himself has suffered being tempted, he is able to succor them that are tempted. (...) For every high priest, being taken from among men, is appointed for men in things pertaining to God, that he may offer both gifts and sacrifices for sins: who can bear gently with the ignorant and erring, for that he himself also is compassed with infirmity; and by reason thereof is bound, as for the people, so also for himself, to offer for sins. And no man takes the honor unto himself, but when he is called of God, even as was Aaron. So Christ also glorified not himself to be made a high priest, but he that spoke unto him, Thou art my Son, This day have I begotten thee: as he said also in another [place,] Thou art a priest for ever After the order of Melchizedek. Who in the days of his flesh, having offered up prayers and supplications with strong crying and tears unto him that was able to save him from death, and having been heard for his godly fear, though he was a Son, yet learned obedience by the things which he suffered; and having been made perfect, he became unto all them that obey him the author of eternal salvation; named of God a high priest after the order of Melchizedek. Of whom we have many things to say, and hard of interpretation, seeing you are become dull of hearing. (...) For if that first [covenant] had been faultless, then would no place have been sought for a second. For finding fault with them, he said, Behold, the days come, said the Lord, That I will make a new covenant with the house of Israel and with the house of Judah; Not according to the covenant that I made with their fathers in the day that I took them by the hand to lead them forth out of the land of Egypt; For they continued not in my covenant, And I regarded them not, said the Lord. For this is the covenant that I will make with the house of Israel After those days, said the Lord; I will put my laws into their mind, and on their heart also will I write them: And I will be to them a God, and they shall be to me a people: And they shall not teach every man his fellow-citizen, and every man his brother, saying, Know the Lord: For all shall know me, From the least to the greatest of them. For I will be merciful to their iniquities, and their sins will I remember no more.

Hebrews 2:10-

Life

Whoever loves father or mother more than me is not worthy of me; and whoever loves son or daughter more than me is not worthy of me; and whoever does not take up the cross and follow me is not worthy of me. Those who find their life will lose it and those who lose their life for my sake will find it."
Matthew 10:37-39

What does it profit them if they gain the whole world, but lose or forfeit themselves?   Luke 9:25

Forgetfulness of self is remembrance of God.
Abu-Yaizd Al-Bistami

Nothing burns in hell but the self.
Theologia Germanica

Who could begin to deny self, if there were not something in man different from self?   *William Law*

Kill me, O my trustworthy friends, for in my being killed is my life. Love is that you remain standing in front of your Beloved. When you are deprived of all your attributes then His attributes become your qualities. Between me and You, there is only me. Take away the me, so only You remain. I am the Supreme Reality.
Al-Hallaj

I die every day.   1st Corinthians 15:31

Can setting cause any harm to the sun or moon? To you, my death seems a setting, but really it is dawn.   *Rumi*

The kingdom of heaven is like treasure hidden in a field, which someone found and hid; then in his joy he goes and sells all

that he has and buys that field. Again, the kingdom of heaven is like a merchant in search of fine pearls; on finding one pearl of great value, he went and sold all that he had and bought it.
Matthew 13:44-46

You know nothing of yourself here in this state. You are like the wax in the honeycomb: what does it know of fire or guttering? When it gets to the stage of the waxen candle and when light is emitted, then it knows. Similarly, you will know that when you were alive you were dead, and only thought yourself alive.
Attar of Nishapur

I'm going to speak some reckless words and I want you to listen to them recklessly... "How do I know that loving life is not a delusion? How do I know that in hating death I am not like a man who, having left home in his youth, has forgotten the way back? Lady Li was the daughter of the border guard Ai. When she was first taken captive and brought to the state of Chin, she wept until her tears drenched the collar of her robe. But later, when she went to live in the palace of the ruler, shared his couch with him, and ate the delicious meats of his table, she wondered why she had ever wept. How do I know that the dead do not wonder why they ever longed for life?"
Chuang Tzu

Men are asleep and when they die they wake.
Hadith of the Prophet Mohammad

Die before you die.   Hadith of the Prophet Mohammad

Would you know whence it is that so many false spirits have appeared in the world, who have deceived themselves and others with false fire and false light, laying claim to information, illumination and openings of the divine Life, particularly to do wonders under extraordinary calls from God? It is this: they have turned to God without turning from themselves; would be alive to God before they are dead to their own nature. Now religion in the hands of the self, or corrupt nature, serves only to discover vices of a worse kind than in nature left to itself. Hence are all the disorderly passions of religious men, which burn in a worse flame than passions only employed about worldly matters; pride, self-exaltation, hatred and persecution, under a cloak of religious zeal, will sanctify actions which nature, left to itself, would be ashamed to own.   *William Law*

    If thou hast seen the devil, look at thine own self.
Jalal-uddin Rumi

    Your own self is your own Cain that murders your own Abel. For every action and motion of self has the spirit of Anti-Christ and murders the divine life within you.
William Law

    Know that when you learn to lose yourself, you will reach the Beloved. There is no other secret to be learned, and more than this is not known to me.   *Ansari of Herat*

    To one of his spiritual children our dear father (St. Francois de Sales) said, "Be patient with everyone, but above all with yourself. I mean, do not be disheartened by your imperfections, but always rise up with fresh courage. I am glad you make a fresh beginning daily; there is no better means of attaining to the spiritual life than by continually beginning again, and never thinking that we have done enough. How are we to be patient in bearing with our neighbor's faults, if we are impatient in bearing with our own? He who is fretted by his own failings will not correct them; all profitable correction comes from a calm, peaceful mind. "
Jean Pierre Camus

    I tell you that no one can experience this birth without a mighty effort. No one can attain this birth unless he can withdraw his mind entirely from things.   *Eckhart*

    The Sufi is absent from himself and present with God.
Hujwiri

> Those who are dead to their lower selves are alive with God.
> *Traditional saying in Sufism*

> Seek Me and live. (...) Seek the Lord and live. (...) Seek good and not evil, that you may live so that the Lord God of hosts will be with you, as you have spoken. Hate evil, love good; establish justice in the gate. It may be that the Lord God of host will be gracious to the remnant of Joseph.   Amos 5:14-15

Truth

Every kingdom divided against itself is laid waste, and no city or house divided against itself will stand. If Satan casts out Satan, he is divided against himself; how then will his kingdom stand.   Matthew 12:25-26

John answered, "Master, we saw someone casting out demons in your name, and we tried to stop him, because he does not follow with us." But Jesus said to him, "Do not stop him; for whoever is not against you is for you."   Luke 9:49-50

Jesus said, "It is impossible for a man to mount two horses or to stretch two bows. And it is impossible for a servant to serve two masters; otherwise, he will honor the one and treat the other contemptuously. No man drinks old wine and immediately desires to drink new wine. And new wine is not put into old wineskins, lest they burst; nor is old wine put into a new wineskin, lest it spoil it. An old patch is not sewn into a new garment, because a tear would result."   Gospel of Thomas 47

Truth is one; only It is called by different names. All people are seeking the same Truth; the variance is due to climate, temperament, and name. A lake has many ghats. From one ghat the Hindus take water in jars and call it *jal*. From another ghat the Muslims take water in leather bags and call it *pani*. From a third the Christians take the same thing and call it "water". Suppose someone says that the thing is not *jal* but *pani*, or that it is not *pani* but water, or that it is not but *jal*. It would indeed be ridiculous. But this very thing is at the root of the friction among sects, their misunderstandings and quarrels. This is why people injure and kill one another, and shed blood, in the name of religion. But this is not good. Everyone is going toward God. They will all realize Him if they have sincerity and longing of heart.   *Ramakrishna*

Four people were given a piece of money. The first was a Persian. He said: "I will buy with this some *angur*." The second was an Arab. He said: "No, because I want *inab*." The third was a Turk. He said: "I don't want *inab*, I want *uzum*." The fourth was a Greek. He said: "I want *stafil*." Because they did not know what lay behind the names of things, these four started to fight. They had information but no knowledge. One man of wisdom present could have reconciled them all, saying: "I can fulfill the needs of all of you, with one and the same piece of money. If you honestly give me your trust, your one coin will become as four; and four at odds will become as one united." Such a man would know that each in his own language wanted the same thing, grapes.   *Jalaludin Rumi*

A royal hawk alighted for a time on the wall of a ruin inhabited by owls. The owls feared him. He said: "This may seem a prosperous place to you, but my place is upon the wrist of a king." Some of the owls shouted to the others: "Do not listen to him! He is using guile to steal our home."   *Jalaludin Rumi*

Teaching, as was his custom, during the ordinary business of life, Sheikh Abu Tahir Harami rode his donkey one day into a market-place, a disciple following behind him. At the sight of him, a man called out: "Look, here comes the ancient unbeliever!" Harami's pupil, his wrath aroused, shouted at the defamer. Before long there was a fierce altercation in progress. The Sufi calmed his disciple, saying: "If you will only cease this tumult, I will show you how you can escape this kind of trouble." They went together to the old man's house. The sheikh told his follower to bring him a box of letters. "Look at these. They are all letters addressed to me. But they are couched in different terms. Here someone calls me Sheikh of Islam; there, Sublime Teacher. Another says I am the "Wise One of the Twin Sanctuaries". And there are others. Observe how each styles in me in accordance with what he considers me to be. But I am none of these things. Each man calls another just what he thinks him to be. This is what the unfortunate one in the market-place has just done. And yet you take exception to it. Why do you do so- since it is the general rule of life?"   Sufism

So what is real truth? It is just a matter of looking back into the purity of your own mind in the course of daily activities, not being influenced by anything wrong. That is because mind is like a monkey, consciousness like a horse: without the chain and bridle of great awareness watching them, it will be truly hard to control them no matter how clever your devices. But when you have whipped and thrashed them into submission, so they merge back into oneness, and all traces of birth and extinction disappear, then you naturally realize basic subtle illumination, thoroughly empty yet uncannily penetrating and effective.
Hui-ching (1528-1598)

O you who believe! Stand out firmly for justice, as witnesses to Allah, even as against yourselves, or your parents, or your kin, and whether it be against rich or poor: for Allah can best protect both. Follow not the lusts of your hearts, lest you swerve, and if you distort justice or decline to do justice, verily Allah is well-acquainted with all that you do.   Quran 4:135

Truth has now arrived and falsehood perished: for Falsehood is by its nature bound to perish.   Quran 17:81

Meditate in this way: Alas! The father and mother, the great storm, the whirlwind, the thunder, the terrifying projections and all these apparent phenomena are illusory in their real nature. However, they appear, they are not real. All substances are false and untrue. They are like a mirage, they are not permanent, they are not changeless. What is the use of desire? What is the use of fear? It is regarding the non-existent as existent. All these are projections of my mind, and since the mind is itself illusory and nonexistent from the beginning, from where externally do they arise like this? I did not understand in this way before, and so I believed the nonexistent to exist, the untrue to be true, the illusion to be real; therefore, I have wandered in samsara for so long. And if I do not realize that they are illusions, I shall still wander in samsara for a long time and certainly fall into the muddy swamp of suffering. Now they are all like dreams, like illusions, like echoes, like cities of the gandharvas, like mirages, like images, like optical illusions, like the moon in water; they are not real, even for a moment. Certainly they are not true but false!   Tibetan Book of the Dead

       Whose [adorning] let it not be the outward adorning of braiding the hair, and of wearing jewels of gold, or of putting on apparel; but [let it be] the hidden man of the heart, in the incorruptible [apparel] of a meek and quiet spirit, which is in the sight of God of great price.   1st Peter 3:3-4

       This is he that came by water and blood, [even] Jesus Christ; not with the water only, but with the water and with the blood. And it is the Spirit that bears witness, because the Spirit is the truth. For there are three who bear witness, the Spirit, and the water, and the blood: and the three agree in one.   1st John 5:6-8

Self-knowledge

O friend, understand: the body is like the ocean rich with hidden treasures. Open your inmost chamber and light its lamp. Within the body are gardens, rare flowers, peacocks, the inner Music; within the body a lake of bliss, on it the white soul-swans take their joy. And in the body, a vast market- go there, trade, sell yourself for a profit you can't spend.   *Mirabai*

Decay is inherent in all component things. Be a lamp unto yourself! Work out your liberation with diligence!   *Buddha*

Therefore, Ananda, be you lamps unto yourselves, be you a refuge to yourselves. Betake yourselves to no external refuge. Hold fast to the Truth as a lamp; hold fast to the Truth as a refuge. Look not for a refuge in anyone beside yourselves. And those, Ananda, who either now or after I am dead shall be a lamp unto themselves, shall betake themselves to no external refuge, but holding fast to the Truth as their refuge, shall not look for refuge to anyone beside themselves- it is they who shall reach the very topmost Height. But they must be anxious to learn.   *Buddha*

Jesus said, "Blessed are they who have been persecuted within themselves. It is they who have truly come to know the father. Blessed are the hungry, for the belly of him who desires will be filled."   Gospel of Thomas 69

He who knows others is clever, he who knows himself has discernment. He who overcomes others has force; he who overcomes himself is strong. He who knows contentment is rich; he who perseveres is a man of purpose; he who does not lose his station will endure; he who lives out his days has a long life.
                    Tao Te Ching

Recognize what is in your sight, and that which is hidden from you will become plain to you. For there is nothing hidden which will not become manifest.   Gospel of Thomas 5

Jesus said, "Let him who seeks, continue seeking until he finds. When he finds, he will become troubled. When he becomes troubled, he will be astonished, and he will rule over the all."
Gospel of Thomas 2

He who knows himself knows his Lord.
Hadith of the Prophet Mohammed

Your medicine is in you, and you do not observe it. Your ailment is from yourself, and you do not register it.   *Hazrat Ali*

Man in ordinary life finds difficulties and seeks happiness. He cannot attain satisfaction or permanently overcome difficulties when he is in a state of ignorance and incapacity. He can, however, arrive at a state in which he believes that his difficulties are gone, or even that he knows things which he does not know. This is the state of those who manipulate their minds, or who allow themselves, because of the tension of their state, to adopt the assurances and techniques of the ignorant. Man is like a swimmer who is fully dressed and hampered every moment by his clinging clothes. He must know why he cannot swim before steps can be taken to make it possible. It is no solution for him to have the impression that he is swimming properly; for this may make him feel better and prevent him from arriving at the farther bank of the river. Such men and women drown.
Latif Ahmad

So long as we assign the causes for our weaknesses to others, we cannot attain perfection in long-suffering.
St. John Cassian

Only take heed to yourself, and keep your soul diligently, lest you forget the things which your eyes have seen, and lest they depart from your heart all the days of your life: but teach them to your sons, and your sons sons.   Deuteronomy 4:9

...the peace of God is with them whose mind and soul are in harmony, who are free from desire and wrath, who know their own soul and in their soul find the light of Brahman.
Bhagavad Gita 5:26

Daiju visited the master Baso in China. Baso asked: "What do you seek?" "'Enlightenment," replied Daiju. "You have your own treasure house. Why do you search outside?" Baso asked. Daiju inquired: "Where is my treasure house?" Baso answered: "What you are asking is your treasure house." Daiju was enlightened! Ever after he urged his friends: "pen your own treasure house and use those treasures."

Jesus said, "Blessed is the man who has suffered and found life."   Gospel of Thomas 58

Jesus said, "That which you have will save you if you bring it forth form yourselves. That which you do not have within you [will] kill you if you do not have it."   Gospel of Thomas 70

So, Ananda, you must be your own lamps, be your own refuges...Hold firm to the truth as a lamp and a refuge and do not look for refuge to anything besides yourselves. A monk becomes his own lamp by continually looking on his body, feelings, perceptions, moods, and ideas in such a manner that he conquers the cravings and depressions of ordinary persons and is always diligent, self-possessed and collected in mind. Whoever among my monks does this, either now or when I am dead, if he is anxious to learn, will reach the summit.   *Buddha*

Do you have the patience to wait until your mud settles and the water is clear? Can you remain unmoving until the right action arises by itself?   Tao Te Ching 15

Shibli was asked: "Who guided you in the Path?" He said: "A dog. One day I saw him, almost dead with thirst, standing by the water's edge. Every time he looked at his reflection in the water he was frightened, and withdrew, because he thought it was another dog. Finally, such was his necessity, he cast away fear and leapt into the water; at which the other dog vanished. The dog found that the obstacle, which was himself, the barrier between him and what he sought, melted away. In this same way my own obstacle vanished, when I knew that it was what I took to be my own self. And my Way was first shown to me by the behavior of- a dog.'"
Sufism

When water is still, it is like a mirror, reflecting the beard and the eyebrows... And if water thus derives lucidity from stillness, how much more the faculties of the mind? The mind of the sage being in repose becomes the mirror of the universe, the speculum of all creation.   *Chuang Tzu*

The most excellent jihad is that for the conquest of self.
Hadith of the Prophet Mohammad

The soul that has not been practiced over a long time and educated fully in knowledge of self is not raised up to knowledge of God. In vain he raises the eye of the heart to see God when he is not yet prepared to see himself. Let a person first learn to see his own invisible things before he presumes he is able to grasp at invisible divine things.   *St. Victor*,   <u>Mystical Ark</u>

Blessed are they who have been persecuted within themselves. It is they who will truly come to know the Father.
Gospel of Thomas

As the light grows, we see ourselves to be worse than we thought. We are amazed at our former blindness as we see issuing forth from our heart a whole swarm of shameful feelings, like filthy reptiles crawling from a hidden cave. But we must be neither amazed nor disturbed. We are not worse than we were; on the contrary, we are better. But while our thoughts diminish, the light we see them by waxes brighter, and we are filled with horror. So long as there is no sign of cure, we are aware of the depth of our disease; we are in a state of blind presumption and hardness, the prey of self-delusion. While we go with the stream, we are unconscious of its rapid course; but when we begin to stem it ever so little, it makes itself felt.   *Fenelon*

Indeed, the saving truth has never been preached by the Buddha, seeing that one has to realize it within oneself.
Sutralamkara

You have spent all your life in the belief that you are wholly devoted to others, and never self-seeking. Nothing so feeds self-conceit as this sort of internal testimony that one is quite free from self-love, and always generously devoted to one's neighbors. But all this devotion that seems to be for others is really for yourself. Your self-love reaches to the point of perpetual self-congratulation that you are free from it; all your sensitiveness is lest you might not be fully satisfied with the self; this is at the root of all your scruples. It is the "I" which makes you so keen and sensitive. You want God as well as man to be always satisfied with you, and you want to be satisfied with yourself in all your dealings with God. Besides, you are not accustomed to be contented with a simple good will- your self-love wants a lively emotion. A reassuring pleasure, some kind of charm or excitement. You are too much used to be guided by imagination and to suppose that your mind and will are inactive, unless you are conscious of their workings. And thus you are dependent upon a certain kind of excitement similar to that which the passions arouse, or theatrical representations. By dint of refinement you fall into the opposite extreme- a real coarseness of imagination. Nothing is more opposed, not only to the life of faith, but also to true wisdom. There is no more dangerous illusion than the fancies by which people try to avoid illusion. It is the imagination which leads us astray; and the certainty which we seek through the imagination, feeling, and taste, is one of the most dangerous sources from which fanaticism springs. This is the gulf of vanity and corruption which God would make you discover in your heart; you must look upon it with the calm and simplicity belonging to true humility. It is mere self-love to be inconsolable at seeing one's own imperfections; but to stand face to face with them, neither flattering nor tolerating them, seeking to correct oneself without becoming pettish- this is to desire what is good for its own sake, and for God's.   *Fenelon*

Faults will turn to good, provided we use them to our own humiliation, without slackening in the effort to correct ourselves. Discouragement serves no possible purpose; it is simply the despair of wounded self-love. The real way of profiting by the humiliation of one's own faults is to face them in their true hideousness, without ceasing to hope in God, while hoping nothing form self.
Fenelon

For twelve years I was the smith of my soul. I put it in the furnace of austerity and burned it in the fire of combat, I laid it on the anvil of reproach and smote it with the hammer of blame until I made of my soul a mirror. Five years I was the mirror of myself and was ever polishing that mirror with divers acts of worship and piety. Then for a year I gazed in contemplation. On my waist I saw a girdle of pride and vanity and self-conceit and reliance on devotion and approbation of my works. I labored for five years more until that girdle became worn out and I professed Islam anew. I looked and saw that all created things were dead. I pronounced four akbirs over them and returned from the funeral of them all, and without intrusion of creatures, through God's help alone, I attained unto God.   *Bayazid of Bistun*

Happy are those who find fault with themselves instead of finding fault with others.
Hadith of the Prophet Mohammad

You ought to know yourself as you really are, so that you may understand of what nature you are, from where you have come to this world, for what purpose you were created, and in what your happiness and misery consist. For within you are combined the qualities of the animals and the wild beasts and also the qualities of the angels, but the spirit is your real essence, and all beside it is, in fact, foreign to you. Strive for knowledge of your origin, so that you may know how to attain to the Divine Presence and the contemplation of the Divine Majesty and Beauty. Deliver yourself from the fetters of lust and passion. God did not create you to be their captive; they should be your servants, under your control for the journey that is before you, to be your steed and your weapon, so that you may use them to pursue your happiness, and when you have not more need of them, then cast them under your feet. A Sufi began to weep in the middle of the night. He said, "The world is like a closed casket in which we are placed and in which, through our own ignorance, we spend our time in folly. When Death opens the lid of the casket, each one who has wings takes his flight to Eternity, but that one who is without wings remains in the casket. Before the lid is taken away from this casket, become a bird of the Way to God. Develop your wings and your feathers. No, rather burn your wings and your feathers and destroy yourself by fire, and so will you arrive at the Goal before all others."   *Attar*

First He pampered me with a hundred favors, then He melted me with the fires of sorrows. After he sealed me with the seal of Love, I became Him. Then, he threw myself out of me.   *Rumi*

I have no Buddhism to give anyone. I just have a sword—whoever comes, I cut down, so their lives cannot go on and their seeing and hearing disappear: then I meet them before their parents gave birth to them. If I see them go forward, I cut them off. However, though the sword is sharp, it does not cut the innocent. Is there anyone who is innocent?   *Chen-ching*

There are not many arts to Zen study: it just requires knowing your own true mind. Now observe that within this body the physical elements combine temporarily, daily heading for extinction: where is the true mind? The flurry of ideas and thoughts arising and passing away without constancy is not the true mind. That which shifts and changes unstably, sometimes good, sometimes bad, is not the true mind. That which wholly depends on external things to manifest, and is not apparent when nothing is there is not the true mind. The heart inside the body cannot see itself, blind to the internal; it is not the true mind. Suppose you turn the light of awareness around to look within, and sense a recondite tranquility and calm oneness; do you consider this the true mind? You still do not realize that this recondite tranquility and calm oneness are due to the perception of the false mind: there is the subjective mind perceiving and the object perceived- so this recondite tranquility and calm oneness totally belong to the realm of inner states. This is what is meant by the Heroic Progress Scripture when it says, "Inwardly keeping to recondite tranquility is still a reflection of discrimination of objects." How could it then be the true mind? So if these are not the true mind, what is the true mind? Try to see what your mind is, twenty-four hours a day. Don't try to figure it out, don't try to interpret it intellectually, don't try to get someone to explain it to you, don't seek some other technique, don't calculate how long it may take, don't calculate the degree of your own strength- just silently pursue this inner investigation on your own: Ultimately what is my own true mind?   *Yuan-hsien*

O living flame of love that wounds so tenderly in my soul's deepest center. As you are no longer oppressive perfect your work in me if it is your will. Break the web of this sweet encounter. Before the divine fire enters the soul and becomes one with its depths, the Holy Spirit wounds it, destroying and consuming the imperfections of its evil habits. The soul suffers greatly in this, for in this state of purification the flame does not burn brightly but in darkness, and if it gives any light at all it is only to show up and make the soul experience its own weakness and defects. It is not a refreshing, peaceful fire, but a consuming and searching one that

makes the soul grieve at the sight of itself. The soul perceives its own smallness in comparison with the immensity of the flame.
St. John of the Cross

But are we not commanded to think of ourselves, to enter into ourselves, to watch over ourselves? Yes, certainly, when beginning to enter into the service of God in order to detach ourselves from the world, to forsake exterior objects, to correct the bad habits we have contracted; but, afterwards, we must forget ourselves to think only of God, forsake ourselves to belong to God alone. But, as for you, you wish to remain always wrapped up in yourself, in your so-called spiritual interests; and God, to draw you out of this last resource of self-love, allows you to find nothing in yourself but a source of fears, doubts, uncertainty, trouble, anxiety and depression, as though this God of goodness said by this: Forget yourself and you will find in me only, peace, spiritual joy, calmness and an absolute assurance of salvation. But again you say: In this forgetfulness of self, far from correcting myself of my sins and imperfections, I do not even know them. An error! An illusion! Ignorance! Never can you more clearly detect your faults than in the clear light of the presence of God. In this way also, better than in any other, all our defects and imperfections are gradually consumed like straw in a fire. *Jean-Pierre de Caussade*

Allah loves those who turn to Him constantly and He loves those who keep themselves pure and clean. Quran 2:222

Let a wise man blow off the impurities of himself, as a smith blows off the impurities of silver, one by one, little by little, and from moment to moment (...) The fault of others is easily perceived, but that of one's self is difficult to perceive; a man winnows his neighbor's faults like chaff, but his own faults he hides, as a cheat hides an unlucky cast of the die. Dhammapada

The Master said, "I suppose I should give up hope. I have yet to meet the man who, on seeing his own errors, is able to take himself to task inwardly."" Analects, Book 5:27

The monk whose body, tongue and mind are quieted, who is collected, and who has rejected the baits of the world- that monk is rightly called quiet. Rouse yourself by yourself, examine yourself by yourself! Thus, self-protected and attentive, you will live happily, O monk! For self is the lord of self, self is the refuge of self. Therefore, curb yourself as the merchant curbs a noble horse.
                                                                Dhammapada

When meditation is mastered, the mind is unwavering like the flame of a lamp in a windless place. In the still mind, in the depths of yoga, the Self reveals itself. Beholding the Self by means of the Self, an aspirant knows the joy and peace of complete fulfillment in a state of truth and union with God (...) Forsaking wholeheartedly all selfish desires and expectations, use your will to control the senses and think of nothing but the Self. Little by little, through patience and repeated effort, the mind will become stilled in the calm peace that comes with being in harmony with the Self dwelling in our hearts.   Bhagavad Gita 6:19-20, 24-25

I am the true Self glowing like a lamp throughout infinity and the beginning, middle and end of all existence. (...) This is true wisdom: to seek the essence of reality. To seek anything else is ignorance. (...) Dwelling in every heart, it is beyond darkness. It is called the light of lights, the object and goal of reality, and knowledge itself shining inherently pure. (...) They alone see truly that all actions are performed by the elements in Prakriti of material and mental substance, while the Self remains unmoved in perfection (...) As the sun lights up the world, the Self dwelling in the field is the source of all light in the field. Those who, with the eye of wisdom, distinguish the field from the Knower and the way to the freedom of the spirit from the bondage of Prakriti, realize the supreme goal and the true goal and source of wisdom and wisdom itself.   Bhagavad Gita 10:20, 13:11,17, 29-30, 33-34

I said, "You are gods, and all of you are children of the Most High. But you shall die like men, and fall like one of the princes."'"   Psalms 82:6-7

Then said Jesus unto his disciples, If any man would come after me, let him deny himself, and take up his cross, and follow me. For whosoever would save his life shall lose it: and whosoever shall lose his life for my sake shall find it. For what shall a man be profited, if he shall gain the whole world, and forfeit his life? or what shall a man give in exchange for his life? For the Son of man shall come in the glory of his Father with his angels; and then shall he render unto every man according to his deeds. Verily I say unto you, there are some of them that stand here, who shall in no wise taste of death, till they see the Son of man coming in his kingdom.
Matthew 16:24-28

Unity

With my own heart I commune on the question how Varuna and I may be united.   Rig Veda

Enlightenment is like the moon reflected on the water. The moon does not get wet, nor is the water broken. Although its light is wide and great, the moon is reflected even in a puddle an inch wide. The whole moon and the entire sky are reflected in dewdrops on the grass, or even in one drop of water. Enlightenment does not divide you, just as the moon does not break the water. You cannot hinder enlightenment, just as a drop of water does not hinder the sky. The depth of the drop is the height of the moon. Each reflection, however long or short its duration, manifests the vastness of the dewdrop, and realizes the limitlessness of the moonlight in the sky.   *Dogen*

Then the king will say to those at his right hand "Come, you that are blessed by my Father, inherit the kingdom prepared for you from the foundation of the world; for I was hungry and you gave me food, I was thirsty and you gave me something to drink, I was a stranger and you welcomed me, I was naked and you gave me clothing, I was sick and you took care of me, I was in prison and you visited me." Then the righteous will answer him, "Lord when was it that we saw you hungry and gave you food, or thirsty and gave you something to drink? And when was it that we saw you a stranger and welcomed you, or naked and gave you clothing? And when was it that we saw you sick or in prison and visited you?" And the king will answer them, "Truly I tell you, just as you did it to one of the least of these who are members of my family, you did it to me." Then he will say to those at his left hand, "You that are accursed, depart from me into the eternal fire prepared for the devil and his angels; for I was hungry and you gave me no food, I was thirsty and you gave me nothing to drink, I was a stranger and you did not welcome me, naked and you did not give me clothing, sick

and in prison and you did not visit me." Then they will also answer, "Lord, when was it that we saw you hungry or thirsty or a stranger or naked or sick or in prison, and did not take care of you?" Then he will answer them. "Truly I tell you, just as you did not do it to one of the least of these, you did not do it to me." And these will go away into eternal punishment, but the righteous into eternal life."
Matthew 25:34-46

Thousand-headed Purusha, thousand eyed, thousand footed- he having pervaded the earth on all sides, still extends ten fingers beyond it. Purusha alone is all this- whatever has been and whatever is going to be. Further, he is the lord of immortality and also of what grows for food. Such is his greatness; greater, indeed, than this is Purusha. All creatures constitute but one quarter of him, his three quarters are the immortal in heaven (..) Being born, he projected himself behind the earth as also before it. When the gods performed the sacrifice with Purusha as the oblation, then the spring was its clarified butter, the summer the sacrificial fuel, and the autumn the oblation. The sacrificial victim Purusha, born at the very beginning, they sprinkled with sacred water upon the sacrificial grass. With him as the oblation the gods performed the sacrifice, and also the Sadhyas and the rishis. From that wholly offered sacrificial oblation were born the verses and the sacred chants; from it were born the meters; the sacrificial formula was born from it. From it horses were born and also those animals who have double rows of teeth; cows were born from it, from it were born goats and sheep. When they divided Purusha, in how many different portions did they arrange him? What became of his mouth, what of his two arms? What were his two thighs and his two feet called? His mouth became the brahman; his two arms were made into the rajanya; his two thighs the vaishyas; from his two feet the shudra were born. The moon was born from the mind, from the eye the sun was born; from the mouth Indra and Agni, from the breath the wind was born. From the navel was the atmosphere made, from the head issued forth heaven; from the two feet was born the earth and the cardinal directions from the ear.

Rig Veda: *The Myth of the Cosmic Giant Purusha*

Who looks with an equal eye upon both the high-born and the low-born, the spark and the blazing sun, the tenderhearted and the cruel, is considered by me to be a sage. One who is always present to my Presence in all, quickly overcomes any tendencies towards rivalry, envy and conceit, which are born of the idea-of "I". Disregarding the contempt and ridicule of friends and acquaintances, and casting aside embarrassment with awareness of the body prostrate sincerely before all: be they outcasts, dogs, asses and cows. Worship everyone in this way in thought, word and deed- and my Presence within all will soon be revealed. That vision, in which the Truth is revealed and Brahman is seen to exist everywhere, will liberate you from all doubts and all effortful striving. This form of worship is the highest: with body, mind, and speech regard all beings as myself.   Uddhava Gita 24:14-19

What the sages sought they have found at last. No more questions have they to ask of life. With self-will extinguished, they are at peace. Seeing the Lord of Love in all around, serving the Lord of Love in all around, they are united with him forever.
From the Mundaka Upanishad

Those who are free from selfish attachments, who have mastered the senses and passions, act not, but are acted through by the Lord. Listen to me now, O son of Kunti, how one who has become an instrument in the hands of the Lord attains Brahman, the supreme consummation of wisdom. Unerring in discrimination, sovereign of the senses and passions, free from the clamor of likes and dislikes, they lead a simple, self-reliant life based on meditation, using speech, body and mind to serve the Lord of Love. Free from self-will, aggressiveness, arrogance, from the lust to possess people or things, they are at peace with themselves and others and enter into the unitive state. United with the Lord, ever joyful, beyond the reach of self-will and sorrow, they serve me in every living creature and attain supreme devotion to me. By loving me they share in my glory and enter into my boundless being.   Bhagavad Gita

Kobun Chino Roshi, a Zen master and a master of kyudo, the way of the bow, was at Esalen with his archery teacher, who was demonstrating Zen archery. He demonstrated a shot at a target and then handed the bow to Kobun and invited him to demonstrate his skill. Esalen is high on a cliff over the Pacific Ocean, so Kobun took an arrow and the bow and with complete concentration released the arrow into the ocean. When it hit the water he said, "Bull's eye!"

Jesus said, "If those who lead you say to you, 'See the kingdom is in the sky', then the birds of the sky will precede you. If they say to you, 'It is in the sea', then the fish will precede you. Rather, the kingdom is inside of you, and it is outside of you. When you come to know yourselves, then you will become known, and you will realize that it is you who are the sons of the living father. But if you will not know yourselves, you dwell in poverty and it is you who are that poverty."   Gospel of Thomas 3

Jesus saw infants being suckled. He said to his disciples, "These infants being suckled are like those who enter the kingdom." They said to him, "Shall we then, as children, enter the kingdom." Jesus said to them, "When you make the two one, and when you make the inside like the outside, and the above like the below, and when you make the male and the female one and the same, so that the male not be male nor the female; and when you fashion eyes in place of an eye, and a hand in place of a hand, and a foot in place of a foot, and a likeness in place of a likeness; then will you enter the kingdom."   Gospel of Thomas 22

Jesus said, "It is I who am the light of which is above them all. It is I who am the call. From me did they all come forth, and unto me did the all extend. Split a piece of wood, and I am there. Lift up the stone, and you will find me there."
                                        Gospel of Thomas 77

Jesus said, "When you make the two one, you will become the sons of man, and when you say, Mountain, move away, it will move away."" Gospel of Thomas

Jesus said, "He who will drink from my mouth will become like me. I myself shall become he, and the things that are hidden will be revealed to him."" Gospel of Thomas 108

His disciples said to him, "When will the kingdom come?" [Jesus said], "It will not come by waiting for it. It will not be a matter of saying 'here it is' or 'there it is'. Rather, the kingdom of the father is spread out on the earth, and men do not see it."
Gospel of Thomas 112

This is the teaching of Uddalaka to Shvetaketu, his son: As by knowing one lump of clay, dear one, we come to know all things made out of clay- that they differ only in name and form, while the stuff of which all are made is clay; as by knowing one gold nugget, dear one we come to know all things made out of gold- that they differ only in name and form, while the stuff of which all are made is gold; (...) So through spiritual wisdom, dear one, we come to know that all of life is one. In the beginning was only Being, one without a second. Out of himself he brought forth the cosmos and entered into everything in it. There is nothing that does not come from him. Of everything he is the inmost Self. He is the truth; he is the Self supreme. You are that, Shvetaketu; you are that.
From the Chandogya Upanishad

All is change in the world of senses, but changeless is the supreme Lord of Love. Meditate on him, be absorbed in him, wake up from this dream of separateness. Know God and all fretters will fall away. No longer identifying yourself with the body, go beyond birth and death. All your desires will be fulfilled in him who is One without a second. Know him to be enshrined within your heart always. Truly there is nothing more to know in life. Meditate and realize the world is filled with the presence of God. Fire is not seen until one fire stick rubs against another, though the fire remains

hidden in the fire stick. So does the Lord remain hidden in the body until he is revealed through the mystic mantrum. Let your body be the lower fire stick; let the mantrum be the upper. Rub them against each other in meditation and realize the Lord. Like oil in sesame seeds, like butter in cream, like water in springs, like fire in a fire stick, so dwells the Lord of Love, the Self, in the very depths of consciousness. Realize him through truth and meditation. The Self is hidden in the hearts of all, as butter lies hidden in cream. Realize the Self in the depths of meditation, the Lord of Love, supreme reality, who is the goal of all knowledge. This is the highest mystical teaching. This is the highest mystical teaching.
From the Shveteshvatara Upanishad

Do not sit at home, do not go into the forest, but recognize mind wherever you are. When one abides in complete and perfect enlightenment, where is Samsara and where is Nirvana? This is myself and this is another. Be free of this bond which encompasses you about, and your own self is thereby released. Do not err in this matter of self and other. Everything is Buddha without exception. Here is that immaculate and final stage, where thought is pure in it's true nature. The fair tree of thought that knows no duality, spreads through the triple world. It bears the flower and fruit of Compassion, and its name is service of others. The fair tree of the Void abounds with flowers, acts of compassion of many kinds, and fruit for others appearing spontaneously, for this joy has no actual thought of another... He who clings to the Void and neglects Compassion, does not reach the highest stage. But he who practices only Compassion does not gain release from toils of existence. He, however, who is strong in practice of both, remains neither in Samsara nor in Nirvana.   *Saraha*

Creation is the extension of God. Creation is God encountered in time and space. Creation is the infinite in the garb of the finite. To attend to creation is to attend to God. To attend to the moment is to attend to eternity. To attend to the part is to attend to the whole. To attend to Reality is to live constructively.
Pirke Avot 6:11

God is unified oneness- one without two, inestimable. Genuine divine existence engenders the existence of all of creation. The sublime, inner essences secretly constitute a chain linking everything from the highest to the lowest, extending from the upper pool to the edge of the universe. There is nothing- not even the tiniest thing- that is not fastened to the links of this chain. Everything is catenated in its mystery, caught in its oneness. God is one, God's secret is one, all the worlds below and above are all mysteriously one. Divine existence is indivisible. The entire chain is one. Down to the last link, everything is linked with everything else; so divine essence is below as well as above, in heaven and on earth. There is nothing else.   *Moses de Leon*

Every particle of the world is a mirror, in each atom lies the blazing light of a thousand suns. Cleave the heart of a rain drop, a hundred pure oceans will flow forth. Look closely at a grain of sand, the seed of a thousand beings can be seen. The foot of an ant is larger than an elephant; in essence, a drop of water is no different than the Nile. In the heart of a barley-corn lies the fruit of a hundred harvests; within the pulp of a millet-seed an entire universe can be found. In the wing of a fly, an ocean of wonder; in the pupil of the eye, an endless heaven. Though the inner chamber of the heart is small, the Lord of both worlds gladly makes His home there.   *Mahmud Shabestari*

Love becomes perfect only when it transcends itself- becoming one with it's object; producing unity of being.
Hakim Jami

One went to the door of the Beloved and knocked. A voice asked: "Who is there?" He answered: "It is I." The voice said: "There is no room here for me and thee." The door was shut. After a year of solitude and deprivation this man returned to the door of the Beloved. He knocked. A voice from within asked: "Who is there?" The man said: "It is Thou." The door was opened for him.   *Rumi*

The Yogi who pure from sin ever prays in this harmony of soul soon feels the joy of Eternity, the infinite joy of union with God. He sees himself in the heart of all beings and he sees all beings in his heart. This is the vision of the Yogi of harmony, a vision which is ever one. And when he sees me in all and he sees all in me, then I never leave him and he never leaves me. He who in this oneness of love, loves me in whatever he sees, wherever this man may live, in truth this man lives in me. And he is the greatest Yogi he whose vision is ever one: when the pleasure and pain of others is his own pleasure and pain.   Bhagavad Gita 6:28-32

As water raining on a mountain-ridge runs down the rocks on all sides, so the man who sees variety of things runs after them on all sides. But as pure water raining on pure water becomes one and the same, so becomes, O Nachiketas, the soul of the sage who knows.
Katha Upanishad

As rivers flowing into the ocean find their final peace and their name and form disappear, even so the wise become free from name and form and enter into the radiance of the Supreme Spirit who is greater than all greatness. In truth, who knows Brahman becomes Brahman.   Mundaka Upanishad

And you are, all of you, sons of God through faith in Jesus Christ... And there are no more distinctions between Jew and Greek, slave and free, male and female, but all of you are one in Jesus Christ. God... is not far from each of us. For in him we live and move and have our being.   Galatians 3

Late have I loved You, O Beauty so ancient and so new; late have I loved You! For behold You were within me, and I outside; and I sought You outside and in my unloveliness fell upon those lovely things that You have made. You were within me and I was not with You. I was kept from You by those things, yet had they not been in You, they would not have been at all. You did send forth Your beams and shine light upon me to chase away my blindness: You did breathe fragrance upon me, and I drew in my breath and do

now pant for You: I tasted You, and now hunger and thirst for You: You did touch me, and I have burned for Your peace.
St. Augustine (354-430)

Where ever you turn, there is the face of God. (...) There is no refuge from God but in Him.   Hadith **of the Prophet Mohammad**

For thirty years God was my mirror, now I am my own mirror. What I was I no longer am, for "I"" and "God" are a denial of God's unity. Since I no longer am, God is his own mirror. He speaks with my tongue, and I have vanished.
Abu-Yazid Al-Bistami (died ca 874)

Behold but One in all things; it is the second that leads you astray.   *Kabir*

To set up what you like against what you dislike- this is the disease of the mind. When the deep meaning of the Way is not understood, peace is disturbed to no purpose. Pursue not the outer entanglements, dwell not in the inner void; be serene in the oneness of things, and dualism vanishes of itself. When you strive to gain quiescence by stopping motion, the quiescence so gained is ever in motion. So long as you tarry in such dualism, how can you realize oneness? And when oneness is not thoroughly grasped, loss is sustained in two ways: the denying of external reality is the assertion of it, and the assertion of Emptiness (the Absolute) is the denying of it... One in all, all in One- if only this is realized, no more worry about not being perfect!   *The Third Patriarch of Zen*

Whatever you see, hear or touch- know that you cannot know it for what it is. Know that whatever your mind makes of it is like a mirage that will fade away. A confused mind sees a world of multiplicities, a world of good and bad. This creates a compulsion to act or to refrain from acting, depending on what will bring gain and what will cause loss. Therefore, control your senses and your mind. See the entire universe as the Self and see this Self in me, its supreme sovereign. In this way you will come to know and realize

that the Self within you is the same Self of all embodied beings. Once you know this your mind will be completely satisfied and all obstacles will be removed. One who has thus transcended good and bad will act for the good and refrain from acting for the bad, but not because of any notion of loss or gain. Rather, these wise ones are like children and act without guile, doing what has to be done.
Uddhava Gita *2:7-11*

The One is the warp and weft of creation. All existence depends upon the One, just as the existence of the cloth rests on its woven threads. This tree of samsara is ancient; as it moves it sends forth fruit and flowers. Good and bad deeds are its seeds; its hundreds of deep roots are desires; rajas, tamas and sattva are its support; and the panchatattva: earth, water, fire, air and space are its five sturdy branches yielding five different kinds of sap- smell, taste, sight, touch and hearing. These five sturdy branches produce ten others which are called the indriyas, the organs of action- the nose, tongue, eyes, ears, skin, the throat, hands, feet, anus, sexual organs, plus the mind. Hidden in its branches it carries the nests of two birds- the supreme One and the ahamkara, the idea of "I". Its three layers of bark are the three humors of the body- wind, bile and phlegm. And it bears two fruits- joy and sorrow. This tree extends farther than the sun. Filled with desires, some people, like vultures will ravage the fruit of sorrow; while those on the path of renunciation, living like swans in the forest, will eat of the fruit of joy. One who truly understands the Vedas and who has gained wisdom through the guru, knows that this tree is the supreme One, which grows through the power of the gunas and the maya which the One has woven. Now, Uddhava, this is my instruction to you: with a quiet and watchful mind, sharpened by service to your guru, take up the axe of awareness and cut this tree down. Thus free the Self and remain totally identified with the Self- only then may you lay down your axe.   Uddhava Gita *7:21-24*

Therefore, cease to identify yourself with the mind which is constantly drawn to objects through the senses, and which then gets caught up in these objects. Instead, identify yourself entirely with that undivided Presence.   Uddhava Gita *8:26*

The one absolute homogenous Truth, which is beyond both the mind and speech, through the power of maya becomes two: the knower and that which is known. These two are Purusha and Prakriti. Prakriti can be said to have a dual nature- it is the unmanifest state and the manifest state of all matter. Purusha is one state of pure consciousness.   Uddhava Gita *19:3-4*

Whatever comes into being- both the small and the great, both the narrow and the wide- everything is both Purusha and Prakriti. But remember, remember: whatever a thing is in the beginning, it returns to being in the end- that is its reality even in the middle. A gold ring is always gold even when it ceases being a ring, and a clay cup is always clay even when it has ceased being a cup. Gold and clay are always their own true nature. Everything that takes form, whether visible or invisible, will have an origin, and as it is transformed will become the next thing- like earthen clay transforming into a cup: the state in which it is a cup has only a relative reality, but the clay earth is its original and final reality.
Uddhava Gita *19:16-18*

When those who are wise perceive an object of the senses, they fully understand that it has no existence of its own and is nothing other than the Self. To the wise, the distinct nature of the object has no more reality than a fading dream to someone waking up. Dear Uddhava, prior to the dawning of wisdom people identify themselves with everything that comes under the domain of the gunas- including all actions taken. But by the cultivation of wisdom such ignorance fades, and the Self alone remains; neither accepted nor rejected, it is that which is.   Uddhava Gita *23:32-33*

When the paintings are hidden, you will see the Painter. O brother, I will tell you the mystery of mysteries. Know, then, that painting and Painter are one! When your faith is made perfect, you will never see yourself, save in Him.   *Attar*

The Lord of Love, omnipresent, dwelling in the heart of every living creature, all mercy, turns every face to himself. He is the supreme Lord, who through his grace moves us to seek him in our own hearts. He is the light that shines forever. He is the inner Self of all, hidden like a flame in the heart. Only by the stilled mind can he be known. Those who realize him become immortal.
From the Shvetashvatara Upanishad

May the Lord of Love, who projects himself into this universe of myriad forms, from whom all beings come and to whom all return, grant us the grace of wisdom. He is fire and the sun, and the moon and the stars. He is the air and the sea, and the Creator, Prajapati. He is this boy, he is that girl, he is this man, too, tottering on his staff. His face is everywhere. He is the blue bird, he is the green bird with red eyes; he is the thundercloud, and he is the seasons and the seas. He has no beginning; he has no end. He is the source from which the worlds evolve. From his divine power comes forth all this magical show of name and from, of you and me, which casts the spell of pain and pleasure. Only when we pierce through this magic veil do we see the One who appears as many. Two birds of beautiful plumage, comrades inseparable, live on the selfsame tree. One bird eats the fruit of pleasure and pain; the other looks on without eating. Forgetting our divine origin, we become ensnared in the world of change and bewail our helplessness. But when we see the Lord of Love in all his glory, adored by all, we go beyond sorrow. What use are the scriptures to anyone who knows not the source from whom they come, in whom all gods and worlds abide? Only those who realize him as ever present within the heart attain abiding joy.   *From the* Shvetashvatara

> Wheresoever you turn, there is the face of Allah.
> Quran *2:23*

> Fear Allah, to Whom you shall be gathered back.
> Quran 5:96

> To Him will be your return- all of you. The promise of Allah is true and sure. It is He who begins the process of creation, and repeats it, that He may reward with justice those who believe and work righteousness; but those who reject Him will have draughts of boiling fluids, and a Penalty grievous, because they did reject Him.
> Quran 10:4

> (After talking with the Buddha and hearing him expound the Dhamma), Ananda and the great assembly perceived that each one's mind was coextensive with the universe, seeing clearly the empty character of the universe as plainly as a leaf or a trifling thing in the hand, and that all things in the universe are alike merely the excellently bright and primeval mind of Bodhi, and that this mind is universally diffused, and comprehends all things in itself. And still reflecting, they beheld their generated bodies, as so many grains of dust in the wide expanse of the universal void, now safe, now lost; or as a bubble of the sea, sprung up from nothing and born to be destroyed. But their perfect and independent soul they beheld as not to be destroyed but remaining ever the same; it is identical with the substance of Buddha... (Buddha speaking): "This unity alone in the world is boundless in reality, and being boundless is yet one. Though in small things, yet it is great; though in great things, yet it is small. Pervading all things, present in every minutest particle of dust, and yet turning the great wheel of the Law; opposed to all sensible phenomena; it is one with Divine Knowledge; it is manifested as the effulgent Nature of the Divine Intelligence of Tathagata."   Surangama Sutra

> Those who wish to attain oneness must practice undiscriminating virtue. They must dissolve all ideas of duality: good and bad, beautiful and ugly, high and low. They will be

obliged to abandon any mental bias born of cultural or religious belief. Indeed, they should hold their minds free of any thought which interferes with their understanding of the universe as a harmonious oneness.   Hua Hu Ching 7

    Empty your mind of all thoughts. Let your heart be at peace. Watch the turmoil of beings, but contemplate their return. Each separate being in the universe returns to the common source. Returning to the source is serenity. If you don't realize the source, you stumble in confusion and sorrow. When you realize where you come from, you naturally become tolerant, disinterested, amused, kindhearted as a grandmother, dignified as a king. Immersed in the wonder of the Tao, you can deal with whatever life brings you and when death comes, you are ready.   Tao te Ching

    To return to the root is to find the meaning, but to pursue appearances is to miss the source. At the moment of inner enlightenment there is a going beyond appearance and emptiness. The changes that appear to occur in the empty world we call real only because of out ignorance. Do not search for the truth; only cease to cherish opinions. Do not remain in the dualistic state; avoid such pursuits carefully. If there is even a trace of this and that, of right and wrong, the Mind-essence will be lost in confusion. Although all dualities come from the One, do not be attached even to this One. (...) When no discriminating thoughts arise, the old mind ceases to exist. When thought objects vanish, the thinking-subject vanishes, as when the mind vanishes, objects vanish. Things are objects because of the mind; the mind is such because of things. Understand the relativity of these two and the basic reality: the unity of emptiness. In this Emptiness the two are indistinguishable and each contains in itself the whole world. If you do not discriminate between coarse and fine you will not be tempted to prejudice and opinion. To live in the Great Way is neither easy nor difficult, but those with limited views are fearful and irresolute: the faster they hurry, the slower they go, and clinging attachment cannot be limited: even to be attached to the idea of enlightenment is to go astray. Just let things be in their own way and there will be neither coming nor going. Obey the nature of things (your own nature) and you will walk freely and undisturbed. When thought is in bondage the truth is hidden, for everything is murky and unclear and the burdensome practice of judging brings annoyance and weariness. What benefit can be derived from distinctions and separations? If you wish to move in the One Way do not dislike even the world of senses and ideas. Indeed, to accept them fully is identical with true Enlightenment. The wise man strives to no goals but the foolish man fetters himself. There is one Dharma, not many; distinctions arise from the clinging needs of the ignorant. To seek Mind with the discriminating mind is the greatest of all mistakes. Rest and unrest derive from passion; with enlightenment there is no liking and disliking. All dualities come from ignorant inference. They are like dreams or flowers in the air: foolish to try to grasp them. Gain and loss, right and wrong: such thoughts must finally be abolished at once. If the eye never sleeps, all dreams will naturally cease. If the mind makes no discriminations, the ten thousand things are as they are, of single essence. To understand the mystery of this One essence is to be released from all entanglements. When all things are seen equally the timeless Self-essence is reached. No comparisons or analogies are possible in this causeless, relation less state. (...) For the unified mind in accord with the Way, all self-centered striving ceases. Doubts and irresolutions vanish and life in true faith is possible. With a single stroke we are free from bondage; nothing clings to us and we hold nothing. All is empty, clear, self-illuminating, with no exertion of the mind's power. Here thought, feeling, knowledge and imagination are of no value. In this world of Suchness there is neither self nor other-than-self. To come directly into harmony with this reality just simply say when doubt arises, "Not two." In this "not two"" nothing is separate, nothing is excluded. No matter when or where, enlightenment means entering this truth. And this truth is beyond extension or diminution in time or space; in it a single thought is ten thousand years. Emptiness here, emptiness there, but the infinite universe stands always before your eyes. Infinitely large and infinitely small; no difference, for definitions have vanished and no boundaries are seen. So too with Being and non-Being. Don't waste time in doubts and arguments that have nothing to do with this. One thing, all things: move among and intermingle, without distinction. To live in this realization is to be without anxiety about non-perfection. To live in this faith is the road to non-duality. Because the non-dual is one with the trusting mind. Words! The Way is beyond language, for in it there is no yesterday, no tomorrow, no today.   *Seng-tsan*

Who sees all beings in his own Self, and his own Self in all beings, loses all fear. When a sage sees this Unity and his Self has become all beings, what delusion and what sorrow can ever be near him?   Isa Upanishad

In the consciousness of Brahman, the universe is and into him it returns.   Maitri Upanishad

Knowledge will remove your bewilderment, and you will see all creation in yourself and me.   Bhagavad Gita 4:35

He sees the atman in all beings, and all beings in the atman, for his heart is firm in Yoga. Who sees me in all things, and all things in me, he is never far from me, and I am never far from him. He worships me and lives in me, whoever he might be, for he has achieved unity of being, he sees me in all things.
Bhagavad Gita 6:29-31

The Yogi who pure from sin ever prays in this harmony of soul soon feels the joy of Eternity, the infinite joy of union with God. He sees himself in the heart of all beings and he sees all beings in his heart. This is the vision of the Yogi of harmony, a vision which is ever one. And when he sees me in all and he sees all in me, then I never leave him and he never leaves me. He who in this oneness of love, loves me in whatever he sees, wherever this man may live, in truth this man lives in me.   Bhagavad Gita 6:28-31

The disunited mind is far from wise; how can it meditate? How be at peace? When you know no peace, how can you know joy? When you let your mind follow the call of the senses, they carry away your better judgment as storms drive a boat off its course. (...)They live in wisdom who see themselves in all and all in them, who have renounced every selfish desire and sense craving tormenting the heart.   Bhagavad Gita 2:66-67, 55

Still your mind in me, still your intellect in me, and without a doubt you will be united with me forever.
Bhagavad Gita 12:8

There are many, free of passion, fear, and anger, at one with me, taking refuge in me, who, refined in the heat of knowledge, have come to my state of being.   Bhagavad Gita 4:10

Sanctify them in the truth: your word is truth. As you did send me into the world, even so sent I them into the world. And for their sakes I sanctify myself, that they themselves also may be sanctified in truth. Neither for these only do I pray, but for them also that believe on me through their word; that they may all be one; even as you, Father, [art] in me, and I in you, that they also may be in us: that the world may believe that you have sent me. And the glory which you have given me I have given unto them; that they may be one, even as we [are] one; I in them, and you in me, that they may be perfected into one; that the world may know that you sent me, and love them, even as You love me. Father, I desire that they also whom you have given me be with me where I am, that they may behold my glory, which you have given me: for you loved me before the foundation of the world. O righteous Father, the world knew you not, but I knew you; and these knew that you didst send me; and I made known unto them your name, and will make it known; that the love wherewith You loved me may be in them, and I in them.   John 17:17-26

Now on the morrow, as they were on their journey, and drew near to the city, Peter went up upon the housetop to pray, about the sixth hour: and he became hungry, and desired to eat: but while they made ready, he fell into a trance; and he beheld the heaven opened, and a certain vessel descending, as it were a great sheet, let down by four corners upon the earth: wherein were all manner of four-footed beasts and creeping things of the earth and birds of the heaven. And there came a voice to him, Rise, Peter; kill and eat. But Peter said, Not so, Lord; for I have never eaten anything that is common and unclean. And a voice [came] unto him again the second time, What God has cleansed, make not thou common. And this was done three times: and straightway the vessel was received up into heaven. (...) And Peter opened his mouth and said, Of a truth I perceive that God is no respecter of persons: but in every nation he that fears him, and works righteousness, is acceptable to him. The word which he sent unto the children of Israel, preaching good tidings of peace by Jesus Christ (He is Lord of all.) -- that saying you yourselves know, which was published throughout all Judaea, beginning from Galilee, after the baptism which John preached; [even] Jesus of Nazareth, how God anointed him with the Holy Spirit and with power: who went about doing good, and healing all that were oppressed of the devil; for God was with him. And we are witnesses of all things which he did both in the country of the Jews, and in Jerusalem; whom also they slew, hanging him on a tree. Him God raised up the third day, and gave him to be made manifest, not to all the people, but unto witnesses that were chosen before of God, [even] to us, who ate and drank with him after he rose from the dead. And he charged us to preach unto the people, and to testify that this is he who is ordained of God [to be] the Judge of the living and the dead. To him bear all the prophets witness, that through his name every one that believes on him shall receive remission of sins. While Peter yet spoke these words, the Holy Spirit fell on all them that heard the word. And they of the circumcision that believed were amazed, as many as came with Peter, because that on the Gentiles also was poured out the gift of the Holy Spirit. For they heard them speak with tongues, and magnify God. Then answered Peter, Can any man forbid the water, that these should not be baptized, who have received the Holy Spirit as well as we? And he commanded them to be baptized in the name of Jesus Christ. Then prayed they him to tarry certain days. (...) And Paul stood in the midst of the Areopagus, and said, You men of Athens, in all things, I perceive that you are very religious. For as I passed along, and observed the objects of your worship, I found also an altar with this inscription, TO AN UNKNOWN GOD. What therefore you worship in ignorance, this I set forth unto you. The God that made the world and all things therein, he, being Lord of heaven and earth, dwells not in temples made with hands; neither is he served by men's hands, as though he needed anything, seeing he himself gives to all life, and breath, and all things; and he made of one every nation of men to dwell on all the face of the earth, having determined [their] appointed seasons, and the bounds of their habitation; that they should seek God, if haply they might feel after him and find him, though he is not far from each one of us: for in him we live, and move, and have our being; as certain even of your own poets have said, For we are also his offspring. Being then the offspring of God, we ought not to think that the Godhead is like unto gold, or silver, or stone, graven by art and device of man. The times of ignorance therefore God overlooked; but now he commands men that they should all everywhere repent: inasmuch as he has appointed a day in which he will judge the world in righteousness by the man whom he has ordained; whereof he has given assurance unto all men, in that he has raised him from the dead.   Acts 10:9-16, 34-48, 17:22-31

For of him, and through him, and unto him, are all things. To him [be] the glory forever. Amen.   Romans 11:36

I therefore, the prisoner in the Lord, beseech you to walk worthily of the calling wherewith you were called, with all lowliness and meekness, with longsuffering, forbearing one another in love; giving diligence to keep the unity of the Spirit in the bond of peace. [There is] one body, and one Spirit, even as also you were called in one hope of your calling; one Lord, one faith, one baptism, one God and Father of all, who is over all, and through all, and in all.

True Self: Atman

Concealed in the heart of all beings is the Atman, the Spirit, the Self; smaller than the smallest atom, greater than the vast spaces. The man who surrenders his human will leaves sorrows behind, and beholds the glory of the Atman by the grace of the Creator... Not even through deep knowledge can the Atman be reached, unless evil ways are abandoned, and there is rest in the senses, concentration in the mind and peace in one's heart.   Katha Upanishad

To set the mind on the flesh is death, but to set the mind on the Spirit is life and peace.   Romans 8:6

Whatever one's duties, one who worships the Self alone and is constant in that worship- knowing that the Self is the Self of all beings- will know me as the Self.   Uddhava Gita *13:44*

...but if by the Spirit you put to death the deeds of the body, you will live. For all who are led by the Spirit of God are children of God.   Romans 8:13-14

The Atman is that by which the universe is pervaded, but which nothing pervades; which causes all things to shine, but which all things cannot make to shine...Who but the Atman can remove the bonds of ignorance, passion, and self-interested action? The Atman is the Witness of the individual mind and its operations. It is absolute knowledge.
    The Crest-Jewel of Wisdom"- *Shankara*

Having realized his own self as the Self of all, a man becomes selfless; and in virtue of selflessness he is to be conceived as unconditioned. This is the highest mystery, betokening emancipation; through selflessness he has no part in pleasure or pain, but attains absoluteness.   Maitrayana Upanishad

Nothing is born, nothing dies and nothing acts. Yet through illusion birth, action and death appear to be a reality- just as it seems that when the log has burned out fire has died. The body knows nine ages: conception, gestation, birth, childhood, youth, adulthood, maturity, old age and death. These states of the body- whether high or low- become the sole identification. But some, with great effort, give up this false identification. You infer you will die because your father died. You infer you were born when you witness your child being born. The Self which witnesses both is subject to neither. One who plants a seed and witnesses its growth, transformation and death, remains distinct from the plant- and from its birth, growth and death. So it is with the Self. The ignorant, who fail to distinguish the Self from its appearance as matter, get lost in the world of appearances and go from death to birth again and again.
Uddhava Gita *17:45-50*

Give up this world of multiplicities experienced through the senses, and see the idea of a duality as nothing more than an illusion. ... rise above all these and discover the Self through the Self.   Uddhava Gita *17:56,58*

As long as the Self sees itself through an undiscriminating intelligence as the body, the senses and the vitality, and limits itself to those, this relative existence, though unreal, will appear to be real. As long as a dream is not disturbed all objects within it appear to be real. Similarly, although this world of experience does not exist anymore than a dream does, as long people identify with it they will continue to undergo these experiences even while their true nature is transcendent to it.   Uddhava Gita *23:12-13*

The Lord is enshrined in the hearts of all. The Lord is the supreme Reality.   Rejoice in him through renunciation. Covet nothing. All belongs to the Lord. Thus working may you live a hundred years. Thus alone will you work in real freedom. Those who deny the Self are born again blind to the Self, enveloped in darkness, utterly devoid of love for the Lord. The Self is one. Ever

still, the Self is swifter than thought, swifter than the senses. Though motionless, he outruns all pursuit. Without the Self, never could life exist. The Self seems to move, but is ever near. He is within all, and he transcends all. Those who see all creatures in themselves and themselves in all creatures know no fear. Those who see all creatures in themselves know no grief. How can the multiplicity of life delude the ones who see its unity? The Self is everywhere. Bright is the Self, indivisible, untouched by sin, wise, immanent and transcendent. He it is that holds the cosmos together. [...] The face of truth is hidden by your orb of gold, O sun. May you remove your orb so that I, who adore the true, may see the glory of truth. O nourishing sun, solitary traveler, controller, source of life for all creatures, spread your light and subdue your dazzling splendor so that I may see your blessed Self. Even that very Self that I am!
from the Isha Upanishad

Know him to be enshrined in your heart always. Truly there is nothing more in life to know. Meditate and realize this world is filled with the presence of God. [...] Like oil in sesame seeds, like butter in cream, like water in springs, like fire in fire sticks, so dwells the Lord of Love, the Self, in the very depths of consciousness. Realize him through meditation. The Self is hidden in the hearts of all, as butter lies hidden in cream. Realize the Self in the depths of meditation- the Lord of Love, supreme Reality, who is the goal of all knowledge.
From the Shvetashvatara Upanishad

Therefore, brethren, everybody whatever, be it past, future, or present: be it inward or outward, gross or subtle, low or high, far or near- everybody should be thus regarded, as it really is, by right insight, - "This is not mine: this is not I: this is not the Self of me." Every feeling whatever, be it past, future or present, gross or subtle, low or high, far or near, -every consciousness, I say, must be thus regarded, as it really is, by right insight: "This is not mine: this is not I: this is not the Self of me." *Buddha*

Atman, the Spirit of vision, is never born and never dies. Before him there was nothing, and he is One for evermore. Never-born and eternal, beyond time gone or to come, he does not die when the body dies. (...) Concealed in the heart of all beings is the Atman, the Spirit, the Self; smaller than the smallest atom, greater than the vast spaces. The man who surrenders his human will leaves sorrows behind and beholds the glory of the Atman by the grace of his Creator. (...) Not through much learning is the Atman reached, not through the intellect and sacred teaching. It is reached by the chosen of him- because they chose him. To his chosen the Atman reveals his glory. Not even through deep knowledge can be reached, unless evil ways are abandoned, and there is rest in the senses, concentration in the mind and peace in one's heart. (...) Know the Atman as Lord of a chariot; and the body as the chariot itself. Know that reason is the charioteer; and the mind indeed is the reins. The horses, they say, are the senses; and their paths are the objects of sense. He who has not right understanding and whose mind is never steady is not the ruler of his life, like a bad driver with wild horses. But he who has right understanding and whose mind is ever steady is the ruler of his life, like a good driver with well-trained horses. (...) The man whose chariot is driven by reason, who watches and holds the reins of his mind, reaches the End of the journey, the supreme everlasting Spirit. Beyond the senses are their objects, and beyond the objects is the mind. Beyond the mind is pure reason, and beyond reason is the Spirit in man.
Katha, Mundaka Upanishad

They say the senses are higher than the flesh; the mind is higher than the senses; the intellect is higher than the mind, and the atman higher than the intellect. Steady the atman in the atman. Strengthened by pure consciousness, destroy the great enemy called kama!   Bhagavad Gita 3:42-43

There is a spirit in man, and the breath of the Almighty gives him understanding.   Job 32:8

Patience, Confidence, and Contentment: Perseverance

Someone asked the sage Abu-Said ibn Abil-Khair what Sufism entailed. He replied, "Whatever you have in mind- forget it; whatever you have in your hand- give it; whatever is to be your fate- face it!"

We know that all things work together for good for those who love God.   Romans 8:28

A powerful king, ruler of many domains, was in a position of such magnificence that wise men were his mere employees. And yet one day he felt himself confused and called the sages to him. He said: 'I do not know the cause, but something impels me to seek a certain ring, one that will enable me to stabilize my state. I must have such a ring. And this ring must be one which, when I am unhappy, will make me joyful. At the same time, if I am happy and look upon it, I must be made sad.' The wise men consulted one another, and threw themselves into deep contemplation, and finally they came to a decision as to the character of this ring which would suit their king. The ring which they devised was one upon which was inscribed the legend: This, too, will pass.   *Attar of Nishapur*

Let nothing disturb you, let nothing frighten you; all things are passing; God never changes; patient endurance obtains all things; who God possesses in nothing is wanted; God alone suffices.
Teresa of Avila (1515-1582)

Riches are not from abundance of worldly goods, but from a contented mind.   God loves those who are content.
Hadith of the Prophet Mohammad

The worth of love does not consist in high feelings, but in detachment, in patience under all trials for the sake of God whom we love.   *St. John of the Cross*

Do what you are doing now, suffer what you are suffering now; to do all this with holiness, nothing need be changed but your hearts. Sanctity consists in willing what happens to us by God's order.   *Jean Pierre de Caussade*

By a man without passions I mean one who does not permit good or evil to disturb his inward economy, but rather falls in with what happens and does not add to the sum of his mortality.
Chuang Tzu

We must not wish anything other than what happens from moment to moment, all the while, however, exercising ourselves in goodness.   *St. Catherine of Genoa*

The soul that is attached to anything, however much good there may be in it, will not arrive at the liberty of divine union. For whether it be a strong wire rope or a slender and delicate thread that holds the bird, it matters not, if it really holds it fast; for, until the cord be broken, the bird cannot fly. So the soul, held by the bonds of human affections, however slight they may be, cannot, while they last, make its way to God.
St. John of the Cross

In the world, when people call anyone simple, they generally mean a foolish, ignorant, credulous person. But real simplicity, so far from being foolish, is almost sublime. All good men like and admire it, are conscious of sinning against it, observe it in others and know what it involves; and yet they could not precisely define it. I should say that simplicity is an uprightness of soul which prevents self-consciousness. It is not the same as sincerity, which is a much humbler virtue. Many people are sincere who are not simple. They say nothing but what they believe to be true, and do not aim at appearing anything but what they are. But they are forever thinking about themselves, weighing their every word and thought, and dwelling upon themselves in apprehension of having done too much or too little. These people are sincere but they are not simple. They are not at their ease with others, nor others with them. There is nothing easy, frank, unrestrained or natural about them. One feels that one would like less admirable people better, who were not so stiff. To be absorbed in the world around and never turn a thought within, as is the blind condition of some who are carried away by what is pleasant and tangible, is one extreme opposed to simplicity. And to be self-absorbed in all matters, whether it be duty to God or man, is the other extreme, which makes a person wise in his own conceit- reserved, self-conscious, uneasy at the least thing which disturbs his inward self-complacency. Such false wisdom, in spite of its solemnity, is hardly less vain and foolish than the folly of those who plunge headlong into worldly pleasures. The one is intoxicated by his outward surroundings, the other by what he believes himself to be doing inwardly; but both are in a state of intoxication, and the last is a worse state than the first, because it seems to be wise, though it is not really, and so people do not try to be cured. Real simplicity lies in a just milieu equally free from thoughtlessness and affectation, in which the soul is not overwhelmed by externals, so as to be unable to reflect, nor yet given up to the endless refinements, which self-consciousness induces. The soul which looks where it is going without losing time arguing over every step, or looking back perpetually, possesses true simplicity. Such simplicity is indeed a great treasure. How shall we attain to it? I would give all I possess for it; it is the costly pearl of Holy Scripture.   *Fenelon*

A drunken man who falls out of a cart, though he may suffer, does not die. His bones are the same as other people's; but he meets his accident in a different way. His spirit is in a condition of security. He is not conscious of riding in the cart; neither is he conscious of falling out of it. Ideas of life, death, fear and the like cannot penetrate his breast; and so, he does not suffer from contact with objective existence. If security is to be got from wine, how much more is it to be got from God?   *Chuang Tzu*

Troubled or still, water is always water. What difference can embodiment or disembodiment make to the Liberated? Whether calm or in tempest, the sameness of the Ocean suffers no change.
Yogavasistha

In this life, there is not purgatory, but only heaven or hell; for he who bears afflictions with patience has paradise, and he who does not has hell.   *St. Philip Neri*

One cannot justify unjust anger; anger plunges a man to his downfall. A patient man need stand firm but for a time, and then contentment comes back to him. ...My son, when you come to serve the Lord, prepare yourself for trials. Be sincere of heart and steadfast, undisturbed in time of adversity. Cling to him, forsake him not; thus will your future be great. Accept whatever befalls you, in crushing misfortune be patient; for in fire gold is tested, and worthy men in the crucible of humiliation. *Sirach 1:19-20, 2:1-5*

Remember the time of hunger in the time of plenty, poverty and want in the day of wealth. Between morning and evening the weather changes; before the Lord all things are fleeting.
Sirach 18: 26-26

The wise should be like a python that does not search out food but takes only what comes its way- whether it is sweet or bitter.   *Uddhava Gita 3:2*

Wealth and vigor build up confidence, but better than either, fear of God. Fear of the Lord leaves nothing wanting; he who has it need seek no other support: the fear of God is a paradise of blessings; its canopy, all that is glorious.   *Sirach 40:26-27*

The greatest contentment comes from devotion alone and not from its rewards, therefore one who has this devotion seeks nothing else.   *Uddhava Gita 15:35*

A dervish was praying silently. A wealthy merchant, observing the dervish's devotion and sincerity, was deeply touched by him. The merchant offered the dervish a bag of gold. "I know that you will use the money for God's sake. Please take it." "Just a moment." The dervish replied. "I'm not sure if it is lawful for me to take your money. Are you a wealthy man? Do you have more money at home?" "Oh yes. I have at least one thousand gold pieces at home," claimed the merchant proudly. "Do you want a thousand gold pieces more?" asked the dervish. "Why yes, of course. Every day I work hard to earn more money." "And do you wish for a thousand gold pieces more beyond that?" "Certainly. Every day I pray that I may earn more and more money." The dervish pushed the bag of gold back to the merchant. ""I am sorry, but I cannot take your gold," he said. "A wealthy man cannot take money from a beggar." "How can you call yourself a wealthy man and me a beggar?" the merchant spluttered. The dervish replied, "I am a wealthy man because I am content with whatever God sends me. You are a beggar, because no matter how much you possess, you are always dissatisfied, and always begging God for more."
Sheikh Muzaffer

Jafar asked Rabia when a devotee might become content with God. She replied, "When is joy in affliction equals his joy in blessing." *Abu Makki*

The Sufi is in this world as a guest, and it ill behooves a guest to make demands of his host; for a well-mannered guest waits, and does not make demands. *Maaruf Karkhi*

The flowers appear on the earth, and the time for pruning has come (Canticles 2:12). The flowers of the heart are good desires. As soon as they appear we must prune away from our conscience all dead and superfluous works. The soul seeking to be a bride of Christ must put off the old self and be clothed with the new self, pruning away everything which comes between it and the love of God. This purging is the foundation of our future health. Ordinary purification and healing of body or soul is accomplished little by

little, slowly and patiently. The soul rising from sin to holiness is like the dawn, which as it rises does not at once dispel darkness, but advances gradually. It is an old saying that a slow cure is a certain cure. The spiritual diseases, like those of the body, come quickly and mounted. They go away on foot and slowly. We must be patient and full of courage. The discipline of purification only ends with life itself. Do not be discouraged by weaknesses; our perfection consists in struggling against them, which we cannot do unless we see them. Nor can we conquer them unless we face up to them. Victory does not lie in ignoring our weaknesses, but in resisting them.
Francis de Sales

At this moment, you are suffering from one of the most dangerous temptations that could assail any soul of goodwill: the temptation to discouragement. I conjure you to resist it with all your might. Have confidence in God, and be convinced he will finish the work he has begun in you. Your foolish fears about the future come from the devil. Think only of the present, abandon the future to Providence. It is the good use of the present that assures the future. Apply yourself to obtaining attachment and conformity to the will of God in all things, and everywhere, even to the smallest things, for in this consists all virtue and perfection. For the rest, God only allows out daily faults to keep us humble. If you know how to gain this fruit and to remain in peace and confidence, then you will be in a better state than if you had not committed any apparent fault, which would only have greatly flattered your self-love. Ought we not to admire and bless the infinite goodness of God who knows how to make our very faults serve for our greater good?
Jean-Pierre de Caussade

If your temptations are altogether interior; if you fear to be carried away by your thoughts and ideas, get rid of that fear also. Do not resist these interior temptations directly; let them fall and resist them indirectly by recollection and the thought of God. And if you are not able to get rid of them in this way, endure them patiently.   *Jean-Pierre de Caussade*

> O ye who believe, seek help with patient perseverance
> and prayer: for Allah is with those who patiently persevere.
> Quran 2:153

> Be firm and patient, in pain or suffering and adversity.
> Quran 2:177

> I can find no particular sin in your conduct, yet I perceive defects and imperfections which might do you great harm if you did not apply a strong remedy. These are uneasiness, foolish fears, depression, weariness, and a discouragement not quite free from deliberation, or at least not combated with sufficient energy, all of which tend to diminish interior peace. But what can I do to prevent them? This: Never retain them willfully; never parlay with them, nor yet combat them with effort, nor violence, which would make them doubly harmful. Drop them as one drops a stone into the water, think of something else, speak to God of other things, then take refuge in the interior silence of respect, submission, confidence and a total abandonment. "But", you say, "supposing that in these or in other matters I commit faults, how ought I to behave?" Well! then you must bear in mind the advice of St. Francis de Sales: do not trouble yourself about your troubles, do not be uneasy about your uneasiness, do not be discouraged because you are discouraged, but return immediately to God without violence, even thanking him for having prevented you from falling into greater faults.
> *Jean-Pierre de Caussade*

> O you who believe, persevere in patience and constancy; vie in such perseverance; strengthen each other; and fear Allah that you may prosper. Quran 3:200

> Seek Allah's help with patient perseverance and prayer: it is hard indeed, except to those who bring a lowly spirit, who bear in mind the certainty that they are to meet their Lord, and that they are to return to Him. Quran 2:45-46

Or do you think that you shall enter the Garden of Bliss without such trials as came to those who passed away before you? They encountered suffering and adversity, and were so shaken in spirit that even the Messenger and those of faith who were with him cried: "When will come the help of Allah?" Ah! Verily, the help of Allah is always near!   Quran 2:214

Our Lord! Pour constancy on us and make our steps firm: help us against those that reject faith.   Quran 2:250

So lose not heart, nor fall into despair: for you must gain mastery if you are true in Faith. If a wound has touched you, be sure a similar wound has touched the others. Such days (of varying fortunes) We give to men and men by turns: that Allah may know those that believe, and that He may take to Himself from your ranks Martyr-witnesses (to Truth). And Allah does not love those that do wrong. Allah's object also is to purge those that are true in Faith and to deprive of blessing those that resist Faith. Did you think that you would enter Heaven without Allah testing those of you who fought hard (in His Cause) and remained steadfast?
Quran 3:139-142

How many of the Prophets fought (in Allah's way), and with them (fought) large bands of godly men? But they never lost heart if they met with disaster in Allah's way, nor did they weaken (in will) nor give in. And Allah loves those who are firm and steadfast. All that they said was: "Our Lord! forgive us our sins and anything we may have done that transgressed our duty: establish our feet firmly, and help us against those that resist Faith."   Quran 3:146-147

Those who patiently persevere, seeking the countenance of their Lord; establish regular prayers; spend out of the gifts We have bestowed for their sustenance, secretly or openly; and turn off Evil with good; for such there is the final attainment of the Eternal Home-   Quran 13: 22

O my son! Establish regular prayer, enjoin what is just, and forbid what is wrong: and bear with patient constancy whatever betide you; for this is firmness of purpose in the conduct of affairs.
                              Quran 31:17

Those who avoid the greater crimes and shameful deeds, and when they are angry even then forgive; those who hearken to their Lord, and establish regular prayer; who conduct their affairs by mutual consultation; who spend out of what We bestow on them for Sustenance; and those who, when an oppressive wrong is inflicted on them, are not cowed but help and defend themselves. The recompense for an injury is an injury equal thereto in degree: but if a person forgives and makes reconciliation, his reward is due from Allah: for Allah does not love those who do wrong. But indeed if any do help and defend themselves after a wrong done to them, against such there is no cause of blame. The blame is only against those who oppress men with wrongdoing and insolently transgress beyond bounds through the land, defying right and justice: for such there will be a penalty grievous. But indeed if any show patience and forgive, that would truly be an exercise of courageous will and resolution in the conduct of affairs.   Quran 42:37-43

Let no man ever cling to what is pleasant, or to what is unpleasant. Not to see what is pleasant is pain, and to see what is unpleasant is pain. Let, therefore, no man be attached to anything; loss of the beloved is evil. Those who are attached to nothing, and hate nothing, have no fetters.
                              Dhammapada

The Master said, "The gentleman is easy of mind, while the small man is ever full of anxiety."   Analects, Book 7:37

Vigilance is the path of freedom beyond life and death; thoughtlessness, the path of death. Those who are vigilant do not die. Those who are thoughtless are as if dead already. (...) When people are vigilant and exert themselves and remain ever mindful, and always do pure deeds, and act with consideration and restraint, and

live according to the law, then their glory will increase. By rousing themselves, by vigilance, by temperance and self-control, wise people make for themselves an island that no flood can overwhelm. Foolish people follow after vanity. Wise people guard vigilance as their greatest treasure. Follow not after vanity, nor after the enjoyment of sensual pleasures of the mind or body! The one who is vigilant and steadfast in a state of pure meditation knows ample joy.
                              Dhammapada

To be elated at success and disappointed at failure is to be the slave of circumstances; how can such a one be called master of himself.   Chinese proverb

Wise ones, after they have listened to the law, become serene, like a deep, clear, still lake. Dhammapada

People don't look at a flowing river for a mirror, they look at still waters, because only what is still stills things and holds them still.   *Chuang Tzu*

Those who go quietly with the flow of nature are not worried by either joy or sorrow. People like these were considered in the past as having achieved freedom from bondage. Those who cannot free themselves are constrained by things.
                              Chuang Tzu

When you are content to be simply yourself and don't compare or compete, everybody will respect you. Fill your bowl to the brim and it will spill. Keep sharpening your knife and it will blunt. Chase after money and security and your heart will never unclench. Care about people's approval and you will be their prisoner. Do your work, then step back. The only path to serenity.
                              Tao te Ching 8-9

The ancient Masters were profound and subtle. Their wisdom was unfathomable. There is no way to describe it; all we can describe is their appearance. They were careful as someone crossing an iced-over stream. Alert as a warrior in enemy territory. Courteous as a guest. Fluid as melting ice. Shapeable as a block of wood. Receptive as a valley. Clear as a glass of water. Do you have the patience to wait till your mud settles and the water is clear? Can you remain unmoving till the right action arises by itself? The Master doesn't seek fulfillment. Not seeking, not expecting, she is present, and can welcome all things.   Tao te Ching 15

   Rushing into action, you fail. Trying to grasp things, you lose them. Forcing a project to completion, you ruin what was almost ripe. Therefore, the Master takes action by letting things take their course. He remains calm at the end as at the beginning. He has nothing, thus he has nothing to lose. What he desires is non-desire; what he learns is to unlearn. He simply reminds people of who they have always been. He cares about nothing but the Tao. Thus he can care for all things.   Tao te Ching 64

   The gods envy these enlightened ones, who have trained their senses as good drivers have tamed their horses, and who are free from lust, greed and pride. Enlightened ones are solid like the earth that endures, steadfast like a well-set column of stone, clear as a lake where all the mud has settled. They are liberated from the world of life, death, and impermanence.
                        Dhammapada

   Not to commit any sin, to do only good, and to purify one's mind: That is the teaching of all the awakened. The awakened say that patience is the best kind of penance; self-control, the greatest good. For no one is a holy hermit who oppresses others, no one is an ascetic who insults others.   Dhammapada

   Like a well-guarded frontier fort, having defenses within and without, guard yourself. Not a moment should escape attention, for those who allow the right moment to pass suffer pain when they are in hell.   Dhammapada

Heat, cold, pain, pleasure- these spring from sensual contact, Arjuna. They begin, and they end. They exist for the time being. Endure them. The man whom these cannot distract, the man who is steady in pain and pleasure, is the man who achieves serenity.   Bhagavad Gita 2:14-15

A little of this dharma removes a world of fear. In this there is only single-minded will; while the efforts of confused people are many-branching and full of contradiction. There is no constancy in the man who runs after pleasure and power, whose reason is robbed by the fool's flattery.   Bhagavad Gita 2:41-42

Be steady in yoga, do whatever you must do; give up attachment, be indifferent to failure and success. This stability is Yoga. Harassed are the seekers of the fruits of action. With this mental poise, you will release yourself from good deeds and ill deeds. Devote yourself to this Yoga: it is the secret of success in work. The steadfast in wisdom, the steadfast of mind, giving up the fruits of action, achieve the perfect state. When your mind is no longer obscured by desire, repose will come to you concerning what is heard and what is yet to be heard. When your mind, so long whirled in conflicting thought, achieves poise, and steadies itself in itself, you will have realized Yoga.
            Bhagavad Gita 2:48-53

You become tranquil when the subdued mind is established in the atman, when anxiety is overcome, and desires abandoned. The flame of the windless lamp is never fitful- a good simile for a controlled yogi, absorbed in Yoga. When the mind is steady in Yoga, and achieves tranquility, and when the atman reveals Brahman, when one is contented in the atman; when perfect calm comes, experienced by the liberated atman (a goal from which there is no straying); and when, having achieved this ineffable state, no anxiety disturbs- Yoga is won! And this is achieved after much hardship. Forsaking desire, and controlling his senses, the yogi must not think of anything else. Success will come by slow degrees. Should his fickle mind stray, he must subdue it, reclaim it, and guide

it by the atman. The supreme bliss is found only by the tranquil yogi, whose passions have been stilled. (...) Arjuna said: You have told me this Yoga of peace and unity of being, but my mind is restless, I do not understand what you say. For the mind Krishna is powerful, violent, uncontrollable. Harnessing the mind is like harnessing the wind. Krishna replied: the mind indeed is all that you say, Arjuna, but determination help; and renunciation curbs it. Without determination, no man can reach Yoga, but the self-disciplined, struggling nobly, can achieve it.
Bhagavad Gita 6:18-27, 33-36

When the sage sees no other worker but the gunas and sees also what is beyond the gunas, he reaches me. The atman which transcends matter-involved gunas is untouched by birth and death, decay and sorrow, and finds immortality. Arjuna asked: "How does one recognize the transcender of the gunas? How does he behave, what does he do with his life" Krishna replied: "He does not dislike light, he does not dislike work, he does not desire them when he is without them; he behaves detachedly; he knows the gunas are working, and he remains steady; he remains serene in pain and joy, or when considering a piece of earth, a stone or a lump of gold; he remains serene in moments of glory and shame."
Bhagavad Gita 14:19-24

Be fearless and pure; never waver in your determination or your dedication to the spiritual life. Give freely. Be self-controlled, sincere, truthful, loving, and full of the desire to serve. Realize the truth of the scriptures; learn to be detached and to take joy in renunciation. Do not get angry or harm any living creature, but be compassionate and gentle; show good will to all. Cultivate vigor, patience, will, purity; avoid malice and pride. Then, Arjuna, you will achieve your divine destiny.   Bhagavad Gita 16:1-3

Comprehensively renouncing desires, which are born out of the intention to produce a particular result, totally restraining the collection of the senses by the mind alone, he should come to rest gently and gradually, with the intelligence held fast; and having fixed the mind in the Self, he should not think of anything at all. Wheresoever the wandering and unsteady mind strays, restraining it, he shall bring it back from that place to control in the self alone. For supreme bliss comes to the yogin whose mind has grown calm, whose passion is stilled, who has become Brahman, without taint. So continually disciplining himself, the stainless yogin easily attains endless bliss, which is the touch of Brahman. The man whose self is disciplined in yoga, whose perception is the same everywhere, sees himself in all creatures and all creatures in himself. For the man who sees me in everything and everything in me, I am not lost for him and he is not lost for me. That yogin grounded in oneness, who honors me as being in all creatures, whatever his mode of life otherwise, exists in me.   Bhagavad Gita 6:24-31

Shall we indeed accept good from God, and not adversity?
Job 2:10

If you would prepare your heart, and stretch out your hands toward Him; if iniquity were in your hand, and you put it far away. And would not let wickedness dwell in your tents; then surely you could lift up your face without spot; yes, you could be steadfast, and not fear; because you would forget your misery, and remember it as waters that have passed away, and your life would be brighter than noonday. Though you were dark, you would be like the morning, and you would be secure because there is hope.
Job11:13-18

Wait on the Lord; be of good courage, and He shall strengthen your heart; wait, I say, on the Lord! (...) The Lord is my strength and my shield; my heart trusted in Him, and I am helped. (...) I waited patiently for the Lord; and He inclined to me.
Psalms 27:14, 28:7, 40:1

Unless the Lord had been my help, my soul would not soon have settled in silence. If I say, "My foot slips," Your mercy, O Lord, will hold me up. In the multitude of my anxieties within me, Your comforts delight my soul.   Psalms 94:17-19

You will keep him in perfect peace, whose mind is stayed on You, because he trusts in You. Trust in the Lord forever, for in YAH, the Lord, is everlasting strength.   Isaiah 26:3-4

In returning and rest you shall be saved; in quietness and confidence shall be your strength. But you would not, and you said, "No, for we will flee on horses"- therefore you shall flee! And, "We will ride on swift horses"- therefore those who pursue you shall be swift! (...) Therefore the Lord will wait, that He may be gracious to you; and therefore, He will be exalted, that He may have mercy on you. For the Lord is a God of justice; blessed are all those who wait for Him.   Isaiah 30:15-16, 18

The work of righteousness will be peace, and the effect of righteousness, quietness and assurance forever.   Isaiah 32:17

So you, by the help of your God, return; observe mercy and justice, and wait on your God continually.
Hosea 12:6

Attachment to things is a bond, here happiness is temporary and sorrow is greater and enjoyment is less. The wise person knowing this to be like a fish-hook in the throat lives alone. (...) In order to attain the supreme good, being strenuous, prudent, industrious, resolute in perseverance, possessed of the power of strength (...) Being diligent, aspiring to the eradication of craving, skilled, learned, mindful, proficient to examine the Dhamma, sure in the path, energetic (...). Like a lion not frightened by noises, like wind not in a net, like a lotus not smeared with the water (...) As a lion, the king of beasts, strong with his teeth, roams overcoming other beasts, living in solitary surroundings (...) practicing loving-kindness, equanimity, compassion, deliverance, and sympathetic joy at the appropriate time, unobstructed by the world.
Khaggavisana Sutta, Sutta Nipata

Confidence is the best wealth to a man in this world. Well-practiced Dhamma brings happiness. Truth is the sweetest of all tastes. Living with wisdom is said to be the noblest kind. (...) One crosses the flood of samsara by confidence. One crosses the sea of existence by vigilance. One transcends unhappiness by strenuous effort. One purifies oneself by wisdom.
     Alavaka Sutta, Sutta Nipata

  Better is the end of a thing than the beginning thereof; [and] the patient in spirit is better than the proud in spirit. Don't be hasty in your spirit to be angry; for anger rests in the bosom of fools.
     Ecclesiastes 7:8-9

  Do you not know that they that run in a race all run, but one receives the prize? Even so run; that you may attain. And every man that strives in the games exercises self-control in all things. Now they [do it] to receive a corruptible crown; but we are incorruptible. I therefore so run, as not uncertainly; so fight I, as not beating the air: but I buffet my body, and bring it into bondage: lest by any means, after that I have preached to others, I myself should be rejected.   1st Corinthians 9:24-27

  Wherefore let him that thinks he stands take heed lest he fall. There has no temptation taken you but such as man can bear: but God is faithful, who will not suffer you to be tempted above that you are able; but will with the temptation make also the way of escape, that you may be able to endure it. (...) Watch, stand fast in the faith, quit you like men, be strong.
    1st Corinthians 10:12-13, 16:13

  And we desire that each one of you may show the same diligence unto the fullness of hope even to the end: that you be not sluggish, but imitators of them who through faith and patience inherit the promises. (...) Cast not away therefore your boldness, which has great recompense of reward. For you have need of patience, that, having done the will of God, you may receive the promise. For yet a very little while, He that comes shall come, and shall not tarry. But my righteous one shall live by faith: And if he shrinks back, my soul has no pleasure in him. But we are not

of them that shrink back unto perdition; but of them that have faith unto the saving of the soul. (...) Be you free from the love of money; content with such things as you have: for himself has said, I will in no wise fail you, neither will I in any wise forsake you. So that with good courage we say, The Lord is my helper; I will not fear: What shall man do unto me? Remember them that had the rule over you, men that spoke unto you the word of God; and considering the issue of their life, imitate their faith. Jesus Christ [is] the same yesterday and to-day, [yea] and forever. Be not carried away by diverse and strange teachings: for it is good that the heart be established by grace; not by meats, wherein they that occupied themselves were not profited.
                Hebrews 6:11-12, 10:35-38, 13:5-9

     One form of gentleness we should practice is towards ourselves. We should never get irritable with ourselves because of out imperfections. It is reasonable to be displeased and sorry when we commit faults, but not fretful or spiteful to ourselves. Some make the mistake of being angry because they have been angry, hurt because they have been hurt, vexed because they have been vexed. They think they are getting rid of anger, that the second remedies the first; actually, they are preparing the way for fresh anger on the first occasion. Besides this, all irritation with ourselves tends to foster pride and springs from self-love, which is displeased at finding we are not perfect. We should regard ourselves with calm, collected and firm displeasure. We correct ourselves better by a quiet persevering repentance than by an irritated, hasty and passionate one. When your heart has fallen raise it gently, humbling yourself before God, acknowledging your fault, but not surprised at your fall. Infirmity is infirm, weakness weak and frailty frail.   *Francis de Sales*

Inner Peace and Harmony

The man who has a good will for all, who is friendly and has compassion; who has no thoughts of "I" or "mine", whose peace is the same in pleasures and sorrows, and who is forgiving; this Yogi of union, ever full of my joy, whose soul is in harmony and whose determination is strong; whose mind and inner vision are set on me- this man loves me, and he is dear to me.   Bhagavad Gita 12:13-14

The man whose love is the same for his enemies or his friends, whose soul is the same in honor and disgrace, who is beyond heat or cold or pleasure or pain, who is free from the chain of attachments; who is balanced in blame and in praise, whose soul is silent, who is happy with whatever he has, whose home is not in this world, and who has love- this man is dear to me. But even dearer to me are those who have faith and love, and who have me as their End Supreme: those who hear my words of Truth, and who come to the waters of Everlasting Life.   Bhagavad Gita 12:18-20

He who hates not light, nor busy activity, nor even darkness, when they are near, neither longs for them when they are far; who unperturbed by changing conditions sits apart and watches and says the powers of nature go round and round, and remains firm and shakes not; who dwells in his inner self, and is the same in pleasure and pain; to whom gold or stones or earth are one, and what is pleasing or displeasing leaves him in peace; who is beyond both praise and blame, and whose mind is steady and quiet; who is the same in honor or disgrace, and has the same love for enemies or friends, who surrenders all selfish undertakings- this man has gone beyond the three. And he who with never-failing love adores me and works for me, he passes beyond the three powers and can be one with Brahman, the One. Quietness of mind, silence, self-harmony, loving-kindness, and a pure heart: this is the harmony of the mind.   Bhagavad Gita 17:16

The soul should take care of the body, just as the pilgrim on his way to Mecca takes care of his camel; but if the pilgrim spends his whole time in feeding and adoring his camel, the caravan will leave him behind, and he will perish in the desert.   *al-Ghazzali*

The Third Patriarch of Zen said, "If you want to attain enlightenment, don't be averse to the objects of the six senses in the course of everyday life, like a duck going into the water without its feathers getting wet."

The Way of Tranquility: The purpose of this discipline is twofold: to bring to a standstill all disturbing thoughts (and all discriminating thoughts are disturbing), to quiet all engrossing moods and emotions, so that it will be possible to concentrate the mind for the purpose of meditation and realization. Secondly, when the mind is tranquillized by stopping all discursive thinking, to practice reflection or meditation, not in a discriminating, analytical way, but in a more intellectual way by realizing the meaning and significance of one's thoughts and experiences. By this twofold practice of stopping and realizing one's faith, which has already been awakened, will be developed, and gradually the two aspects of this practice will merge into one another- the mind perfectly tranquil, but most active in realization. In the past one naturally had confidence in one's faculty of discrimination, but this is now to be eradicated and ended. Those who are practicing "stopping" should retire to some quiet place and there, sitting erect, earnestly seek to tranquilize and concentrate the mind. While one may at first think of one's breathing, it is not wise to continue this practice very long, nor to let the mind rest on any particular appearances, or sights, or conceptions, arising from the senses, such as the primal elements of earth, water, fire and ether, nor to let it rest on any of the mind's perceptions, particularizations, discriminations, moods or emotions. All kinds of ideation are to be discarded as fast as they arise; even the notions of controlling and discarding are to be got rid of. One's mind should become like a mirror, reflecting things, but not judging them or retaining them. Conceptions of themselves have no substance; let them arise and pass away unheeded. Conceptions arising from the senses and lower mind will not take form of themselves, unless they are grasped by the

attention; if they are ignored, there will be no appearing and no disappearing. The same is true of conditions outside the mind; they should not be allowed to engross one's attention and so to hinder one's practice. The mind cannot be absolutely vacant, and as the thoughts arising from the senses and the lower mind are discarded and ignored, one must supply their place with right mentation. The question then arises: what is right mentation? The reply is: right mentation is the realization of mind itself, of its pure undifferentiated Essence, there should be no lingering notions of the self, even of the self in the act of realizing, nor of realization as a phenomenon.
Ashvaghosha

The wise man therefore, instead of trying to prove this or that point by logical disputation, sees all things in the light of direct intuition. He is not imprisoned by the limitations of the "I", for the viewpoint of direct intuition is both "I" and "Not-I." Hence, he sees that on both sides of every argument there is both right and wrong. He also sees that in the end they are reducible to the same thing, once they are related to the pivot of Tao. When the wise man grasps this pivot, he is in the center of the circle, and there he stands while "Yes" and "No" pursue each other around the circumference. The pivot of Tao passes through the center where all affirmations and denials converge. He who grasps the pivot is at the still-point from which all movements and oppositions can be seen in their right relationship. Hence he sees the limitless possibilities of both "Yes" and "No." Abandoning all thought of imposing a limit or taking sides, he rests in direct intuition. Therefore I said: "Better to abandon disputation and seek the true light!"" *Chuang Tzu*

God created everything to partake of his own nature, to have some degree and share of his own life and happiness. Nothing can be good or evil, happy or unhappy, but as it does or does not stand in the same degree of divine life in which it was created, receiving in God and from God all that good that it is capable of, and co-operating with him according to the nature of its powers and perfections. As soon as it turns to itself and would, as it were, have a sound of its own, it breaks off from the divine harmony and falls

into the misery of its own discord; and all its workings then are only so many sorts of torment or ways of feeling its own poverty. The redemption of mankind can then only be effected, the harmony of the creation can then only be restored when the will of God is the will of every creature. For this reason, our blessed Lord, having taken upon him a created nature, so continually declares against the doing of anything of himself and always appeals to the will of God as the only motive and end of everything he did, saying that it was his meat and drink to do the will of him that sent him.
William Law

The great principle of the interior life is the peace of the soul, and it must be preserved with such care that the moment it is attacked all else must be put aside and every effort made to try and regain this holy peace. Peace and tranquility of mind alone give great strength to the soul to enable it to do all that God wishes, while anxiety and uneasiness make the soul feeble and languid, and as though sick. Then one feels neither taste for, nor attraction to virtue, but on the contrary, disgust and discouragement of which the devil does not fail to take advantage. For this reason, he uses all his cunning to deprive us of peace, and under a thousand specious pretexts at one time about self-examination, or sorrow for sin, at another about the way we continually neglect grace, or that by our own fault we make no progress; that God will, at last, forsake us. This is why masters of spiritual life lay down this great principle to distinguish the true inspirations of God from those of the devil; that the former are always sweet and peaceful, inducing to confidence and humility, while the latter are intense, restless and violent, leading to discouragement and mistrust, or else to presumption and self-will.   *Jean-Pierre de Caussade*

Strive to keep your soul limpid and pure before God, undisturbed by thoughts of one thing or another.
St. John of the Cross

Men and women who wish to be aware of the whole truth should adopt the practices of the Integral Way. These time-honored disciplines calm the mind and bring one into harmony with all things.   Hua Hu Ching 2

Do you imagine the universe is agitated? Go into the desert at night and look out at the stars. This practice should answer the question. The superior person settles her mind as the universe settles the stars in the sky. By connecting her mind with the subtle origin, she calms it. Once calmed, it naturally expands, and ultimately her mind becomes as vast and immeasurable as the night sky.
Hua Hu Ching 5

Keep your mind free of divisions and distinctions. When your mind is detached, simple, quiet, then all things can exist in harmony, and you can begin to perceive the subtle truth.
Hua Hu Ching 11

The breath of the Tao speaks, and only those who are in harmony with it hear quite clearly.   Hua Hu Ching 81

Perfect balance is found in still waters. Such water should be an example to us all. Inner harmony is protected and nothing external affects it. Virtue is the result of true balance. Virtue has no shape or form yet nothing can be without it, said Confucius.
The Book of Chuang Tzu

If powerful men and women could remain centered in the Tao, all things would be in harmony. The world would become a paradise. All people would be at peace, and the law would be written in their hearts.   Tao te Ching 32

The great Way is easy, yet people prefer the side paths. Be aware when things are out of balance. Stay centered within the Tao.   Tao te Ching 53

As in the ocean's midmost depths no wave is born, but all is still, so let practitioners be still, be motionless, and nowhere should they swell.   Sutta Nipata

The peace of God is with them whose mind and soul are in harmony, who are free from desire and wrath, who know their own soul.   Bhagavad Gita 5:26

Oh, that you had heeded My commandments! Then your peace would have been like a river, and your righteousness like the waves of the sea.   Isaiah 48:18

The goods of God, which are beyond all measure, can only be contained in an empty and solitary heart.
St. John of the Cross

The Spiritual life is nothing else but the working of the Spirit of God within us, and therefore our own silence must be a great part of our preparation for it, and much speaking or delight in it will be often no small hindrance of that good which we can only have from hearing what the Spirit and voice of God speaks within us.... Rhetoric and fine language about the things of the spirit is a vainer babble than in other matters; and he that thinks to grow in true goodness by hearing or speaking flaming words or striking expressions, as is now much the way of the world, may have a great deal of talk, but will have little of his conversation in heaven.
William Law

This should be the purpose of the heart: not to be trapped by convention, nor to be concerned with adornments; not to be thoughtless in treating others, nor to be in opposition to the crowd; to want the whole world to live in peace and balance for the sake of the people's unity, to look to the needs of others as well as yourself.
Chuang Tzu

Love

That one I love who is incapable of ill will, who is friendly and compassionate. Living beyond the reach of I and mine and of pleasure and pain, patient, contented, self-controlled, firm in faith, with all his heart and all his mind given to me- with such a one I am in love. Not agitating the world or by it agitated, he stands above the sway of elation, competition, and fear: he is my beloved. He is detached, pure, efficient, impartial, never anxious, selfless in all his undertakings; he is my devotee; very dear to me.
Bhagavad Gita 12:13-16

You shall do no unrighteousness in judgment: you shall not be partial to the poor, nor honor the person of the mighty: but in righteousness judge your neighbor. You shall not go up and down as a talebearer among your people: neither shall you stand against the blood of your neighbor: I am the LORD. You shall not hate your brother in your heart: you shall not in any way rebuke your neighbor, and not suffer sin upon him. You shall not avenge, nor bear any grudge against the children of your people, but love your neighbor as yourself: I am the LORD.   Leviticus 19:15-18

Hear, O Israel: The Lord our God, the Lord is one! You shall love the Lord your God with all your heart, with all your soul, and with all your strength.   Deuteronomy 6:4-5

He who covers a transgression seeks love, but he who repeats a matter separates friends. (...) A friend loves at all times, and a brother is born for adversity. (...) A merry heart does good, like medicine, but a broken spirit dries the bones. (...) What is desired in a man is kindness, and a poor man is better than a liar.
Proverbs 17:9,17,22, 19:22

You have heard that it was said, "An eye for an eye and a tooth for a tooth." But I tell you not to resist an evil person. But whoever slaps you on your right cheek, turn the other to him also. If anyone wants to sue you and take away your tunic, let him have your cloak also. And whoever compels you to go one mile, go with him two. Give to him that asks, and from him who wants to borrow from you do not turn away. You have heard that it was said, "You shall love your neighbor and hate your enemy." But I say to you, love your enemies, bless those who curse you, do good to those who hate you, and pray for those who spitefully use you and persecute you, that you may sons of your Father in heaven; for He makes His sun rise on the evil and on the good, and sends rain on the just and on the unjust. For if you love those who love you, what reward have you? Do not even the tax collectors do the same? And if you greet your brethren only, what do you do more than others? Do not even the tax collectors do so? Therefore you shall be perfect, just as your Father in heaven is perfect.   Matthew 5:43-48

    Hatred stirs up strife, but love covers all sins.
                                  Proverbs 10:12

    Let love be genuine; hate what is evil, hold fast to what is good; love one another with mutual affection; outdo one another in showing honor. Do not lag in zeal, be ardent in spirit, serve the Lord. Rejoice in hope be patient in suffering, persevere in prayer. Contribute to the needs of the saints; extend hospitality to strangers. Bless those who persecute you; bless and do not curse them. Rejoice with those who rejoice, weep with those who weep. Live in harmony with one another; do not be haughty, but associate with the lowly; do not claim to be wiser than you are. Do not repay anyone evil for evil, but take thought for what is noble in the sight of all. If it is possible, so far as it depends on you, live peaceably with all. Beloved, never avenge yourselves, but leave room for the wrath of God; for it is written, "Vengeance is mine, I will repay you, says the Lord." No, if your enemies are hungry, feed them; if they are thirsty, give them something to drink; for by doing this you will heap burning coal on their heads. Do not be overcome by evil, but overcome evil with good.
                                Romans 12:9-21

    Do not hate the sinner. Become a proclaimer of God's grace, seeing that God provides for you even though you are unworthy.

Although your debt to him is very great, there is no evidence of him exacting any payment from you, whereas in return for the small ways in which you do manifest good intention, he rewards you abundantly. Do not speak of God as "just", for his justice is not in evidence in his actions towards you. How can you call God just when you read the gospel lesson concerning the hiring of the workmen in the vineyard? How can someone call God just when he comes across the story of the prodigal son who frittered away all his belongings in riotous living- yet merely in response to his contrition his father ran and fell on his neck, and gave him authority over all his possessions? In these passages, it is not someone else speaking about God; had that been the case, we might have had doubts about God's goodness. No, it is God's own Son who testifies about him in this way. Where then is this "justice" in God, seeing that, although we were sinners, Christ died for us? If he is so compassionate in this, we have faith that he will not change.
Isaac of Syria

Then came Peter and said to him, Lord, how often shall my brother sin against me, and I forgive him? until seven times? Jesus said unto him, I say not unto you, Until seven times; but, Until seventy times seven. Therefore is the kingdom of heaven likened unto a certain king, who would make a reckoning with his servants. And when he had begun to reckon, one was brought unto him, that owed him ten thousand talents. But forasmuch as he had not [wherewith] to pay, his lord commanded him to be sold, and his wife, and children, and all that he had, and payment to be made. The servant therefore fell down and worshipped him, saying, Lord, have patience with me, and I will pay thee all. And the lord of that servant, being moved with compassion, released him, and forgave him the debt. But that servant went out, and found one of his fellow-servants, who owed him a hundred shillings: and he laid hold on him, and took [him] by the throat, saying, Pay what you owe me. So, his fellow-servant fell down and besought him, saying, Have patience with me, and I will pay you. And he would not: but went and cast him into prison, till he should pay that which was due. So when his fellow-servants saw what was done, they were exceeding sorry, and came and told unto their lord all that was done. Then his lord called him unto him, and said to him, You wicked servant, I forgave you all that debt, because you besought me: should not you also have had mercy on thy fellow-servant, even as I had mercy on you? And his lord was wroth, and delivered him to the tormentors, till he should pay all that was due. So shall also my heavenly Father do unto you, if you forgive not everyone his brother from your hearts.   Matthew 18:21-35

Teacher, which is the great commandment in the law? And he said unto him, You shall love the Lord your God with all your heart, and with all your soul, and with all your mind. This is the great and first commandment. And a second like [unto it] is this, You shall love your neighbor as yourself. On these two commandments the whole law hangs, and the prophets.
Matthew 22:36-40

But I say unto you that hear, Love your enemies, do good to them that hate you, bless them that curse you, pray for them that despitefully use you. To him that strikes you on the [one] cheek offer also the other; and from him that takes away your cloak withhold not your coat also. Give to everyone that asks of you; and of him that takes away thy goods ask them not again. And as you would that men should do to you, do you also to them likewise. And if you love them that love you, what thanks should you have for even sinners love those that love them? And if you do good to them that do good to you, what thanks have you? for even sinners do the same. And if you lend to them of whom you hope to receive, what thanks have you? even sinners lend to sinners, to receive again as much. But love your enemies, and do [them] good, and lend, never despairing; and your reward shall be great, and you shall be sons of the Most High: for he is kind toward the unthankful and evil. Be you merciful, even as your Father is merciful.   Luke 6:27-36

And behold, a certain lawyer stood up and made trial of him, saying, Teacher, what shall I do to inherit eternal life? And he said unto him, What is written in the law? how readest thou? And he answering said, You shall love the Lord your God with all your heart, and with all your soul, and with all your strength, and with all your mind; and your neighbor as yourself. And he said unto him, You have answered right: this do, and you shall live. But he, desiring to justify himself, said unto Jesus, And who is my neighbor? Jesus made answer and said, A certain man was going down from Jerusalem to Jericho; and he fell among robbers, who both stripped him and beat him, and departed, leaving him half dead. And by chance a certain priest was going down that way: and when he saw him, he passed by on the other side. And in like manner a Levite also, when he came to the place, and saw him, passed by on the other side. But a certain Samaritan, as he journeyed, came where he was: and when he saw him, he was moved with compassion, and came to him, and bound up his wounds, pouring on [them] oil and wine; and he set him on his own beast, and brought him to an inn, and took care of him. And on the morrow, he took out two shillings, and gave them to the host, and said, Take care of him; and whatsoever you spend more, I, when I come back again, will repay you. Which of these three, do you think, proved neighbor unto him that fell among the robbers? And he said, He that showed mercy on him.' And Jesus said unto him, Go, and do likewise.

Luke 10:25-37

Who shall separate us from the love of Christ? shall tribulation, or anguish, or persecution, or famine, or nakedness, or peril, or sword? Even as it is written, For your sake we are killed all the day long; We were accounted as sheep for the slaughter. Nay, in all these things we are more than conquerors through him that loved us. For I am persuaded, that neither death, nor life, nor angels, nor principalities, nor things present, nor things to come, nor powers, nor height, nor depth, nor any other creature, shall be able to separate us from the love of God, which is in Christ
Jesus our Lord.   Romans 8:35-39

When therefore he was gone out, Jesus said, Now is the Son of man glorified, and God is glorified in him; and God shall glorify him in himself, and straightway shall he glorify him. Little children, yet a little while I am with you. You shall seek me: and as I said unto the Jews, Whither I go, you cannot come; so now I say unto you. A new commandment I give unto you, that you love one another; even as I have loved you, that you also love one another. By this shall all men know that you are my disciples, if you have love one to another.   John 13:31-35

And he came forth and saw a great multitude, and he had compassion on them, because they were as sheep not having a shepherd: and he began to teach them many things.   Mark 6:34

Let love be without hypocrisy. Abhor that which is evil; cleave to that which is good. In love of the brethren be tenderly affectioned one to another; in honor preferring one another; in diligence, not slothful; fervent in spirit; serving the Lord; rejoicing in hope; patient in tribulation; continuing steadfastly in prayer; communicating to the necessities of the saints; given to hospitality. (...) Be not overcome of evil, but overcome evil with good.
Romans 12:9-13, 21

Owe no man anything, save to love one another: for he that loves his neighbor has fulfilled the law. For this, You shall not commit adultery, You shall not kill, You shall not steal, You shall not covet, and if there be any other commandment, it is summed up in this word, namely, You shall love your neighbor as yourself. Love works no ill to his neighbor: love therefore is the fulfillment of the law.   Romans 13:8-10

All things are lawful; but not all things are expedient. All things are lawful; but not all things edify. Let no man seek his own, but each his neighbor's good.   1st Corinthians 10:23-24

Hereby know we love, because he laid down his life for us: and we ought to lay down our lives for the brethren. But who so has the world's goods, and beholds his brother in need, and shuts up his compassion from him, how does the love of God abide in him? [My] Little children, let us not love in word, neither with the tongue; but in deed and truth. Hereby shall we know that we are of the truth, and shall assure our heart before him: because if our heart condemns us, God is greater than our heart, and knows all things. Beloved, if our heart condemns us not, we have boldness toward God; and whatsoever we ask we receive of him, because we keep his commandments and do the things that are pleasing in his sight. And this is his commandment, that we should believe in the name of his Son Jesus Christ, and love one another, even as he gave us commandment. And he that keeps his commandments abides in him, and he in him. And hereby we know that he abides in us, by the Spirit which he gave us.   1st John 3:16-24

	Beloved, let us love one another: for love is of God; and every one that loves is begotten of God, and knows God. He that loves not knows not God; for God is love. Herein was the love of God manifested in us, that God has sent his only begotten Son into the world that we might live through him. Herein is love, not that we loved God, but that he loved us, and sent his Son [to be] the propitiation for our sins. Beloved, if God so loved us, we also ought to love one another. No man has beheld God at any time: if we love one another, God abides in us, and his love is perfected in us: hereby we know that we abide in him and he in us, because he has given us of his Spirit. And we have beheld and bear witness that the Father has sent the Son [to be] the Savior of the world. Whosoever shall confess that Jesus is the Son of God, God abides in him, and he in God. And we know and have believed the love which God has in us. God is love; and he that abides in love abides in God, and God abides in him. Herein is love made perfect with us, that we may have boldness in the day of judgment; because as he is, even so are we in this world. There is no fear in love: but perfect love casts out fear, because fear has punishment; and he that fears is not made perfect in love. We love, because he first loved us. If a man says, I love God, and hates his brother, he is a liar: for he that loves not his brother whom he has seen, cannot love God whom he has not seen. And this commandment have we from him, that he who loves God

love his brother also. Whosoever believes that Jesus is the Christ is begotten of God: and whosoever loves him that begat loves him also that is begotten of him. Hereby we know that we love the children of God, when we love God and do his commandments.
1st John 4:7- 5:2

I went to a wilderness, love had rained and had covered earth, as feet penetrate snow, found my feet covered with love.
Bayazid Bistami

Worship

He who utters the name of God while walking gets the merit of a sacrifice at every step. His body becomes a place of pilgrimage. He who repeats God's Name while working always finds perfect peace. He who utters the Name of God while eating gets the merit of a fast even though he has taken his meals. Even if one were to give in charity the whole earth encircled by the seas it would not equal the merit of repeating the Name. By the power of the Name one will know what cannot be known, one will see what cannot be seen, one will speak what cannot be spoken, one will meet what cannot be met. Tuka says, incalculable is the gain that comes from repeating the Name of God.   *Tukaram*

O Sadhu! The simple union is the best. Since the day when I met with my Lord, there has been no end to the sport of our love. I shut not my eyes, I close not my ears, I do not mortify my body; I see with eyes open and smile, and behold His beauty everywhere: I utter His Name, and whatever I see, it reminds me of Him; whatever I do, it becomes His worship. The rising and setting are one to me; all contradictions are solved. Wherever I go, I move round Him, all I achieve is His service: when I lie down, I lie prostrate at His feet. He is the only adorable one to me: I have none other. My tongue has left off impure words, it sings His glory day and night: whether I rise or sit down, I can never forget Him; for the rhythm of His music beats in my ears. Kabir says: "My heart is frenzied, and I disclose in my soul what is hidden. I am immersed in that one great bliss which transcends pleasure and pain." *Kabir*

Guard strictly your habit of prayers, especially the Middle Prayer, and stand before Allah in a devout frame of mind.
                              Quran 2:238

Call upon Allah, or call upon Rahman: by whatever name you call upon Him, it is well: for to Him belong the Most Beautiful Names. Neither speak your Prayer aloud, nor speak it in a low tone, but seek a middle course between.   Quran 17:110

    "Sacrifice as if present" is taken to mean "sacrifice to the gods as if the gods were present." The Master, however, said, "unless I enter into the spirit of a sacrifice, it is as if I did not sacrifice."   Analects, Book 3:12

    The Master said, "Unless a man has the spirit of the rites, in being respectful he will wear himself out, in being careful he will become timid, having courage he will become unruly, and in being forthright he will become unrelenting."   Analects, Book 8:2

    Do not go about worshiping deities and religious institutions as the source of the subtle truth. To do so is to place intermediaries between yourself and the divine, and to make of yourself a beggar who looks outside for a treasure that is hidden in his own breast. If you want to worship the Tao, first discover it in your own heart. Then your worship will be meaningful.   Hua Hu Ching 17

    Dualistic thinking is a sickness. Religion is a distortion. Materialism is cruel. Blind spirituality is unreal. Chanting is no more holy than listening to the murmur of a stream, counting prayer beads no more sacred than simply breathing, religious robes no more spiritual than work clothes. If you wish to attain oneness with the Tao, don't get caught up in spiritual superficialities. Instead, live a quiet and simple life, free of ideas and concepts. Find contentment in the practice of undiscriminating virtue, the only true power. Giving to others selflessly and anonymously, radiating light throughout the world and illuminating your own darkness, your virtue becomes a sanctuary for yourself and all beings. This is what is meant by embodying the Tao.   Hua Hu Ching 47

    Not by shaving his head does an undisciplined, lying person become a monk. Can a person be a monk who is still held captive by desires and greed?   Dhammapada

We praise you with our thoughts, O God. We praise you even as the sun praises you in the morning: may we find joy in being your servants. Keep us under your protection. Forgive our sins and give us your love. God made the rivers to flow. They feel no weariness, they cease not from flowing. They fly swiftly like birds in the air. May the stream of my life flow into the river of righteousness. Loose the bonds of sin that bind me. Let not the thread of my song be cut while I sing; and let not my work end before its fulfillment.   Rig Veda II. 28

When a man is speaking, he cannot be breathing: this is the sacrifice of breath to speech. And when a man is breathing he cannot be speaking: this is the sacrifice of speech to breath. These are the two never-ending immortal offerings of man, whether he is awake of whether he is asleep.   Kaushitaki Upanishad

A man is a living sacrifice.   Chandogya Upanishad

I satisfy all, whatever the form of worship. My path is the path all follow, in different ways.   Bhagavad Gita 4:11

Those who adhere to the words of the Vedas are doomed to constant rebirth. But those who worship me and my unity in all beings are the truly persevering, and to these I give what they do not have and increase what they have. Even the worshipers of images, in reality worship me; their faith is real, though their means are poor. (...) I will accept any gift, a fruit, a flower, a leaf, even water, if it is offered purely, and devoutly, and with love. Whatever you do, Arjuna, whatever you sacrifice, whatever you give in charity, whatever penance you perform, do it for my sake. This will free you from the fetters of work, and you will come to me, with your heart steady in Yoga.   Bhagavad Gita 9:21-28

Ritual which is sattvika is work performed selflessly, satisfying for its own sake, not for reward. Ritual which is rajasika is work for reward, performed for the sake of fame and success. Ritual which is tamasika is without mantra, without shraddha (faith), without any kind of dedication, work that goes against moral principles.   Bhagavad Gita 17:11-13

Give me your mind and give me your heart, give me your offerings and your adoration; and thus, with your soul in harmony, and making me your goal supreme, you shall in truth come to me.
Bhagavad Gita 9:34

Thou God from the beginning, God in man since man was. Thou Treasure supreme of this vast universe. Thou the One to be known and the Knower, the final resting place. Thou infinite Presence in whom all things are.   Bhagavad Gita 11:38

Neither knowledge of the Vedas, nor austerity, nor charity, nor sacrifice can bring the vision you have seen. But through unfailing devotion, Arjuna, you can know me, see me, and attain union with me. Whoever makes me the supreme goal of all his work and acts without selfish attachment, who devotes himself to me completely and is free from ill will for any creature, enters into me.
Bhagavad Gita 11:53-55

All these, who know what sacrifice is, have their imperfections obliterated by sacrifice. (...) Incinerator of the Foe, the sacrifice of knowledge is better than the sacrifice of material substance. There is no action whatsoever, Partha, which is not concluded in knowledge.   Bhagavad Gita 4:30,33

Even those who in faith worship other gods, because of their love they worship me, although not in the right way.
Bhagavad Gita 9:23

He who offers to me with devotion only a leaf, or a flower, or a fruit, or even a little water, this I accept from that yearning soul, because with a pure heart it was offered with love. Whatever you do, or eat, or give, or offer in adoration, let it be an offering to me; and whatever you suffer, suffer it for me.   Bhagavad Gita 9:26-27

God, if I worship You in fear of hell, burn me in hell. And if I worship You in hope of Paradise, exclude me from Paradise; but if I worship You for Thine own sake, withhold not Thine everlasting Beauty.   *Rabia*

For where two or three are gathered together in my name, there am I in the midst of them.   Matthew 18:20

But above all things, my brethren, swear not, neither by the heaven, nor by the earth, nor by any other oath: but let your yes be yes, and your no, no; that you fall not under judgment. Is any among you suffering? Let him pray. Is any cheerful? Let him sing praise. Is any among you sick? Let him call for the elders of the church; and let them pray over him, anointing him with oil in the name of the Lord: and the prayer of faith shall save him that is sick, and the Lord shall raise him up; and if he has committed sins, it shall be forgiven him. Confess therefore your sins one to another, and pray one for another, that ye may be healed. The supplication of a righteous man avails much in its working. Elijah was a man of like passions with us, and he prayed fervently that it might not rain; and it rained not on the earth for three years and six months. And he prayed again; and the heaven gave rain, and the earth brought forth her fruit.   James 5:12-18

I beseech you therefore, brethren, by the mercies of God, to present your bodies a living sacrifice, holy, acceptable to God, [which is] your spiritual service. And be not fashioned according to this world: but be transformed by the renewing of your mind, and you may prove what is the good and acceptable and perfect will of God   .Romans 12:1-2

Someone told Uwais el-Qarni that a certain dervish sat on a tomb, dressed in a shroud and weeping. Qarni said: "Tell him that the method has become an idol; he must transcend the practice, for it is an obstacle."   Sufism

These are the three adorations of the all-conquering Kaushitaki: at the rising of the sun he said, "You who give liberty, make me free from my sins." When the sun was mid-way in heaven he said, "You who are on high and give liberty, set me on high and make me free from my sins." At the hour of sunset, he uttered this prayer, "You who give full liberty, make me fully free from my sins."   Kaushitaki Upanishad

Worship is the submission of all of our nature to God.
Archbishop *William Temple*

The Way of prayer is twofold: it comprises practice of the virtues and contemplation. (...) Persevere with patience in your prayer, and repulse the cares and doubts that arise within you. They disturb and trouble you, and so slacken the intensity of your prayer. (...) If you patiently accept what comes, you will always pray with joy. (...) When an angel comes to us, all who trouble us withdraw at once; then the intellect is completely calm and prays soundly. But at other times, when the attacks of the demons are particularly strong, the intellect does not have a moments respite. This is because it is weakened by the passions to which it has succumbed in the past. But if it goes on searching, it will find; and if it knocks, the door will be opened. (...) Pure undistracted prayer is the highest intellection of the intellect. Prayer is the ascent of the intellect to God. (...) If your intellect is still distracted during prayer, you do not yet know what it is to pray as a monk; but your prayer is still worldly, embellishing the outer tabernacle. (...) Stand on guard and protect your intellect from thoughts while you pray. Then your intellect will complete its prayer and continue in the tranquility that is natural to it. In this way, He who has compassion on the ignorant will come to you, and you will receive the blessed gift of prayer. You cannot attain pure prayer while entangled in material things and agitated by constant cares. For prayer mean the shedding of thoughts.
St. Evagrios the Solitary

Realization, Enlightenment and Watchfulness: Metanoia

The intellect's great gain from stillness is this: all the sins which formerly beat upon the intellect as thoughts and which, once admitted by the mind, were turned into outward acts of sin, are now cut off by mental watchfulness. For, with the help of our Lord Jesus Christ, this watchfulness does not allow these sins to enter our inner self and so to burgeon into outward acts of evil.   *St Hesychios*

Do you think you can clear your mind by sitting constantly in silent mediation? This makes your mind narrow, not clear. Integral awareness is fluid and adaptable, present in all places and at all times. That is true meditation.   Hua Hu Ching 52

Come, come! What you must do is put down your previous knowledge and views of Buddhism all at once; then the mental stamp of your own cosmic Buddha will be clear through and through.   *Chen-ching*

There is no greater mystery than this, that we keep seeking reality when in fact we are reality. We think that there is something hiding reality and that this must be overcome before reality is gained. How ridiculous! A day will dawn when you will laugh at all your past efforts. That day that you laugh is already here and now.
Ramana Maharshi

Be soft in your practice. Think of the method as a fine silvery stream, not a raging waterfall. Follow the stream, have faith in its course. It will go its own way, meandering here, trickling there. It will find the grooves, the cracks, the crevices. Just follow it. Never let it out of your sight. It will take you.
Sheng-yen

Don't try to make clarity of mind with severe practice. Every mind comes to hate severity, and where is clarity in mortification? So an ancient once said, "Clear a passageway through severe practice."   *Kyong Ho*

Because there is no attainment, the bodhisattvas, supported by the Perfection of Understanding, find no obstacles for their minds. Having no obstacles, they overcome fear, liberating themselves forever from illusion and realizing perfect Nirvana.
The Heart of the Prajnaparamita

Layman Pang was sitting in his grass-thatched hut. All of a sudden he said, "Difficult, difficult. It's like trying to cover a tree with ten cups of sesame oil." His wife heard him and said, "Easy, easy. It's like a hundred grass tips on top of the ancestor's mind." His daughter said, "Not difficult, not easy. It's like eating rice when hungry, sleeping when tired."

The true man of God sits in the midst of his fellow-men, and rises and eats and sleeps and marries and buys and sells and gives and takes in the bazaars and spends the days with other people, and yet never forgets God even for a single moment.
Abu Sa'id Ibn Abi'l Khayr (967-1049)

The Buddha way is, basically, leaping clear of the many and the one; thus there are birth and death, delusion and realization, sentient beings and Buddhas. Yet in attachment blossoms fall, and in aversion weeds spread. To carry yourself forward and experience myriad things is delusion. That myriad things come forth and experience themselves is awakening. ...When you see forms, or hear sounds fully engaging body-and-mind, you grasp things directly. Unlike things and their reflections in the mirror, and unlike the moon and its reflection in the water, when one side is illumined and the other is dark.   *Dogen*

Zen students are with their masters at least ten years before they presume to teach others. Nan-in was visited by Tenno, who, having passed his apprenticeship, had become a teacher. The day happened to be rainy, so Tenno wore wooden clogs and carried an umbrella. After greeting him Nan-in remarked: "I suppose you left your wooden clogs in the vestibule. I want to know if your umbrella is on the right or left side of the clogs. Tenno, confused, had no instant answer. He realized that he was unable to carry his Zen every minute. He became Nan-in's pupil, and he studied six more years to accomplish his every-minute

If you attempt to fix a picture of the Tao in your mind, you will lose it. This is like pinning a butterfly: the husk is captured, but the flying is lost.   *Hua Hu Ching*

The image of God is found essentially and personally in all mankind. Each possesses it whole, entire and undivided, and all together not more than one alone. In this way, we are all one, intimately united in our eternal image, which is the image of God and the source in us of all our life. Our created essence and our life are attached to it without meditation as to their external cause.
Ruysbroeck

There is nothing true anywhere, the True s nowhere to be found. If you say you see the True, this seeing is not the true one. When the True is left to itself, there is nothing false in it, for it is Mind itself. When Mind in itself is not liberated from the false, there is nothing true; nowhere is the True to be found.
Hui Neng

The truth has never been preached by the Buddha, seeing that one has to realize it within oneself.   Sutralamkara

Jejune and barren speculations may unfold the plicatures of Truth's garment, but they cannot discover her lovely face.   *John Smith, the Platonist*

With the lamp of word and discrimination one must go beyond word and discrimination and enter upon the path of realization.   Lankavatara Sutra

So long as you seek Buddhahood, specifically exercising yourself for it, there is no attainment for you.
Yung-chia Ta-shih

How shall I grasp it? Do not grasp it. That which remains when there is no more grasping is the Self.   *Panchadasi*

Before, I imagined you outside of myself: I envisaged you waiting at the end of my journey; I know, now I've found you, it was you I abandoned with my very first step.   *Dhul-Nun*

Mystic understanding of truth is not perception or cognition. That is why it is said that you arrive at the original source by stopping the mind, so it is called the enlightened state of being as is, the ultimately independent free individual.   *Nan-ch'uan (748-834)*

What is disturbing you and making you uneasy is that there are things outside and mind inside. Therefore even when the ordinary and the holy are one reality, there still remains a barrier of view. So it is said that as long as views remain you are ordinary; when feelings are forgotten you're a buddha. I advise you, don't seek reality, just stop having views.   *Fa-yen (885-958)*

One day a student asked Taiga Ike, "What is the most difficult part of painting?" Taiga said, "The part of the paper where nothing is painted is the most difficult."

Thirty spokes share one hub. Adapt the nothing therein to the purpose in hand, and you will have the use of the cart. Knead clay in order to make a vessel. Adapt the nothing therein to the purpose in hand, and you will have the use of the vessel. Cut out the doors and windows in order to make a room. Adapt the nothing therein to the purpose in hand, and you will have the use of the room. Thus, what we gain is Something, yet it is by virtue of Nothing that this can be put to use.   Tao Te Ching

The best way of dealing with idle thoughts is not to combat them and still less to be anxious and troubled about them, but just to let them drop like a stone into the sea. Gradually the habit of acting thus will become easy.   *Jean-Pierre de Caussade*

Tung-shan was asked, "The normal mind is the way; what is the normal mind?" He replied, ""Not picking things up along the road."

You must detach from forms and labels before you can learn the way. When your learning reaches the effortless knowledge that is not learned, the path is not a fixed path- the mind itself is the Buddha-mind. Maximum capacity becomes accessible; not from formal externals, but experienced directly.   *P'u-an*

An ancient said, "If people want to know the realm of Buddhahood, they should make their minds clear as open space, detaching from all false thoughts and all grasping, making their minds unobstructed wherever they turn." What is the realm of Buddhahood? Basically, it is the normal course of one's own mind in everyday life it's just that one daily buries one's head in things and events and is swept along under the influence of objects. If you want to harmonize with the realm of Buddhahood, if you can just keep mindful twenty-four hours a day, not giving up through every state of mind, one day it will be like meeting an old friend in a busy city: "Oh! So here you are!" When you get to this state, errant thoughts and all grasping melt right away, and everything becomes your own subtle function.   *Ch'ih-chueh*

Buddhahood is only attained after permanent cessation of ignorance by means of purity of panoramic awareness.
    Scripture of Complete Enlightenment

"Miserable," said Lao. "All blocked up! Tied in knots! Try to get untied! If your obstructions are from the outside, do not attempt to grasp them one by one and thrust them away. Impossible! Learn to ignore them. If they are within yourself, you cannot destroy them piecemeal, but you can refuse to let them take effect. If they are both inside and outside, do not try to hold on to Tao- just hope that Tao will keep hold of you. (...) Can you rest where there is rest? Do you know when to stop? Can you mind your own business without cares, without desiring reports of how others are progressing? Can you stand on your own feet? Can you duck? Can you be like an infant that cries all day without getting a sore throat or clenches his fist all day without getting a sore hand or gazes all day without eyestrain? You want the first elements? The infant has them. Free from care, unaware of self, he acts without reflection, stays where he is put, does not know why, does not figure things out, just goes along with them, is part of the current. These are the first elements!" The disciple asked: "Is this perfection?" Lao replied: "Not at all. It is only the beginning. This melts the ice. This enables you to unlearn, so that you can be led by Tao, be a child of Tao. If you persist in trying to attain what is never attained, if you persist in making effort to obtain what effort cannot get; if you persist in reasoning about what cannot be understood, you will be destroyed by the very thing you seek. To know when to stop, to know when you can get no further by your own action, this is the right beginning.""   *Chuang Tzu*

There was a man who was so disturbed by the sight of his own shadow and so displeased with his own footsteps that he determined to get rid of them both. The method he hit upon was to run away from them. So he got up and ran. But every time he put his foot down there was another step, while his shadow kept up with him without the slightest difficulty. He attributed his failure to the fact that he was not running fast enough. So he ran faster and faster, without stopping, until he finally dropped dead. He failed to realize that if he merely stepped into the shade, his shadow would vanish, and if he sat down and stayed still, there would be no more footsteps.   *Chuang Tzu*

By rousing himself, by earnestness, by restraint and control, the wise man can make for himself an island which no flood can overwhelm. (...) A bhikshu who delights in earnestness, who looks with fear on thoughtlessness, moves about like fire, burning all his fetters, small or large.   Dhammapada

As a fletcher makes straight his arrow, a wise man makes straight his trembling and unsteady thought, which is difficult to guard, difficult to hold back. (...) It is good to tame the mind, which is difficult to hold in and flighty, rushing wherever it lists; a tamed mind brings happiness. Let the wise man guard his thoughts, for they are difficult to perceive, very subtle, and restless; thoughts well-guarded bring happiness. Those who bridle their mind, which travels far, moves about alone, is incorporeal, and hides in the chamber of the heart, will be free from the bonds of Mara, the tempter. If a man's faith is unsteady, if he does not know the true law, if his peace of mind is troubled, his knowledge will never be perfect.   If a man's thoughts are not scattered, if his mind is not perplexed, if he has ceased to think of good or evil, then there is no fear for him while he is watchful.   Knowing that his body is fragile like a jar, and making his thought firm like a fortress, one should attack Mara, the tempter, with the weapon of knowledge; one should watch him when conquered, and should never rest.   Dhammapada

Each moment is fragile and fleeting. The moment of the past cannot be kept, however beautiful. The moment of the present cannot be held, however enjoyable. The moment of the future cannot be caught, however desirable. But the mind is desperate to fix the river in place: possessed by ideas of the past, preoccupied with images of the future, it overlooks the plain truth of the moment. The one who can dissolve her mind will suddenly discover the Tao at her feet, and clarity at hand.   Hua Hu Ching 21

The Master gives himself up to whatever the moment brings. He knows that he is going to die, and he has nothing to hold on to: no illusions in his mind, no resistances in his body. He doesn't think about his actions; they flow from the core of his being. He holds nothing back from life; therefore, he is ready for death, as a man is ready for sleep after a good day's work.   Tao te Ching 50

    As fletchers make straight their arrows, wise ones make straight their trembling, unsteady minds, which are difficult to guard, difficult to hold back. Like a fish taken from the water and thrown on the dry ground, our mind quivers all over in its effort to escape the dominion of Mara. It is good to tame the mind, which is flighty and difficult to restrain, rushing wherever it will. A tamed mind brings happiness. Let wise ones monitor the mind, which is difficult to perceive and restless. A well monitored mind brings happiness. Those who bridle their mind, which, being insubstantial, would travel far on its own, hidden away in the body, are free from the bonds of Mara. If one's mind is unsteady, if one does not know the true law, one's wisdom will never be perfect. (...) Knowing that one's body is fragile like a clay pot, and making one's mind firm like a fortress, one should attack Mara with the weapon of wisdom. One should then never falter in watching the conquered Mara.   Dhammapada

    The one who knows that this body is like froth, as unsubstantial as a mirage, will break the flower-tipped arrow of Mara and never see the king of death. Death carries off a person who is gathering flowers with a distracted mind, just as a flood carries off a sleeping village.   Dhammapada

    Having abandoned covetousness for the world, he dwells with a mind free from covetousness; he purifies his mind from covetousness. Having abandoned ill will and hatred, he dwells with a benevolent mind, sympathetic for the welfare of all living beings; he purifies his mind from ill will from ill will and hatred. Having abandoned dullness and drowsiness, he dwells perceiving light, mindful, and clearly comprehending; he purifies his mind from dullness and drowsiness. Having abandoned restlessness and worry, he dwells at ease within himself, with a peaceful mind; he purifies his mind from restlessness and worry. Having abandoned doubt, he dwells as one who has passed beyond doubt, unperplexed about wholesome states; he purifies his mind from doubt.   Digha Nikaya

Do not pursue the past, do not lose yourself in the future. The past no longer is. The future has not yet come. Looking deeply at life as it is in the very here and now, the practitioner dwells in stability and freedom. We must be diligent today. To wait until tomorrow is too late. Death comes unexpectedly. How can we bargain with it? The sage calls the person who knows how to dwell in mindfulness night and day 'one who knows the better way to live alone.
Bhaddekaratta Sutta

To actualize the blessedness of meditation you should practice with pure intention and firm determination. Your meditation room should be clean and quiet. Do not dwell in thoughts of good or bad. Just relax and forget that you are meditating. Do not desire realization since that thought will keep you confused. (...) Many thoughts will crowd into your mind, ignore them, letting them go. If they persist be aware of them with the awareness which does not think.   *Dogen*

The clouds that wander through the sky have no roots, no home, nor do the distinctive thoughts floating through the mind. Once the Self-mind is seen, discrimination stops.
Song Of Mahamudra- *Tilopa*

When the five senses and the mind are still, and reason itself rests in silence, then begins the path supreme. This calm steadiness of the senses is called Yoga. Then one should become watchful, because Yoga comes and goes.   Katha Upanishad

Even as fire without fuel finds peace in its resting place, when thoughts become silence the soul finds peace in its own source. And when a mind which longs for truth finds the peace of its own source, then those false inclinations cease which were the result of former actions done in the delusion of the senses. Samsara, the transmigration of life, takes place in one's own mind. Let one therefore keep the mind pure, for what a man thinks that he becomes: this is a mystery of Eternity.   Maitri Upanishad

>Beware lest there be a wicked thought in your heart.
>Deuteronomy 15:9

He who gives up anger which has arisen, completely destroyed lust, has completely destroyed cravings like drying up a once swiftly flowing river, He who has completely destroyed pride like a weak bridge of reeds swept away by a mighty flood, He who does not see any substantiality in forms of becoming as one who does not find flowers on a fig tree, He who has no ill-temper within him and who has overcome all forms of becomings. He who has destroyed speculations, who is well-prepared without remainder, He who is neither restless nor indolent and who has overcome all such impediments, He who is neither restless nor indolent and knows that all the world is unsubstantial, He who has no unhealthy tendencies whatsoever and has completely destroyed the roots of evil. He has no anxieties whatsoever which are the causes of entering this world, He who has no cravings whatsoever which cause attachment to becoming, He who has eradicated the five hindrances (sensuality, ill-will, physical and mental laziness, restlessness and worry, skepticism), freed from confusion, having overcome doubts and sorrow, that monk gives up the cycle of existence as a snake sheds its old decayed skin.   Sutta Nipata

>Arise! Sit up! What advantage is there in your sleeping; what sleep is there to those who are afflicted with disease, pierced by the arrow of suffering? Arise! Sit up! Train yourselves resolutely to attain Peace. Do not let the king of evil (Mara) knowing you are negligent, delude you and place you under his control. Overcome this craving to which gods and men remain attached and seek pleasure. Do not let the opportune moment (khana) pass. Those who let khana pass will grieve when they are consigned to woe. Negligence is a taint and so is the taint which falls continuously, from negligence to negligence, by earnestness and knowledge let one pluck out his dust of passions.
>Uttana Sutta, Sutta Nipata

Strive first for the kingdom of God and his righteousness, and all these things (food, clothing, drink) will be given to you as well.   Matthew 6:33

Is there anyone among you who, if your child asks for a fish, will give you a snake instead of a fish? Or if a child asks for an egg, will you give a scorpion? If you then, who are evil, know how to give good gifts to your children, how much more will the heavenly Father give the Holy Spirit to those who ask him!   Luke 11:11-13

Ask, and it will be given to you; seek, and you will find; knock, and it will be opened to you. For everyone who asks receives, and he who seeks finds, and to him who knocks it will be opened. Or what man is there among you who, if his son asks for bread, will give him a stone? Or if he asks for a fish, will give him a serpent? If you then, being evil, know how to give good gifts to your children, how much more will your Father who is in heaven give good things to those who ask Him! Therefore, whatever you want men to do to you, do also to them, for this is the Law and the Prophets. Enter by the narrow gate; for wide is the gate and broad is the way that leads to destruction, and there are many who go in by it. Because narrow is the gate and difficult is the way which leads to life, and there are few who find it.   Matthew 7:7-14

Scripture says, "No one knows the Father but the Son." Therefore, if you want to know God, you must not only be like the Son, you must be the Son. *St. Thomas Aquinas* (1225-1274)

Go not on a way that is set with snares, and let not the same thing trip you twice. Be not too sure even of smooth roads, be careful on all your paths. Whatever you do, be on your guard, for in this way you will keep the commandments.   Sirach *32:20-23*

The disciple's attempt to purify the heart is like the person ordered to uproot a tree. However much he reflects and struggles to do so, he is unable. So he says to himself, "I'll wait until I'm more powerful

and then uproot it." But the longer he waits and leaves the tree to grow, the larger and stronger it becomes while he only becomes weaker, and its uprooting becomes more difficult.
Abu Uthman al-Maghribi

This process of controlling the mind can be likened to taming a wild horse: little by little learning when to slacken the reins and when to draw them in. This practice is the first step towards the highest Yoga.   Uddhava Gita *14:21*

Only by bringing the mind under control can the senses be controlled. Unable to conquer the formidable foe called mind, whose urges tears us apart to the very depths of our being, people begin to evaluate this world in terms of friends and enemies. This body, which is a production of the mind, becomes their sole identification: "I" and "mine" seem different from that which is another. Thus deluded they stumble about in a world of utter darkness. Even if other people are the cause of my happiness or distress, of what concern can that be to the Self, which is the Self of all people? It is the bodies interacting here that are the cause of both pleasure and pain- the Self is neither happy nor unhappy. For if a man were to bite his own tongue with which should he get angry- the tongue or the teeth?   Uddhava Gita *18:48-51*

And what brethren, is right effort? Herein, brethren, a brother generates the will to inhibit the arising of evil immoral conditions that have not yet arisen: he makes an effort, he sets energy afoot, he applies his mind and struggles. Likewise, (he does the same) to reject evil immoral conditions that have already arisen. Likewise, (he does the same) to cause the arising of good conditions that have not yet arisen. Likewise, he does the same to establish, to prevent the corruption, to cause the increase, the practice, the fulfillment of good conditions that have already arisen. This brethren is called right effort.   *Digha Nikaya,*

Whoever believes he can reach God by his own efforts toils in vain; whoever imagines he can reach God without effort is merely a traveler on the road of intent.   *Abu Said Kharraz*

People learning the way should first empty and quiet their minds. This is because the mind must be empty and quiet before it can mystically understand the subtle principle. If the mind is not emptied, it is like a pitcher full of donkey milk- how can you also fill it with lion's milk? If the mind is not quiet, it is like a lamp in the wind, or like turbulent water- how can it reflect myriad forms? Therefore, learners should first stop cogitation and minimize their objects of attention, making the mind empty and quiet. After that you have a basis for attaining the way. As Te-shan said, "Just have no mind on things and no things in your mind, and you will naturally be empty and spiritual, tranquil and sublime." Nevertheless, you should not settle in empty quietude, sitting relaxed and untrammeled in nothingness. You must be truly attentive, investigating diligently, before you can break through the barrier of illusion and accomplish the great task. People's forces of habit, accumulated since beginningless time, are deep-seated; if you want to uproot them today, it will not be easy. You need to have a firm will constantly spurring you on. Strive to make progress in the work, without thinking about how much time it may take. When you have practiced for a long time, you will naturally become peaceful and whole. Why seek any other particular method?   *Yuan-hsien*

If you really want to attain the Way, you must die completely once; only then can you realize it.   *Daiyu*

Watch and pray, that you enter not into temptation: the spirit indeed is willing, but the flesh is weak.   Matthew 26:41

Take heed, watch and pray: for you know not when the time is. [It is] as [when] a man, sojourning in another country, having left his house, and given authority to his servants, to each one his work, commanded also the porter to watch. Watch therefore: for you know not when the lord of the house comes, whether at evening, or at midnight, or at cock crowing, or in the morning; lest coming suddenly he find you sleeping. And what I say unto you I say unto all, Watch!   Mark 13:33-37

Strive to enter in by the narrow door: for many, I say unto you, shall seek to enter in, and shall not be able. When once the master of the house is risen up, and has shut to the door, and you begin to stand without, and to knock at the door, saying, Lord, open to us; and he shall answer and say to you, I know you not whence you are; then shall you begin to say, We did eat and drink in your presence, and you did teach in our streets; and he shall say, I tell you, I know not whence you are; depart from me, all you workers of iniquity. There shall be the weeping and the gnashing of teeth, when you shall see Abraham, and Isaac, and Jacob, and all the prophets, in the kingdom of God, and yourselves cast forth without. And they shall come from the east and west, and from the north and south, and shall sit down in the kingdom of God. And behold, there are last who shall be first, and there are first who shall be last.   Luke 13:24-30

And he said, A certain man had two sons: and the younger of them said to his father, Father, give me the portion of your substance that falls to me. And he divided unto them his living. And not many days after, the younger son gathered all together and took his journey into a far country; and there he wasted his substance with riotous living. And when he had spent all, there arose a mighty famine in that country; and he began to be in want. And he went and joined himself to one of the citizens of that country; and he sent him into his fields to feed swine. And he would fain have filled his belly with the husks that the swine did eat: and no man gave unto him. But when he came to himself he said, How many hired servants of my father's have bread enough and to spare, and I perish here with hunger! I will arise and go to my father, and will say unto him, Father, I have sinned against heaven, and in your sight: I am no more worthy to be called your son: make me as one of your hired servants. And he arose, and came to his father. But while he was yet afar off, his father saw him, and was moved with compassion, and ran, and fell on his neck, and kissed him. And the son said unto him, Father, I have sinned against heaven, and in your sight: I am no more worthy to be called your son. But the father said to his servants, Bring forth quickly the best robe, and put it on him; and put a ring on his hand, and shoes on his feet: and bring the fatted calf, [and] kill it, and let us eat, and make merry: for this my son was dead, and is alive again; he was lost, and is found. And they began to be merry. Now his elder son was in the field: and as he came and drew nigh to the house, he heard music and dancing. And he called to him one of the servants, and inquired what these things might be. And he said unto him, Your brother is come; and your father has killed the fatted calf, because he has received him safe and sound. But he was angry, and would not go in: and his father came out, and entreated him. But he answered and said to his father, Lo, these many years do I serve you, and I never transgressed a commandment of yours; and you never gave me a kid, that I might make merry with my friends: but when this your son came, who has devoured your living with harlots, you kill for him the fatted calf. And he said unto him, Son, you are always with me, and all that is mine is thine. But it was meet to make merry and be glad: for this your brother was dead, and is alive; and lost, and is found. (...) And when he was at the place, he said unto them, Pray that you enter not into temptation.   Luke 15:11-32, 22:40

And this, knowing the season, that already it is time for you to awake out of sleep: for now is salvation nearer to us than when we [first] believed. The night is far spent, and the day is at hand: let us therefore cast off the works of darkness, and let us put on the armor of light. Let us walk becomingly, as in the day; not in reveling and drunkenness, not in chambering and wantonness, not in strife and jealousy. But put ye on the Lord Jesus Christ, and make not provision for the flesh, to [fulfill] the lusts [thereof].
.   Romans 13:11-14

The Gift of discrimination is nothing worldly or insignificant. It is the greatest gift of God's grace. A monk must seek this gift with all his strength and diligence, and acquire the

ability to discriminate between the spirits that enter him and to assess them accurately. Otherwise he will not only fall into the foulest pits of wickedness as he walks around in the dark, but he will even stumble when his path is clear and laid out smooth and straight before him. (...) The light of the body is the eye; if therefore your eye is pure, your whole body will be full of light. But if your eye is evil, your whole body will be full of darkness (Matt 6:22-23). And this is just what we find; for the power of discrimination, scrutinizing all the thoughts and actions of a man, distinguishes and sets aside everything that is base and not pleasing to God, and keeps him free from delusion..
St. John Cassian

Finally, brethren, farewell. Be perfected; be comforted; be of the same mind; live in peace: and the God of love and peace shall be with you.   2nd Corinthians 13:11

My little children, of whom I am again in travail until Christ be formed in you.   Galatians 4:19

And he gave some [to be] apostles; and some, prophets; and some, evangelists; and some, pastors and teachers; for the perfecting of the saints, unto the work of ministering, unto the building up of the body of Christ: till we all attain unto the unity of the faith, and of the knowledge of the Son of God, unto a full grown man, unto the measure of the stature of the fullness of Christ: that we may be no longer children, tossed to and fro and carried about with every wind of doctrine, by the sleight of men, in craftiness, after the wiles of error; but speaking truth in love, we may grow up in all things into him, who is the head, [even] Christ; from whom all the body fitly framed and knit together through that which every joint supplieth, according to the working in [due] measure of each several part, makes the increase of the body unto the building up of itself in love. This I say therefore, and testify in the Lord, that you no longer walk as the Gentiles also walk, in the vanity of their mind, being darkened in their understanding, alienated from the life of God, because of the ignorance that is in them, because of the hardening of their heart; who being past feeling gave themselves up to lasciviousness, to work all uncleanness with greediness. But you did not so learn Christ; if so be that you heard him, and were taught in him, even as truth is in Jesus: that you put away, as concerning your former manner of life, the old man, that waxes corrupt after the lusts of deceit; and that you be renewed in the spirit of your mind, and put on the new man, that after God has been created in righteousness and holiness of truth. Wherefore, putting away falsehood, speak you truth each one with his neighbor: for we are members one of another. Be angry, and sin not: let not the sun go down upon your wrath: neither give place to the devil. Let him that stole steal no more: but rather let him labor, working with his hands the thing that is good, that he may have whereof to give to him that has need. Let no corrupt speech proceed out of your mouth, but such as is good for edifying as the need may be, that it may give grace to them that hear. And grieve not the Holy Spirit of God, in whom you were sealed unto the day of redemption. Let all bitterness, and wrath, and anger, and clamor, and railing, be put away from you, with all malice: and be kind one to another, tenderhearted, forgiving each other, even as God also in Christ forgave you. Be therefore imitators of God, as beloved children; and walk in love, even as Christ also loved you, and gave himself up for us, an offering and a sacrifice to God for an odor of a sweet smell. But fornication, and all uncleanness, or covetousness, let it not even be named among you, as becomes saints; nor filthiness, nor foolish talking, or jesting, which are not befitting: but rather giving of thanks. For this you know of a surety, that no fornicator, nor unclean person, nor covetous man, who is an idolater, has any inheritance in the kingdom of Christ and God. Let no man deceive you with empty words: for because of these things comes the wrath of God upon the sons of disobedience. Be not therefore partakers with them; For you were once darkness, but are now light in the Lord: walk as children of light (for the fruit of the light is in all goodness and righteousness and truth), proving what is well-pleasing unto the Lord; and have no fellowship with the unfruitful works of darkness, but rather even reprove them; for the things which are done by them in secret it is a shame even to speak of. But all things when they are reproved are made manifest by the light: for everything that is made manifest is light. Wherefore [he] saith, Awake, you that sleep, and arise from the dead, and Christ shall shine upon thee.   Ephesians 4:11- 5:14

    Finally, be strong in the Lord, and in the strength of his might. Put on the whole armor of God, that you may be able to stand against the wiles of the devil. For our wrestling is not against flesh and blood, but against the principalities, against the powers, against the world-rulers of this darkness, against the spiritual [hosts] of wickedness in the heavenly [places]. Wherefore take up the whole armor of God, that you may be able to withstand in the evil day, and, having done all, to stand. Stand therefore, having girded your loins with truth, and having put on the breastplate of righteousness, and having shod your feet with the preparation of the gospel of peace;

withal taking up the shield of faith, wherewith you shall be able to quench all the fiery darts of the evil [one]. And take the helmet of salvation, and the sword of the Spirit, which is the word of God: with all prayer and supplication praying at all seasons in the Spirit, and watching thereunto in all perseverance and supplication for all the saints.   Ephesians 6:10-18

Wherefore, even as the Holy Spirit says, Today if you shall hear his voice, Harden not your hearts, as in the provocation, Like as in the day of the trial in the wilderness, Where your fathers tried [me] by proving [me,] And saw my works forty years. Wherefore I was displeased with this generation, And said, They do always err in their heart: But they did not know my ways; As I swore in my wrath, They shall not enter into my rest. Take heed, brethren, lest haply there shall be in any one of you an evil heart of unbelief, in falling away from the living God: but exhort one another day by day, so long as it is called Today; lest anyone of you be hardened by the deceitfulness of sin: for we are become partakers of Christ, if we hold fast the beginning of our confidence firm unto the end: while it is said, Today if you shall hear his voice, Harden not your hearts, as in the provocation.   Hebrews 3:7-15

Follow after peace with all men, and the sanctification without which no man shall see the Lord: looking carefully lest [there be] any man that falls short of the grace of God; lest any root of bitterness springing up trouble [you], and thereby the many be defiled;   Hebrews 12:14-15

Wherefore girding up the loins of your mind, be sober and set your hope perfectly on the grace that is to be brought unto you at the revelation of Jesus Christ; as children of obedience, not fashioning yourselves according to your former lusts in [the time of] your ignorance: but like as he who called you is holy, be you yourselves also holy in all manner of living; because it is written, You shall be holy; for I am holy. And if you call on him as Father, who without respect of persons judges according to each man's work, pass the time of your sojourning in fear: knowing that you were redeemed, not with corruptible things, with silver or gold, from your vain manner of life handed down from your fathers;

but with precious blood, as of a lamb without spot, [even the blood] of Christ: who was foreknown indeed before the foundation of the world, but was manifested at the end of times for your sake, who through him are believers in God, that raised him from the dead, and gave him glory; so that your faith and hope might be in God. Seeing you have purified your souls in your obedience to the truth unto unfeigned love of the brethren, love one another from the heart fervently: having been begotten again, not of corruptible seed, but of incorruptible, through the word of God, which is alive and abides. For, all flesh is as grass, And all the glory thereof as the flower of grass. The grass withers, and the flower falls: But the word of the Lord abides forever. And this is the word of good tidings which was preached unto you.   1st Peter 1:13-25

      Be sober, be watchful: your adversary the devil, as a roaring lion, walks about, seeking whom he may devour, whom withstand steadfast in your faith, knowing that the same sufferings are accomplished in your brethren who are in the world. And the God of all grace, who called you unto his eternal glory in Christ, after that you have suffered a little while, shall himself perfect, establish, strengthen you. To him [be] the dominion forever and ever. Amen.   1st Peter 5:8-11

      This is now, beloved, the second epistle that I write unto you; and in both of them I stir up your sincere mind by putting you in remembrance; that you should remember the words which were spoken before by the holy prophets, and the commandments of the Lord and Savior through your apostles: knowing this first, that in the last days mockers shall come with mockery, walking after their own lusts, and saying, Where is the promise of his coming? for, from the day that the fathers fell asleep, all things continue as they were from the beginning of the creation. For this they willfully forget, that there were heavens from of old, and an earth compacted out of water and amidst water, by the word of God; by which means the world that then was, being overflowed with water, perished: but the heavens that now are, and the earth, by the same word have been stored up for fire, being reserved against the day of judgment and destruction of ungodly men. But forget not this one thing, beloved, that one day is with the Lord as a thousand years, and a thousand years as one day. The Lord is not slack concerning his promise, as some count slackness; but is longsuffering to you-ward, not wishing that any should perish, but that all should come to repentance. But the day of the Lord will come as a thief; in the which the heavens shall pass away with a great noise, and the elements shall be dissolved with fervent heat, and the earth and the works that are therein shall be burned up. Seeing that these things are thus all to be dissolved, what manner of persons ought you to be in [all] holy living and godliness, looking for and earnestly desiring the coming of the day of God, by reason of which the heavens being on fire shall be dissolved, and the elements shall melt with fervent heat? But, according to his promise, we look for new heavens and a new earth, wherein dwelleth righteousness. Wherefore, beloved, seeing that you look for these things, give diligence that you may be found in peace, without spot and blameless in his sight. And account that the longsuffering of our Lord is salvation; even as our beloved brother Paul also, according to the wisdom given to him, wrote unto you.   2 Peter 3:1-15

>Man can have nothing but what he strives for.
>Quran 53:39

>Struggle to preserve unimpaired the light that shines within your intellect. If passion begins to dominate you when you look at things, this means that the Lord has left you in darkness; He has dropped the reins with which He has been guiding you, and the light of your eyes is gone from you. Yet even if this happens, do not despair or give up, but pray to God with the words of David: "O send out Your light and Your truth to me in my gloom, for Thou art the salvation of my countenance and my God" (Ps 43:3,5); Thou shalt send forth Your Spirit and they shall be created; and You shall renew the face of the earth' (Ps 104:30).   *St. John of Karpathos*

The Way of the Word

Where is the way to the dwelling of light? (...) Who has put wisdom in the mind? Or who has given understanding to the heart?
Job 38:19, 36

Therefore, whoever hears these sayings of Mine, and does them, I will liken him to a wise man who built his house on the rock; and the rain descended, the floods came, and the winds blew and beat on that house; and it did not fall, for it was founded on the rock. But everyone who hears these sayings of Mine, and does not do them, will be like a foolish man who built his house on the sand: and the rain descended, the floods came, and the winds blew and beat on that house; and it fell. And great was its fall.
Matthew 7:24-27

About unbelievers Allah's says: thenceforth your hearts were hardened: they became like a rock and even worse in hardness. For among rocks there are some from which rivers gush forth; others there are which when split asunder send forth water; and others which sink for fear of Allah. And Allah is not unmindful of what you do.   Quran 2:74

The parable of those who take protectors other than Allah is that of the Spider, who builds to itself a house; but truly the flimsiest of houses is the Spider's house; -if they but knew.
Quran 29:41

Allah does not cause to stray, except those who forsake the path.   Quran 2:26

We have indeed made the Signs clear to anyone who holds firmly to the Faith in their hearts.   Quran 2:18

When My servants ask you concerning Me, I am indeed close to them: I listen to the prayer of every supplicant when he calls on Me: let them also, with a will, listen to My call, and believe Me: that they may walk in the right way.   Quran 2:186

The book of all books is in your own heart, in which are written and engraven the deepest lessons divine instruction; learn therefore to be deeply attentive to the presence of God in your hearts, who is always speaking, always instructing, always illuminating that heart that is attentive to him. Here you will meet the divine light in its proper place, in that depth of your souls, where the birth of the Son of God and the proceeding of the Holy Ghost are always ready to spring up in you. And be assured of this, that so much as you have of inward love and adherence to his holy light and spirit within you, so much as you have of real unaffected humility and meekness, so much as you are dead to your own will and self-love, so much as you have purity of heart, so much, and no more, nor any further, do you see and know the truths of God.
William Law

All our salvation consists in the manifestation of the nature, life and spirit of Jesus Christ in our inward new man. This alone is Christian redemption, this alone redeems, renews and regains the first life of God in the soul of man. Everything besides this is self, is fiction, is propriety, is own will, and however colored is only your old man, with all his deeds. Enter therefore with all your heart into this truth, let your eye be always upon it, do everything in view of it, try everything by the truth of it, love nothing but for the sake of it. Wherever you go, whatever you do, at home or abroad, in the field or at church, do all in a desire of union with Christ, in imitation of his tempers and inclinations, and look upon all as nothing but that which exercises and increases the spirit and life of Christ in your soul.   *William Law*

Do not all Christians desire to have Christ to be their Savior? Yes. But here is the deceit; all would have Christ to be their Savior in the next world and to help them into heaven when they die by his power and merits with God. But this is not willing Christ to be your

Savior; for his salvation, if it is to be had, must be had in this world; if he saves you it must be done in this life by changing all that is within you, by helping you to a new heart, as he helped the blind to see, the lame to walk and the dumb to speak. For to have salvation from Christ is nothing else but to be made like unto him; it is to have his humility and meekness, his mortification and self-denial, his renunciation of the spirit, wisdom and honors of this world, his love of God, his desire of doing God's will and seeking only his honor. To have these tempers formed and begotten in your heart is to have salvation from Christ. But if you will not have these tempers brought forth in you, if your faith and desire does not seek and cry to Christ for them in the same reality as the lame asked to walk and the blind to see, then you must be said to be unwilling to have Christ to be your Savior.   *William Law*

If a soul is seeking God, its Beloved is seeking it still more. When the soul reflects that God is the guide of its blind self, then its main preoccupation will be to see that it sets no obstacle in the way of its guide, the Holy Spirit, upon the road by which God is leading it. The soul then must walk with loving advertence to God, without making specific acts, and exerting no effort on its own part. It must keep a simple, pure and loving awareness, like one who gazes with the awareness of love. The soul must be attached to nothing, whether of sense or spirit, which would introduce noise into the deep silence. There the voice of God speaks to the heart in this secret place, in utmost peace and tranquility.   *St. John of the Cross*

Those who have gauged the depths of their own nothingness can no longer retain any kind of confidence in themselves, nor trust in any way to their works in which they can discover nothing but misery, self-love and corruption. This absolute distrust and complete disregard of self is the source from which alone flow those delightful consolations of souls wholly abandoned to God, and form their unalterable peace, holy joy and immoveable confidence in God only. Oh! if you but knew the gift of God, the value, merit, power, peace and holy assurance of salvation hidden in this state of abandonment, you would soon be delivered from all your fears and anxieties. But you imagine you will be lost directly you think of abandoning yourself; and yet the most efficacious means of salvation is to practice this total and perfect abandonment. I have never yet come across any who have so set themselves against making this act of abandonment to god, as you. Nevertheless, you will necessarily have to come to it, at least at the hour of death. Everyone is absolutely compelled to abandon self to the very great mercy of God.   *Jean-Pierre de Caussade*

"But", you say, "if I had lived a holy life and performed some good works, I might think myself authorized to practice this abandonment, and to divest myself of my fears." An illusion, my dear sister. Such language can only have been inspired by your unhappy self-love, which desires to be able to trust entirely to itself, whereas you ought to place your confidence only in God and in the infinite merits of Jesus Christ. You have never really thoroughly fathomed this essential point but have always stopped short to examine into your fears and doubts instead of rising above them, and throwing yourself heart and soul into the hands of God, and upon his fatherly love. In other words, you always want to have a distinct assurance based on yourself in order to abandon yourself better. Most certainly this is anything but an abandonment to God in complete confidence in him only, but, rather, a secret desire of being able to depend on yourself before abandoning yourself to his infinite goodness. This is to act like a state criminal who, before abandoning himself to the clemency of the king, wishes to be assured of his pardon. Can this be called depending on God, hoping only in God? Judge for yourself.
Jean-Pierre de Caussade

Fear me that I may complete my favors on you, and ye may consent to be guided.   Quran 2:150

Allah beckons by His grace to the Garden and makes His Signs clear to mankind: that they may receive admonition.
Quran 2:221

Behold! the angels said: "O Mary! Allah gives you glad tidings of a Word from Him: his name will be Jesus Christ.
Quran 3:45

Abraham was not a Jew nor yet a Christian; but he was true in Faith and he bowed his will to Allah's.   Quran 3:67

Allah guides not a people unjust.   Quran 3:86

Whoever holds firm to Allah will be shown a way that is straight.   Quran 3:101

Fear Me; and that I may complete my favors, and you may consent to be guided (...) then you remember Me; I will remember you. Be grateful to Me and do not reject Faith O you who believe!   Seek help with patient perseverance and prayer: for Allah is with those who patiently persevere. (...) They are those on whom descend blessings from Allah and Mercy, and they are the ones that receive guidance.   Quran 2:150-157

Behold! The angles said: O Mary! Allah gives you glad tidings of a Word from Him: his name will be Christ Jesus, the son of Mary, held in honor in this world and the Hereafter and of the company of those nearest to Allah; (...) And Allah will teach him the Book and Wisdom, the Law and the Gospel, and appoint him a Messenger to the Children of Israel (..) I have come to you to attest the Law which was before me. And to make lawful to you part of what was before forbidden to you; I have come to you with a Sign from your Lord. So, fear Allah, and obey me. It is Allah Who is my Lord and your Lord; then worship Him. This is a Way that is straight.   Quran 3:45-51

The Truth comes from Allah alone; so be not of those who doubt.   Quran 3:60

True guidance is the guidance of Allah.
Quran 3:73

Who can do better in religion than one who submits his whole self to Allah, does good, and follows the way of Abraham the true in faith? For Allah took Abraham for a friend.
Quran 4:124

O People of the Book! Commit no excesses in your religion: nor say of Allah anything but the truth. Christ Jesus the son of Mary was a Messenger of Allah, and His Word, which we bestowed on Mary, and a Spirit proceeding from Him: so, believe in Allah and His Messengers.   Quran 4: 171

O People of the Book! There has come to you Our Messenger, revealing to you much that you used to hide in the Book, and passing over much (that is now unnecessary): There has come to you from Allah a (new) light and a perspicuous Book,- wherewith Allah guides all who seek His good pleasure to ways of peace and safety, and leads them out of darkness, by His Will unto the light, - guides them to a Path that is Straight.   Quran 5: 15-16

O you who believe! If you fear Allah, He will grant you a Criterion to judge between right and wrong, remove from you all evil that may afflict you, and forgive you: for Allah is the Lord of grace unbounded.   Quran 8:29

Those who believe and work righteousness, - their Lord will guide them because of their Faith: beneath them will flow rivers in Gardens of Bliss.   Quran 10:9

Truly Allah leaves to stray whom He will; but He guides to Himself those who turn to Him in penitence, - those who believe and whose hearts find satisfaction in the remembrance of Allah; for without a doubt in the remembrance of Allah do hearts find satisfaction.   Quran 13:27-28

Don't you see how Allah sets forth a parable? - a goodly Word like a goodly tree, whose root is firmly fixed, and its branches reach to the heavens, - It brings forth its fruit at all times, by the leave of its Lord.   So, Allah sets forth parables for men, in order that they may receive admonition.   And the parable of an evil Word is that of an evil tree: it is torn up by the root from the surface of the earth: it has no stability.   Allah will establish in strength those who believe, with the Word that stands firm, in this world and in the Hereafter; but Allah will leave, to stray, those who do wrong: Allah does what He wills.   Quran 14: 24-27

(...) thus Adam disobeyed his Lord and allowed himself to be seduced.   But his Lord chose him for His Grace: He turned to him, and gave him guidance.   He said: "Get you down, both of you, - all together, from the Garden, with enmity one to another: but if, as is sure, there comes to you guidance from Me, whosoever follows My guidance, will not lose his way, nor fall into misery."
                              Quran 20:121-123

Allah is the Light of the heavens and the earth.   The parable of His Light is as if there were a Niche and within it a Lamp: the Lamp enclosed in Glass: the glass as it were a brilliant star: lit from a blessed Tree, an Olive, neither of the East nor of the West, whose Oil is well-nigh Luminous, though fire scarce touched it: Light upon Light! Allah guides whom He will to His Light: Allah sets forth Parables for men: and Allah knows all things.   Quran 24:35

Or the Unbelievers state is like the depths of darkness in a vast deep ocean, overwhelmed with billow topped by billow, topped by dark clouds: depths of darkness, one above another: if a man stretches out his hand, he can hardly see it!   For any to whom Allah does not give light, there is no light.   Quran 24:40

To those who receive guidance, He increases the light of Guidance, and bestows on them their Piety and Restraint from evil.
Quran 47:17

If anyone believes in Allah, Allah guides his heart aright.
Quran 64:11

O you who believe! Celebrate the praises of Allah, and do this often; and glorify Him morning and evening. He it is Who sends blessings on you, as do His angels, that He may bring you out from the depths of Darkness into Light: and He is full of Mercy to the Believers.   Quran 33:41-43

By the Sky and the Night-Visitant therein; - and what will explain to you what the Night Visitant is? It is the Star of piercing brightness; - there is no soul but has a protector over it. Now let man but think from what he is created! He is created from a drop emitted-proceeding from between the backbone and the ribs: surely Allah is able to bring him back to life! The Day that all hidden things shall be made manifest, man will have no power and no helper. By the Firmament which returns in its round, and by the Earth which opens out for the gushing of springs or the sprouting of vegetation, - behold this is the Word that distinguishes Good from Evil.
Quran 86:1-13

Ananda, dwell having self for island, self for refuge and no other refuge; having Dhamma for island, Dhamma for refuge and no other refuge.   Samyutta-Nikaya

He who sees Dhamma sees the Lord.
Samyutta-Nikaya

The gentleman devotes his efforts to the roots, for once the roots are established, the way will grow therefrom. Being good as a son and obedient as a young man is, perhaps, the root of a man's character.   Analects, Book 1:2

His disciples said, "Show us the place where you are, for we must seek it." He said to them, "Whoever has ears ought to listen. There is light within an enlightened person, and it shines on the whole world. If the light does not shine, it is dark."
                        Gospel of Thomas 24

If you allow your mind to guide you, who then can be said to be without a teacher? Why is it thought that only the one who understands change and whose heart approves this can be a teacher? Surely the fool is just the same. But if you ignore your mind but insist you know right from wrong, you are like the saying, Today I set off for Yueh and arrived yesterday.' *Chuang Tzu*

By the light shining out of chaos, the sage is guided; he does not make use of distinctions but is led on by the light.
                        Chuang Tzu

The one who knows how to stop at what he knows is best. Who knows the arguments that needs no words, and the Tao that cannot be named? To those who do, this is called the Treasury of Heaven. Pour into it and it is never full; empty it and it is never empty. We do not know where it comes from originally, and this is called our Guiding Light. *Chuang Tzu*

The essence of the perfect Tao is hidden in darkness, lost in silence. Nothing seen; nothing heard. Embrace the spirit in quietness, the body with its own rightness. Be still, be pure, do not make your body struggle, do not disturb your essence. All this will result in a long life. The eye does not see, the ear does not hear, the heart knows nothing, yet your spirit will guard your body and your body will have a long life. Guard what is within, block that which is outside, for much knowledge is dangerous. *Chuang Tzu*

The Tao is called the Great Mother, empty yet inexhaustible, it gives birth to multiple worlds. It is always within you. You can use it any way you want.   Tao te Ching 6

Colors blind the eye. Sounds deafen the ear. Flavors numb the taste. Thoughts weaken the mind. Desires wither the heart. The Master observes the world but trusts his inner vision. He allows things to come and go. His heart is open as the sky.
                                        Tao te Ching 12

The Master keeps her mind always at one with the Tao; that is what gives her radiance. The Tao is ungraspable. How can her mind be at one with it? Because she doesn't cling to ideas.
                                        Tao te Ching 21

Confucius was sightseeing in Lu Liang, where the waterfall is thirty fathoms high and the river races along for forty miles, so fast that neither fish nor any other creature can swim in it. He saw one person dive in and he assumed that this person wanted to embrace death, perhaps because of some anxiety, so he placed his followers along the bank and they prepared to pull him out. However, the swimmer, having gone a hundred yards, came out, and walked nonchalantly along the bank, singing a song with water dripping off him. Confucius pursued him and said, "I thought you were a ghost, but now I see, Sir, that you are a man. I wish to enquire; do you have a Tao for swimming under the water?" He said, "No, I have no Tao. I started with what I knew, matured my innate nature and allow destiny to do the rest. I go in with the currents and go out with the flow, just going with the Tao of the water and never being concerned. That is how I survive.'"   *Chuang Tzu*

Yeh Chueh asked Pi I about the Tao, and Pi I said, "Attend to your body, concentrate upon the One, and the perfect harmony of Heaven will be yours. Rein in your understanding, unify your stance and the spirit will dwell within you. Virtue will be your beauty and the Tao will be your dwelling place."   *Chuang Tzu*

Look within. Be still. Free from fear and attachment, know the sweet joy of the way.   Dhammapada

Therefore, Ananda, be lamps unto yourselves, be a refuge to yourselves. Betake yourselves no external refuge. Hold fast to the Truth as a lamp; hold fast to the Truth as a refuge. Look not for a refuge in anyone beside yourselves. And those, Ananda, who either now or after I am dead shall be a lamp unto themselves, shall betake themselves to no external refuge, but holding fast to the Truth as their lamp, and holding fast to the truth as their refuge, shall not look for refuge to anyone beside themselves- it is they who shall reach the very topmost Height. But they must be anxious to learn.   Mahaparinibbana Sutta

Remember the clear light, the pure clear white light from which everything in the universe comes, to which everything in the universe returns; the original nature of your own mind. The natural state of the universe unmanifest. Let go into the clear light, trust it, merge with it. It is your own true nature, it is home. The visions you experience exist within your consciousness; the forms they take are determined by your past attachments, your past desires, your past fears, your past karma. These visions have no reality outside your consciousness. No matter how frightening some of them may seem they cannot hurt you. Just let them pass through your consciousness. They will all pass in time. No need to become involved with them; no need to be repulsed by the frightening ones. No need to be seduced or excited by the sexual ones. No need to be attached to them at all. Just let them pass. If you become involved with these visions, you may wander for a long time confused. Just let them pass through your consciousness like clouds passing through an empty sky. Fundamentally they have no more reality than this. Remember these teachings, remember the clear light, the pure bright shining white light of your own nature, it is deathless. If you can look into the visions you can experience and recognize that they are composed of the same pure clear white light as everything else in the universe. No matter where or how far you wander, the light is only a split second, a half breath away. It is never too late to recognize the clear light.   The Tibetan Book of the Dead

I will tell you the Word that all the Vedas glorify, and all self-sacrifice expresses, all sacred studies and holy life seek. That Word is OM. That Word is the everlasting Brahman: that Word is the highest End. When that sacred Word is known, all longings are fulfilled. It is the supreme means of salvation: it is the help supreme. When that great Word is known, one is great in the heaven of Brahman.   Katha Upanishad

Always dwelling within all beings is the Atman, the Purusha, the Self, a little flame in the heart. Let one with steadiness withdraw him from the body even as an inner stem is withdrawn from its sheath. Know this pure immortal light; know in truth this pure immortal light.   Katha Upanishad

Do not follow the ideas of others, but learn to listen to the voice within yourself. Your body and mind will become clear and you will realize the unity of all things.   *Dogen*

There is a Spirit who is among the things of this world and yet he is above the things of this world. He is clear and pure, in the peace of a void of vastness. He is beyond the life of the body and the mind, never-born, never-dying, everlasting, ever One in his own greatness. He is the Spirit whose power gives consciousness to the body: he is the driver of the chariot.   Maitri Upanishad

When a wise man has withdrawn his mind from all things without, and when his spirit of life has peacefully left inner sensations, let him rest in peace, free from the movements of will and desire. Since the living being called the spirit of life has come from that which is greater than the spirit of life, let the spirit of life surrender itself into what is called turya, the fourth condition of consciousness. For it has been said: there is something beyond our mind which abides in silence within our mind. It is the supreme mystery beyond thought. Let one's mind and one's subtle body rest upon that and not rest on anything else.   Maitri Upanishad

The breath of life is the consciousness of life, and the consciousness of life is the breath of life.
Kaushitaki Upanishad

There is a light that shines beyond all things on earth, beyond us all, beyond the heavens, beyond the highest, the very highest heavens. This is the Light that shines in our heart.
Chandogya Upanishad

The white light of the skandha of form in its basic purity, the mirror-like wisdom, dazzling white, luminous, and clear, will come towards you from the heart of Vajrasattva and his consort and pierce you so that your eyes cannot bear to look at it. At the same time, together with the wisdom light, the soft smoky light of hell-beings will also come towards you and pierce you. At that time, under the influence of aggression, you will be terrified and escape from the brilliant white light, but you will feel an emotion of pleasure towards the soft smoky light of the hell-beings. At that time, do not be afraid of the sharp, brilliant, luminous and clear white light, but recognize it as wisdom. (...) Do not take pleasure in the soft smoky light of the hell-beings. This is the inviting path of your neurotic veils, accumulated by violent aggression. If you are attracted to it you will fall down into hell, and sink into the muddy swamp of unbearable suffering from which there is never any escape. It is an obstacle blocking the path of liberation, so do not look at it, but give up aggression. Do not be attracted to it, do not yearn for it. Feel longing for the luminous, brilliant, white light.
Tibetan Book of the Dead

But, like the sun, knowledge reveals Brahman to those whose ignorance is removed by self-realization. Washed in the light of knowledge, and never born again, are those whose minds are engrossed in the atman, whose fulfillment is in the atman.
                    Bhagavad Gita 5:16-17

   I am the source of everything, everything evolves from me-thinking in this manner, the learned concentrate on me. Their minds in me, their senses in me, instructing each other and singing my glory, they are happy. And I enlighten them, and they come to me, for they are devoted and steadfast. I dwell in their heart, and my compassion like a glowing lamp of wisdom scatters their ignorant darkness.   Bhagavad Gita 10:8-11

   Brahman is Om Tat Sat, the Truth That Is.
                    Bhagavad Gita 17:23

   He is the Light of all lights, which shines beyond all darkness. It is vision, the end of vision, to be reached by vision, dwelling in the heart of all.   Bhagavad Gita 13:17

   The intelligent, filled with my state of being, share in me, knowing that I am the origin of all this, and that everything unrolls from me. Their thoughts on me, their life breath directed towards me, enlightening each other and constantly talking of me, they are gratified and rejoice. To those who are continuously disciplined, who worship me full of joy, I grant the discipline of intelligence by which they come to me. Situated in their being, out of compassion for them I put to flight the darkness born of their ignorance with the bright lamp of knowledge.   Bhagavad Gita 10:8-11

   Listen and I shall explain now, Arjuna, how one who attains perfection attains Brahman, the supreme consummation of wisdom. Unerring in his discrimination, sovereign of his senses and passions, free from the clamor of likes and dislikes, he leads a simple, self-reliant life based on meditation, controlling his speech, body and mind. Free from self-will, aggressiveness, arrogance, anger, and the

lust to possess people or things, he is at peace with himself and others and enters into the unitive state. United with Brahman, ever joyful, beyond the reach of desire and sorrow, he has equal regard for every living creature and attains supreme devotion to me. By loving me he comes to know me truly; then he knows my glory and enters into my boundless being. All his acts are performed in my service, and through my grace he wins eternal life. Make every act an offering to me; regard me as your only protector. Relying on interior discipline, meditate on me always. Remembering me, you shall overcome all difficulties through my grace. But if you will not heed me in your self-will, nothing will avail you. (...) The Lord dwells in the hearts of all creatures and whirls them around upon the wheel of maya. Run to him for refuge with all your strength, and peace profound will be yours through his grace. (...) Be aware of me always, adore me, make every act an offering to me, and you shall come to me; this I promise, for you are dear to me. Abandon all supports and look to me for protection. I shall purify you from the sins of the past; do not grieve.
                      Bhagavad Gita 18:50-58, 61-62, 65-66

It is called the light of lights beyond darkness- knowledge, the object of knowledge, and the goal of knowledge, inherent in the heart of everyone. (...) Just as the one sun lights up this entire world, so, Bharata, the owner of the field lights the entire field.
                      Bhagavad Gita 13: 17,33

He might make you know that man shall not live by bread alone; but man lives by every word that proceeds from the mouth of the Lord.   Deuteronomy 8:3,   Matthew 4:4

There is a reality even prior to heaven and earth; indeed, it has no form much less a name; eyes fail to see it; It has no voice for ears to detect. To call it Mind or Buddha violates its nature for then it becomes like a visionary flower in the air. It is not Mind nor Buddha. Absolutely quiet, and yet illuminating in a mysterious way, It allows itself to be perceived only by the clear-eyed. It is Dharma truly beyond form and sound. It is Tao having nothing to do with words. Wishing to entice the blind, the Buddha has playfully let words escape his golden mouth. Heaven and earth are ever since filled with entangling briars. O my good worthy friends gathered here, if you desire to listen to the thunderous voice of the Dharma, exhaust your words, empty your thoughts, for then you may come to recognize this One Essence. Says Hui the Brother, "The Buddha's Dharma is not to be given up to mere human sentiments." Dai-o Kokushi "On Zen"

    For this commandment which I command you today is not too mysterious for you, nor is it far off. It is not in heaven, that you should say, "Who will ascend into heaven for us and bring it to us, that we may hear it and do it?" Nor is it beyond the sea, that you should say, "Who will go over the sea for us and bring it to us, that we may hear it and do it?" But the word is very near to you, in your mouth and in your heart, that you may do it. See, I have set before you today life and death, good and evil, in that I command you today to love the Lord your God, to walk in His ways, and to keep His commandments, His statutes, and His judgments, that you may live and multiply; and the Lord your God will bless you in the land which you go to possess. But if your heart turns away so that you do not hear, and are drawn away, and worship other gods and serve them, I announce to you today that you shall surely perish; you shall not prolong your days in the land which you cross over the Jordan to go in and possess, I call heaven and earth as witnesses today against you, that I have set before you life and death, blessing and cursing; therefore, choose life, that both you and your descendants may live; that you may love the Lord your God, that you may obey His voice, and that you may cling to Him, for He is your life and the length of your days; and that you may dwell in the land which the Lord swore to your fathers, to Abraham, Isaac, and Jacob, to give them.
                                                Deuteronomy 30:11-20

    The light of the wicked indeed goes out, and the flame of his fire does not shine. The light is dark in his tent, and his lamp beside him is put out.   Job 18:5-6

    God will redeem my soul from going down to the pit, and my life shall see the light. Behold, God works all these things, twice, in fact, three times with a man, to bring back his soul from the Pit, that he may be enlightened with the light of life. (...) The spirit within me compels me.   Job 33:28-30, 32:18

As for me, I will see Your face in righteousness; I shall be satisfied when I awake in Your likeness. I will love You, O Lord, my strength. The Lord is my rock and my fortress and my deliverer; my God, my strength, in whom I will trust; my shield and the horn of my salvation, my stronghold. I will call upon the Lord, who is worthy to be praised; so, shall I be saved from my enemies. The pangs of death surrounded me, and the floods of ungodliness made me afraid. The sorrows of Sheoul surrounded me; the snares of death confronted me. In my distress, I called upon the Lord, and cried out to my God; he heard my voice from His temple, and my cry came before Him, even to His ears.   Psalms 17:15, 18:1-6

For You will light my lamp; the Lord my God will enlighten my darkness. For by You I can run against a troop, by my God I can leap over a wall. As for God, His way is perfect; the word of the Lord is proven; he is a shield to all who trust in Him. (...) The heavens declare the glory of God; and the firmament shows His handiwork. Day unto day utters speech, and night unto night reveals knowledge. There is no speech nor language where their voice is not heard. Their line has gone out through all the earth, and their words to the end of the world. (...) The law of the Lord is perfect, converting the soul; the testimony of the Lord is sure, making wise the simple; the statutes of the Lord are right, rejoicing the heart; the commandment of the Lord is pure, enlightening the eyes; the fear of the Lord is clean, enduring forever; the judgments of the Lord are true and righteous altogether. More to be desired are they than gold, yea, than much fine gold; sweeter also than honey and the honeycomb. Moreover, by them Your servant is warned, and in keeping them there is great reward.
Psalms 18:28-30, 19:1-4, 7-11

The Lord is my shepherd; I shall not want. He makes me to lie down in green pastures; he leads me beside the still waters. He restores my soul; he leads me in the paths of righteousness for His name's sake. Yea, though I walk through the valley of the shadow of death, I will fear no evil; for You are with me; Your rod and Your staff, they comfort me. You prepare a table before me in the

presence of my enemies; you anoint my head with oil; my cup runs over. Surely goodness and mercy shall follow me all the days of my life; and I will dwell in the house of the Lord forever.
Psalm 23

Good and upright is the Lord; therefore, He teaches the sinners in the way. The humble He guides in justice, and the humble He teaches His way. All the paths of the Lord are mercy and truth, to such as keep His covenant and His testimonies. For your name's sake, O Lord, pardon my iniquity, for it is great. (...) The Lord is my light and my salvation: whom shall I fear? The Lord is the strength of my life; of whom shall I be afraid?   Psalm 25:8-11, 27:1

To him who orders his conduct aright I will show the salvation of God.   Psalms 50:23

Deal bountifully with Your servant, that I may live and keep Your word. Open my eyes, that I may see wondrous things from Your law. (...) My soul clings to the dust. Revive me according to Your word. (...) Remember the word to Your servant, upon which You have caused me to hope. This is my comfort in my affliction, for Your word has given me life. (...) Forever, O Lord, Your word is settled in heaven. Your faithfulness endures to all generations. (...) Your word is a lamp to my feet and a light to my path.
Psalms 119:17-18, 25, 49-50, 89-90, 105

Wisdom calls aloud outside; she raises her voice in the open squares. She cries out in the chief concourses, at the openings of the gates in the city she speaks her words: "How long, you simple ones, will you love simplicity? For scorners delight in their scorning, and fools hate knowledge. Turn at my rebuke; surely I will pour out my spirit on you; I will make my words known to you. Because I have called and you refused, I have stretched out my hand and no one regarded, because you disdained all my counsel, and would have none of my rebuke, I also will laugh at your calamity; I will mock when your terror comes like a storm, and your destruction comes like a whirlwind, when distress and anguish come upon you. Then they will call on me, but I will not answer; they will seek me diligently, but they will not find me. Because they hated knowledge and did not choose the fear of the Lord, they would have none of my counsel and despised my every rebuke. Therefore, they shall eat the fruit of their own way, and be filled to the full with their own fancies. For the turning away of the simple will slay them, and the complacency of fools will destroy them; but whoever listens to me will dwell safely, and be secure, without fear of evil. My son, if you receive my words, and treasure my commands within you, so that you incline your ear to wisdom, and apply your heart to understanding; yes, if you cry out for discernment, and lift up your voice for understanding, if you seek her as silver, and search for her as for hidden treasures; then you will understand the fear of the Lord, and find the knowledge of God. For the Lord gives wisdom; from His mouth come knowledge and understanding; he stores up sound wisdom for the upright; He is a shield to those who walk uprightly; He guards the paths of justice, and preserves the ways of the saints. Then you will understand righteousness and justice, equity and every good path. When wisdom enters your heart, and knowledge is pleasant to your soul, discretion will preserve you; understanding will keep you, to deliver you from the way of evil, from the man who speaks perverse things, from those who leave the paths of righteousness to walk in darkness. (...) Trust in the Lord with all your heart, and lean not on your own understanding; in all your ways acknowledge Him, and He shall direct your paths. (...) Happy is the man who finds wisdom, and the man who gains understanding; for her proceeds are better than the profits of silver, and her gain than fine gold. She is more precious than rubies, and all the things you may desire cannot compare with her. Length of days is in her right hand, in her left-hand riches and honor. Her ways are ways of pleasantness, and all her paths are peace. She is a tree of life to those who take hold of her, and happy are all who retain her. The Lord by wisdom founded the Earth; by understanding He established the heavens; by His knowledge the depths were broken up, and clouds drop down the dew. My son, let them not depart from your eyes- keep sound wisdom and discretion; so they will be life to your soul and grace to your neck. Then you

will walk safely in your way, and your foot will not stumble. When you lie down, you will not be afraid; yes, you will lie down and your sleep will be sweet. Do not be afraid of sudden terror, nor of trouble from the wicked when it comes; for the Lord will be your confidence, and will keep your foot from being caught.
Proverbs 1:20-33, 2:1-13, 3:13-26

The path of the just is like the shining sun, that shines brighter unto the perfect day. The way of the wicked is like darkness; they do not know what makes them stumble. (...) Keep your heart with all diligence, for out of it spring the issues of life. (...) For the commandment is a lamp, and the law a light; reproofs of instruction are the way of life.   Proverbs 4:18-19, 23, 6:23

Does not wisdom cry out, and understanding lift up her voice? She takes her stand on the top of the high hill, beside the way, where the paths meet. She cries out by the gates, at the entry of the city, at the entrance of the doors: "To you, O men, I call, and my voice is to the sons of men. O you simple ones, understand prudence, and you fools, be of an understanding heart. (...) All the words of my mouth are with righteousness; nothing crooked or perverse is in them. (...) "I wisdom, dwell with prudence, and find out knowledge and discretion. The fear of the Lord is to hate evil. (...) I love those who love me, and those who seek me diligently will find me. (...) Now therefore, listen to me, my children, for blessed are those who keep my ways. Hear instruction and be wise, and do not disdain it. Blessed is the man who listens to me, watching daily at my gates, watching at the posts of my doors. For whoever finds me finds life, and obtains favor from the Lord; but he who sins against me wrongs his own soul; all those who hate me love death."
Proverbs 8:1-5, 8, 12-13, 17, 32-36

He who despises the word will be destroyed, but he who fears the commandment will be rewarded. The law of the wise is a fountain of life, to turn one away from the snares of death.
Proverbs 13:13-14

He who heeds the word wisely will find good, and whoever trusts in the Lord, happy is he. (...) Understanding is a wellspring of life to him who has it. But the correction of fools is folly. The heart of the wise teaches his mouth, and adds learning to his lips.
Proverbs 16:20, 22-23

The spirit of a man is the lamp of the Lord, searching all the inner depths of his heart. (...) The lamp of the wicked will be put out.   Proverbs 20:27, 24:20

By wisdom a house is built, and by understanding it is established; by knowledge the rooms are filled with all precious and pleasant riches.   Proverbs 24:3-4

The poor man and the oppressor have this in common: the Lord gives light to the eyes of both. (...) Every word of God is pure; He is a shield to those who put their trust in Him.
Proverbs 29:13, 30:5

God gives wisdom and knowledge and joy to a man who is good in His sight.   Ecclesiastes 2:26

Blessed is the man who trusts in the Lord, and whose hope is the Lord. For he shall be like a tree planted by the waters, which spreads out its roots by the river, and will not fear when heat comes; but its leaf will be green, and will not be anxious in the year of the drought, nor will cease from yielding fruit. (...) Those who depart from Me shall be written in the earth, because they have forsaken the Lord, the fountain of living waters.   Jeremiah 17:7-8,13

Behold, the days are coming, says the Lord, when I will make a new covenant with the house of Israel and with the house of Judah- not according to the covenant that I made with their fathers in the day that I took them by the hand to lead them out of the land of Egypt, My covenant which they broke, though I was a husband to them, says the Lord. But this is the covenant that I will make with the house of Israel after those days, says the Lord: I will put My law in their minds and write it on their hearts; and I will be their God, and they shall be My people. No more shall every man teach his neighbor, and every man his brother saying, "Know the Lord," for they all shall know Me, from the least of them to the greatest of them, says the Lord. For I will forgive their iniquity, and their sin I will remember no more. Jeremiah 31:31-34

Agree with your adversary quickly, while you are on the way with him, lest your adversary deliver you to the judge, the judge hand you over to the officer, and you be thrown into prison. Assuredly, I say to you, you will be no means get out of there until you have paid the last penny.
Matthew 5:25-26

Ask, and it will be given to you; seek, and you will find; knock, and it will be opened to you. For everyone who asks receives, and he who seeks finds, and to him who knocks it will be opened. Or what man is there among you who, if his son asks for bread, will give him a stone? Or if he asks for a fish, will he give him a serpent? If you then, being evil, know how to give good gifts to your children, how much more will your Father who is in heaven give good things to those who ask Him! Therefore, whatever you want men to do to you, do also to them, for this is the Law and the prophets. Enter by the narrow gate; for wide is the gate and broad is the way that leads to destruction, and there are many who go in by it. Because narrow is the gate and difficult is the way which leads to life, and there are few who find it. (...) Therefore whoever hears these sayings of mine, and does them, I will liken him to a wise man who built his house on the rock: and the rain descended, the floods came, and the winds blew and beat on his house; and it did not fall, for it was founded in the rock. But everyone who hears these sayings of mine, and does not do them, will be like a foolish man who built his house on the sand: and the rain descended, the floods came, and the winds blew and beat on that house; and it fell. And great was its fall. Matthew 7:7-14, 24-27

The lamp of the body is the eye. If therefore your eye is good, your whole body will be full of light. But if your eye is bad, your whole body will be full of darkness. If therefore the light that is in you is darkness, how great is that darkness!   Matthew 6:22-2

You are the salt of the earth; but if the salt loses its flavor, how shall it be seasoned? It is then good for nothing but to be thrown out and trampled underfoot by men. You are the light of the world. A city that is set on a hill cannot be hidden. Nor do they light a lamp and put it under a basket, but on a lamp stand, and it gives light to all who are in the house. Let your light so shine before men, that they may see your good works and glorify your Father in heaven.   Matthew 5:13-16

All things have been delivered to Me by My Father, and no one knows the Son except the Father, nor does anyone know the Father except the Son, and the one to whom the Son wills to reveal Him. Come to Me, all you who labor and are heavy laden, and I will give you rest; take my yoke upon you and learn from Me, for I am gentle and lowly in heart, and you will find rest for your souls. For My yoke is easy and My burden is light.   Matthew 11:28-30

Behold, a sower went out to sow. And as he sowed, some seed fell by the wayside; and the birds came and devoured them. Some fell on stony places, where they did not have much earth. But when the sun was up they were scorched, and because they had not root they withered away. And some fell among thorns, and the thorns sprang up and choked them. But others fell on good ground and yielded a crop: some a hundredfold, some sixty, some thirty. He who has ears to hear, let him hear. (...) For to whoever has, to him more will be given, and he will have abundance; but whoever does not have, even what he has will be taken away from him. (...) Therefore hear the parable of the sower: when anyone hears the word of the kingdom, and does not understand it, then the wicked one comes and snatches away what was sown in his heart. This is he who received seed by the wayside. But he who received the seed on stony places, this is he who hears the word and immediately receives it with joy,
             Matthew 13:3-9

If you desire wisdom, keep the commandments and the Lord will lavish her upon you. For the fear of the Lord is wisdom and discipline, fidelity and humility are his delight.   Sirach 1:26-27

Wisdom teaches her children and gives help to those who seek her. Whoever loves her loves life, and those who seek her from early morning are filled with joy. Those who serve her minister to the Holy One; and the Lord loves those who love her. If they remain faithful, they will inherit her. If they go astray she will forsake them, and hand them over to ruin.   Sirach 4:11-12

For thirty years I sought God. But when I looked carefully I found that in reality God was the seeker and I the sought.
Bayazid of Bistami

Hear the commandments of life, O Israel; give ear, and learn wisdom! Why is it, O Israel, that you are in the land of your enemies (...), that you are counted among those in Hades? You have forsaken the fountain of wisdom. If you have walked in the way of God, you would be living in peace forever. Learn where there is wisdom, where there is strength, where there is understanding, so that at the same time discern where there is length of days and life, and where there is light for the eyes and peace. (...) She is the book of commandments of God, the law that endures forever. All who hold her fast will live and those who forsake her will die.
Baruch 3:9-10, 12-13, 4:1

Which of you, having a hundred sheep, if he loses one of them, does not leave the ninety-nine in the wilderness, and go after the one which is lost until he finds it. And when he has found it, he lays it on his shoulders, rejoicing. And when he comes home, he calls together his friends and neighbors saying to them, "Rejoice with me, for I have found my sheep which was lost!" I say to you likewise there will be more joy in heaven over one sinner who repents than over ninety-nine just persons who need no repentance. Or what woman, having ten silver coins, if she loses one coin, does not light a lamp, sweep the house, and search carefully until she finds it, and in finding it also calls together her friends and neighbors saying, "Rejoice with me, for I have found the piece which I lost!" Likewise, I say to you, there is joy in the presence of the angels of God over one sinner who repents.   Luke 15:4-10

And Jesus came to them and spoke unto them, saying, All authority has been given unto me in heaven and on earth. Go therefore, and make disciples of all the nations, baptizing them into the name of the Father and of the Son and of the Holy Spirit: teaching them to observe all things whatsoever I commanded you: and lo, I am with you always, even unto the end of the world.
Matthew 28:18-20

And the devil said unto him, if you are the Son of God, command this stone that it become bread. And Jesus answered unto him, It is written, Man shall not live by bread alone. And he led him up, and showed him all the kingdoms of the world in a moment of time. And the devil said unto him, To you will I give all this authority, and the glory of them: for it has been delivered unto me; and to whomsoever I will I give it. If you therefore will worship before me, it shall all be yours. And Jesus answered and said unto him, It is written, You shall worship the Lord your God, and him only shall you serve.   Luke 4:3-8

And he answered and said unto them, Go and tell John the things which ye have seen and heard; the blind receive their sight, the lame walk, the lepers are cleansed, and the deaf hear, the dead are raised up, the poor have good tidings preached to them. And blessed is he, whosoever shall find no occasion of stumbling in me.
Luke 7:22-23

The sower went forth to sow his seed: and as he sowed, some fell by the way side; and it was trodden under foot, and the birds of the heaven devoured it. And other fell on the rock; and as soon as it grew, it withered away, because it had no moisture. And other fell amidst the thorns; and the thorns grew with it, and choked it. And other fell into the good ground, and grew, and brought forth fruit a hundredfold. As he said these things, he cried, He that has ears to hear, let him hear. (...) Now the parable is this: The seed is the word of God. And those by the way side are they that have heard; then comes the devil, and takes away the word from their heart, that they may not believe and be saved. And those on the rock [are] they who, when they have heard, receive the word with joy; and these have no root, who for a while believe, and in time of temptation fall away. And that which fell among the thorns, these are they that have heard, and as they go on their way they are choked with cares and riches and pleasures of [this] life, and bring no fruit to perfection. And that in the good ground, these are such as in an honest and good heart, having heard the word, hold it fast, and bring forth fruit with patience. And no man, when he has lighted a lamp, covers it with a vessel, or puts it under a bed; but he puts it on a stand, that they that enter in may see the light. For nothing is hid, that shall not be made manifest; nor secret, that shall not be known and come to light. Take heed therefore how you hear: for whosoever has, to him shall be given; and whosoever has not, from him shall be taken away even that which he thinks he has. And there came to him his mother and brethren, and they could not come at him for the crowd. And it was told him, Your mother and brothers stand outside, desiring to see you. But he answered and said unto them, My mother and my brethren are these that hear the word of God, and do it.   Luke 8:5-8,11-21

All things have been delivered unto me of my Father: and no one knows who the Son is, save the Father; and who the Father is, save the Son, and he to whomsoever the Son wills to reveal.   Luke 10:22

And he said unto them, Which of you shall have a friend, and shall go unto him at midnight, and say to him, Friend, lend me three loaves; for a friend of mine is come to me from a journey, and I have nothing to set before him; and he from within shall answer and say, Trouble me not: the door is now shut, and my children are with me in bed; I cannot rise and give thee? I say unto you, Though he will not rise and give him because he is his friend, yet because of his importunity he will arise and give him as many as he needs. And I say unto you, Ask, and it shall be given you; seek, and you shall find; knock, and it shall be opened unto you. For every one that asks receives; and he that seeks finds; and to him that knocks it shall be opened. And of which of you that is a father shall his son ask a loaf, and he give him a stone? or a fish, and he for a fish give him a serpent? Or [if] he shall ask an egg, will he give him a scorpion? If you then, being evil, know how to give good gifts unto your children, how much more shall [your] heavenly Father give the Holy Spirit to them that ask him?   Luke 11:5-13

The men of Nineveh shall stand up in the judgment with this generation, and shall condemn it: for they repented at the preaching of Jonah; and behold, a greater than Jonah is here. No man, when he has lighted a lamp, puts it in a cellar, neither under the bushel, but on the stand, that they which enter in may see the light. The lamp of your body is your eye: when your eye is single, your whole body also is full of light; but when it is evil, your body also is full of darkness. Look therefore whether the light that is in you be not darkness. If therefore thy whole body be full of light, having no part dark, it shall be wholly full of light, as when the lamp with its bright shining does give you light.   Luke 11:33-36

And why even of yourselves judge you not what is right? For as you are going with your adversary before the magistrate, on the way give diligence to be quit of him; lest haply he drag you unto the judge, and the judge shall deliver you to the officer, and the officer shall cast you into prison. I say unto you, you shall by no means come out thence, till you have paid the very last mite.
                              Luke 12:57-59

He said therefore, Unto what is the kingdom of God like? and whereunto shall I liken it? It is like unto a grain of mustard seed, which a man took, and cast into his own garden; and it grew, and became a tree; and the birds of the heaven lodged in the branches thereof. And again he said, Whereunto shall I liken the kingdom of God? It is like unto leaven, which a woman took and hid in three measures of meal, till it was all leavened. And he went on his way through cities and villages, teaching, and journeying on unto Jerusalem. And one said unto him, Lord, are they few that are saved? And he said unto them, Strive to enter in by the narrow door: for many, I say unto you, shall seek to enter in, and shall not be able. When once the master of the house is risen up, and has shut to the door, and you begin to stand without, and to knock at the door, saying, Lord, open to us; and he shall answer and say to you, I know you not whence you are; then shall you begin to say, We did eat and drink in your presence, and you did teach in our streets; and he shall say, I tell you, I know not whence you are; depart from me, all you workers of iniquity. There shall be the weeping and the gnashing of teeth, when you shall see Abraham, and Isaac, and Jacob, and all the prophets, in the kingdom of God, and yourselves cast forth without. And they shall come from the east and west, and from the north and south, and shall sit down in the kingdom of God. And behold, there are last who shall be first, and there are first who shall be last.
Luke 13:18-30

In the beginning was the Word, and the Word was with God, and the Word was God. The same was in the beginning with God. All things were made through him; and without him was not anything made that has been made. In him was life; and the life was the light of men. And the light shined in the darkness; and the darkness comprehended it not. There came a man, sent from God, whose name was John. The same came for witness, that he might bear witness of the light, that all might believe through him. He was not the light, but came that he might bear witness of the light. There was the true light, which lights every man that comes into the world. He was in the world, and the world was made through him, and the world knew him not. He came unto his own, and they that were his own received him not. But as many as received him, to them gave he the right to become children of God, [even] to them that believe on his name: who were born, not of blood, nor of the will of the flesh, nor of the will of man, but of God. And the Word became flesh, and dwelt among us (and we beheld his glory, glory as of the only begotten from the Father), full of grace and truth. John bears witness of him, and cries, saying, "This was he of whom I said, He that comes after me is become before me: for he was before me." For of his fullness we all received, and grace for grace. For the law was given through Moses; grace and truth came through Jesus Christ. No man has seen God at any time; the only begotten Son, who is in the bosom of the Father, he has declared [him]. And this is the witness of John, when the Jews sent unto him from Jerusalem priests and Levites to ask him, "Who are you?" And he confessed, and denied not; and he confessed, "I am not the Christ." And they asked him, "What then? Are you Elijah?" And he said, "I am not." "Are you the prophet?" And he answered, "No." They said therefore unto him, "Who are you? that we may give an answer to them that sent us. What do you say of yourself?" He said, "I am the voice of one crying in the wilderness, Make straight the way of the Lord, as said Isaiah the prophet." And they had been sent from the Pharisees. And they asked him, and said unto him, "Why then do you baptize, if you are not the Christ, neither Elijah, neither the prophet?" John answered them, saying, "I baptize in water: in the midst of you stands one whom you know not, he that comes after me, the latchet of whose shoe I am not worthy to unloose." These things were done in Bethany beyond the Jordan, where John was baptizing. On the morrow, he saw Jesus coming unto him, and said, "Behold, the Lamb of God, that takes away the sin of the world! This is he of whom I said, After me comes a man who is become before me: for he was before me. And I knew him not; but that he should be made manifest to Israel, for this cause came I baptizing in water." And John bare witness, saying, "I have beheld the Spirit descending as a dove out of heaven; and it abode upon him. And I knew him not: but he that sent me to baptize in water, he said unto me, Upon whomsoever you shall see the Spirit descending, and abiding upon him, the same is he that baptizes in the Holy Spirit. And I have seen, and have borne witness that this is the Son of God." John 1:1-34

John answered and said, A man can receive nothing, except it have been given him from heaven. You yourselves bear me witness, that I said, I am not the Christ, but, that I am sent before him. He that has the bride is the bridegroom: but the friend of the bridegroom, that stands and hears him, rejoices greatly because of the bridegroom's voice: this my joy therefore is made full. He must increase, but I must decrease. He that comes from above is above all: he that is of the earth is of the earth, and of the earth he speaks: he that comes from heaven is above all. What he has seen and heard, of that he bears witness; and no man receives his witness. He that has received his witness has set his seal to [this], that God is true. For he whom God has sent speaks the words of God: for he gives not the Spirit by measure. The Father loves the Son, and has given all things into his hand. He that believes on the Son has eternal life; but he that obeys not the Son shall not see life, but the wrath of God abides on him. John 3:27-36

So he came to the city of Samaria, called Sychar, near to the parcel of ground that Jacob gave to his son Joseph: and Jacob's well was there. Jesus therefore, being wearied with his journey, sat thus by the well. It was about the sixth hour. There came a woman of Samaria to draw water: Jesus said unto her, Give me to drink. For his disciples were gone away into the city to buy food. The Samaritan woman therefore said unto him, How is it that you, being a Jew, ask a drink of me, who am a Samaritan woman? (For Jews have no dealings with Samaritans.) Jesus answered and said unto her, If you knew the gift of God, and who it is that says to you, Give me to drink; you would have asked of him, and he would have given you living water. The woman said unto him, Sir, you have nothing to draw with, and the well is deep: whence then have you that living water? Are you greater than our father Jacob, who gave us the well, and drank thereof himself, and his sons, and his cattle? Jesus answered and said unto her, Every one that drinks of this water shall thirst again: but whosoever drinks of the water that I shall give him shall never thirst; but the water that I shall give him shall become in him a well of water springing up unto eternal life. The woman said unto him, Sir, give me this water, that I thirst not, neither come all the way hither to draw. Jesus said unto her, Go, call your husband, and come hither. The woman answered and said unto him, I have no husband. Jesus said unto her, You said right, I have no husband: for you have had five husbands; and he whom you now have is not your husband: this have you said truly. The woman said unto him, Sir, I perceive that you are a prophet. Our fathers worshiped in this mountain; and you say, that in Jerusalem is the place where men ought to worship. Jesus said unto her, Woman, believe me, the hour comes, when neither in this mountain, nor in Jerusalem, shall you worship the Father. You worship that which you know not: we worship that which we know; for salvation is from the Jews. But the hour comes, and now is, when the true worshipers shall worship the Father in spirit and truth: for such does the Father seek to be his worshipers. God is a Spirit: and they that worship him must worship in spirit and truth. The woman said unto him, I know that the Messiah comes (he that is called Christ): when he is come, he will declare unto us all things. Jesus said unto her, I that speak unto you am he.

John 4:5-26

But Jesus answered them, My Father works even until now, and I work. For this cause, therefore the Jews sought the more to kill him, because he not only broke the Sabbath, but also called God his own Father, making himself equal with God. Jesus therefore answered and said unto them, Verily, verily, I say unto you, The Son can do nothing of himself, but what he sees the Father doing: for what things so ever he does these the Son also does in like manner. For the Father loves the Son, and shows him all things that he does himself: and greater works than these will he show him, that you may marvel. For as the Father raises the dead and gives them life, even so the Son also gives life to whom he will. For neither does the Father judge any man, but he has given all judgment unto the Son; that all may honor the Son, even as they honor the Father. He that honors not the Son honors not the Father that sent him. Verily, verily, I say unto you, He that hears my word, and believes him that sent me, has eternal life, and comes not into judgment, but has passed out of death into life. Verily, verily, I say unto you, The hour comes, and now is, when the dead shall hear the voice of the Son of God; and they that hear shall live. For as the Father has life in himself, even so gave he to the Son also to have life in himself: and he gave him authority to execute judgment, because he is a son of man. Marvel not at this: for the hour comes, in which all that are in the tombs shall hear his voice, and shall come forth; they that have done good, unto the resurrection of life; and they that have done evil, unto the resurrection of judgment. I can of myself do nothing: as I hear, I judge: and my judgment is righteous; because I seek not mine own will, but the will of him that sent me. If I bear witness of myself, my witness is not true. It is another that bears witness of me; and I know that the witness which he witnesses of me is true. You have sent unto John, and he has borne witness unto the truth. But the witness which I receive is not from man: howbeit I say these things, that you may be saved. He was the lamp that burns and shines; and you were willing to rejoice for a season in his light. But the witness which I have is greater than [that of] John; for the works which the Father has given me to accomplish, the very works that I do, bear witness of me, that the Father hath sent me. And the Father that sent me, he has borne witness of me. You have neither heard his voice at any time, nor seen his form. And you have not his word abiding in you: for whom he sent, him you believe not. You search the scriptures, because you think that in them you have eternal life; and these are they which bear witness of me; and you will not come to me, that you may have life. I receive not glory from men. But I know you, that you have not the love of God in yourselves. I am come in my Father's name, and you receive me not: if another shall come in his own name, him you will receive. How can you believe, who receive glory one of another, and the glory that [comes] from the only God you seek not? Think not that I will accuse you to the Father: there is one that accuses you, Moses, on whom you have set your hope. For if you believed Moses, you would believe me; for he wrote of me. But if

you believe not his writings, how shall you believe my words?
John 5:17-47

Jesus answered them and said, "Verily, verily, I say unto you, you seek me, not because you saw signs, but because you ate of the loaves, and were filled. Work not for the food which perishes, but for the food which abides unto eternal life, which the Son of man shall give unto you: for him the Father, even God, has sealed." They said therefore unto him, "What must we do, that we may work the works of God?" Jesus answered and said unto them, "This is the work of God, that you believe on him whom he has sent." They said therefore unto him, "What then will you do for a sign, that we may see, and believe you? what do you work? Our fathers ate the manna in the wilderness; as it is written, He gave them bread out of heaven to eat." Jesus therefore said unto them, "Verily, verily, I say unto you, It was not Moses that gave you the bread out of heaven; but my Father gives you the true bread out of heaven. For the bread of God is that which comes down out of heaven, and gives life unto the world." They said therefore unto him, "Lord, evermore give us this bread." Jesus said unto them. "I am the bread of life: he that comes to me shall not hunger, and he that believes on me shall never thirst. But I said unto you, that you have seen me, and yet believe not. All that which the Father gives me shall come unto me; and him that comes to me I will in no way cast out. For I am come down from heaven, not to do mine own will, but the will of him that sent me. And this is the will of him that sent me, that of all that which he has given me I should lose nothing, but should raise it up at the last day. For this is the will of my Father, that every one that beholds the Son, and believes on him, should have eternal life; and I will raise him up at the last day." The Jews therefore murmured concerning him, because he said, I am the bread which came down out of heaven. And they said, "Is not this Jesus, the son of Joseph, whose father and mother we know? how does he now say, I am come down out of heaven?" Jesus answered and said unto them, "Murmur not among yourselves. No man can come to me, except the Father that sent me draw him: and I will raise him up in the last day. It is written in the prophets, And they shall all be taught of

God. Every one that has heard from the Father, and has learned, comes unto me. Not that any man has seen the Father, save he that is from God, he has seen the Father. Verily, verily, I say unto you, He that believes has eternal life. I am the bread of life. Your fathers ate the manna in the wilderness, and they died. This is the bread which comes down out of heaven, that a man may eat thereof, and not die. I am the living bread which came down out of heaven: if any man eat of this bread, he shall live forever: yea and the bread which I will give is my flesh, for the life of the world." The Jews therefore strove one with another, saying, "How can this man give us his flesh to eat?" Jesus therefore said unto them, "Verily, verily, I say unto you, Except you eat the flesh of the Son of man and drink his blood, you have not life in yourselves. He that eats my flesh and drinks my blood has eternal life: and I will raise him up at the last day. For my flesh is meat indeed, and my blood is drink indeed. He that eats my flesh and drinks my blood abides in me, and I in him. As the living Father sent me, and I live because of the Father; so he that eats me, he also shall live because of me. This is the bread which came down out of heaven: not as the fathers ate, and died; he that eats this bread shall live forever." These things said he in the synagogue, as he taught in Capernaum. Many therefore of his disciples, when they heard [this], said, "This is a hard saying; who can hear it?" But Jesus knowing in himself that his disciples murmured at this, said unto them, "Does this cause you to stumble? [What] then if you should behold the Son of man ascending where he was before? It is the spirit that gives life; the flesh profits nothing: the words that I have spoken unto you are spirit, are life. But there are some of you that believe not." For Jesus knew from the beginning who they were that believed not, and who it was that should betray him. And he said, "For this cause have I said unto you, that no man can come unto me, except it be given unto him of the Father."   John 6:26-65

The world cannot hate you; but me it hates, because I testify of it, that its works are evil.   John 7:7

Now on the last day, the great [day] of the feast, Jesus stood and cried, saying, If any man thirst, let him come unto me and drink. He that believes on me, as the scripture has said, from within him shall flow rivers of living water.   John 7:37-38

Again therefore Jesus spoke unto them, saying, I am the light of the world: he that follows me shall not walk in the darkness, but shall have the light of life.(...) Jesus therefore said to those Jews that had believed him, If you abide in my word, [then] are you truly my disciples; (...) Verily, verily, I say unto you, If a man keep my word, he shall never see death. (...) Jesus answered, If I glorify myself, my glory is nothing: it is my Father that glorifies me; of whom you say, that he is your God; and you have not known him: but I know him; and if I should say, I know him not, I shall be like unto you, a liar: but I know him, and keep his word. Your father Abraham rejoiced to see my day; and he saw it, and was glad. The Jews therefore said unto him, You are not yet fifty years old, and you have seen Abraham?   Jesus said unto them, Verily, verily, I say unto you, Before Abraham was born, I am.
John 8:12, 31, 54-58

And Jesus said, For judgment came I into this world, that they that see not may see; and that they that see may become blind. Those of the Pharisees who were with him heard these things, and said unto him, Are we also blind? Jesus said unto them, If you were blind, you would have no sin: but now you say, We see: your sin remains. Verily, verily, I say unto you, He that enters not by the door into the fold of the sheep, but climbs up some other way, the same is a thief and a robber. But he that enters in by the door is the shepherd of the sheep. To him the porter opens; and the sheep hear his voice: and he calls his own sheep by name, and leads them out. When he has put forth all his own, he goes before them, and the sheep follow him: for they know his voice. And a stranger will they not follow, but will flee from him: for they know not the voice of strangers. This parable spoke Jesus unto them: but they understood not what things they were which he spoke unto them. Jesus therefore said unto them

again, Verily, verily, I say unto you, I am the door of the sheep. All that came before me are thieves and robbers: but the sheep did not hear them. I am the door; by me if any man enters in, he shall be saved, and shall go in and go out, and shall find pasture. The thief comes not, but that he may steal, and kill, and destroy: I came that they may have life, and may have [it] abundantly. I am the good shepherd: the good shepherd lays down his life for the sheep. He that is a hireling, and not a shepherd, whose own the sheep are not, sees the wolf coming, and leaves the sheep, and flees, and the wolf snatches them, and scatters [them]: because he is a hireling, and cares not for the sheep. I am the good shepherd; and I know mine own, and mine own know me, even as the Father knows me, and I know the Father; and I lay down my life for the sheep. And other sheep I have, which are not of this fold: them also I must bring, and they shall hear my voice: and they shall become one flock, one shepherd. Therefore does the Father love me, because I lay down my life, that I may take it again. No one takes it away from me, but I lay it down of myself. I have power to lay it down, and I have power to take it again. This commandment received I from my Father.
John 9:39-10:18

Jesus answered, Are there not twelve hours in the day? If a man walk in the day, he stumbles not, because he sees the light of this world. But if a man walk in the night, he stumbles, because the light is not in him.   John 11:9-10

Jesus said unto her, I am the resurrection, and the life: he that believes on me, though he dies, yet shall he live; and whosoever lives and believes on me shall never die.   John 11:25-26

Jesus answered them, I told you, and you believe not: the works that I do in my Father's name, these bear witness of me. But you believe not, because you are not of my sheep. My sheep hear my voice, and I know them, and they follow me: and I give unto

them eternal life; and they shall never perish, and no one shall snatch them out of my hand. My Father, who has given [them] unto me, is greater than all; and no one is able to snatch [them] out of the Father's hand. I and the Father are one. The Jews took up stones again to stone him. Jesus answered them, Many good works have I showed you from the Father; for which of those works do you stone me? The Jews answered him, For a good work we stone you not, but for blasphemy; and because that you, being a man, makes yourself God. Jesus answered them, Is it not written in your law, I said, you are gods? If he called them gods, unto whom the word of God came (and the scripture cannot be broken), say you of him, whom the Father sanctified and sent into the world, You blasphemy; because I said, I am [the] Son of God? If I do not the works of my Father, believe me not. But if I do them, though you believe not me, believe the works: that you may know and understand that the Father is in me, and I in the Father.
John 10:25-38

Jesus answered and said, This voice has not come for my sake, but for your sakes. Now is the judgment of this world: now shall the prince of this world be cast out. And I, if I be lifted up from the earth, will draw all men unto myself. But this he said, signifying by what manner of death he should die. The multitude therefore answered him, We have heard out of the law that the Christ abides forever: and how say you, The Son of man must be lifted up? who is this Son of man? Jesus therefore said unto them, Yet a little while is the light among you. Walk while you have the light, that darkness overtakes you not: and he that walks in the darkness knows not whither he goes. While you have the light, believe on the light, that you may become sons of light. These things spoke Jesus, and he departed and hid himself from them.
John 12:30-36

And Jesus cried and said, He that believes on me, believes not on me, but on him that sent me. And he that sees me beholds him that sent me. I am come a light into the world, that whosoever believes on me may not abide in the darkness. And if any man hears my sayings, and keeps them not, I judge him not: for I came not to judge the world, but to save the world. He that rejects me, and receives not my sayings, has one that judges him: the word that I spoke, the same shall judge him in the last day. For I spoke not from myself; but the Father that sent me, he has given me a commandment, what I should say, and what I should speak. And I know that his commandment is life eternal: the things therefore which I speak, even as the Father has said unto me, so I speak.

John 12:44-50

Jesus said unto him, I am the way, and the truth, and the life: no one comes unto the Father, but by me. If you had known me, you would have known my Father also: from henceforth you know him, and have seen him. Philip said unto him, Lord, show us the Father, and it will suffice us. Jesus said unto him, Have I been so long time with you, and do you not know me, Philip? he that has seen me has seen the Father; how do you say, Show us the Father? Do you not believe that I am in the Father, and the Father in me? the words that I say unto you I speak not from myself: but the Father abiding in me does his works. Believe me that I am in the Father, and the Father in me: or else believe me for the very works' sake. Verily, verily, I say unto you, he that believes on me, the works that I do shall he do also; and greater [works] than these shall he do; because I go unto the Father. And whatsoever you shall ask in my name, that will I do, that the Father may be glorified in the Son. If you shall ask anything in my name, that will I do. If you love me, you will keep my commandments. And I will pray the Father, and he shall give you another Comforter, that he may be with you forever, [even] the Spirit of truth: whom the world cannot receive; for it beholdeth him not, neither knows him: you know him; for he abides with you, and shall be in you. I will not leave you desolate: I come unto you. Yet a little while, and the world beholds me no more; but you behold me: because I live, you shall live also. In that day, you shall know that I am in my Father, and you in me, and I in you. He that has my commandments, and keeps them, he it is that loves me: and he that loves me shall be loved of my Father, and I will love him, and will manifest myself unto him. Judas (not Iscariot) said unto him, Lord, what is come to pass that you will manifest yourself unto us, and not unto the world? Jesus answered and said unto him, If a man loves me, he will keep my word: and my Father will love him, and we will come unto him, and make our abode with him. He that loves me not keeps not my words: and the word which you hear is not mine, but the Father's who sent me. These things have I spoken unto you, while [yet] abiding with you. But the Comforter, [even] the Holy Spirit, whom the Father will send in my name, he shall teach you all things, and bring to your remembrance all that I said unto you. Peace I leave with you; my peace I give unto you: not as the world gives, give I unto you. Let not your heart be troubled, neither let it be fearful. You heard how I said to you, I go away, and I come unto you. If you loved me, you would have rejoiced, because I go unto the Father: for the Father is greater than I. And now I have told you before it come to pass, that, when it is come to pass, you may believe. I will no more speak much with you, for the prince of the world comes: and he has nothing in me; but that the world may know that I love the Father, and as the Father gave me commandment, even so I do. Arise, let us go hence. I am the true vine and my Father is the husbandman. Every branch in me that bears not fruit, he takes it away: and every [branch] that bears fruit, he cleanses it, that it may bear more fruit. Already you are clean because of the word which I have spoken unto you. Abide in me, and I in you. As the branch cannot bear fruit of itself, except it abide in the vine; so neither can you, except you abide in me. I am the vine, you are the branches: He that abides in me, and I in him, the same bears much fruit: for apart from me you can do nothing. If a man abides not in me, he is cast forth as a branch, and is withered; and they gather them, and cast them into the fire, and they are burned. If you abide in me, and my words abide in you, ask whatsoever you will, and it shall be done unto you. Herein is my Father glorified, that you bear much fruit; and [so] shall you be my disciples. Even as the Father has loved me, I also have loved you: abide you in my love. If you keep my commandments, you shall abide in my love; even as I have kept my Father's commandments, and abide in his love. These things have I spoken unto you, that my joy may be in you, and [that] your joy may be made full. This is my commandment, that you love one another, even as I have loved you. Greater love has no man than this, that a man lay down his life for his friends. You are my friends, if you do the things which I command you. No longer do I call you servants; for the servant knows not what his lord does: but I have called you friends; for all things that I heard from my Father, I have made known unto you. You did not choose me, but I chose you, and appointed you, that you should go and bear fruit, and [that] your fruit should abide: that whatsoever you shall ask of the Father in my name, he may give it you. These things I command you, that you may love one another. If the world hates you, you know that it has hated me before [it hated] you. If you were of the world, the world would love its own: but because you are not of the world, but I chose you out of the world, therefore the world hates you. Remember the word that I said unto you, A servant is not greater than his lord. If they persecuted me, they will also persecute you; if they kept my word, they will keep yours also. But all these things will they do unto you for my name's sake, because they know not him that sent me. If I had not come and spoken unto them, they had not had sin: but now they have no excuse for their sin. He that hates me hates my Father also. If I had not done among them the works which none other did, they had not had sin: but now have they both seen and hated both me and my Father. But [this comes to pass], that the word may be fulfilled that is written in their law, They hated me without a cause. But when the Comforter is come, whom I will send unto you from the Father, [even] the Spirit of truth, which proceeds from the Father, he shall bear witness of me: and you also bear witness, because you have been with me from the beginning. These things have I spoken unto you, that you should not be caused to stumble. They shall put you out of the synagogues: yea, the hour comes, that whosoever kills you shall think that he offers service unto God. And these things will they do, because they have not known the Father, nor me. But these things have I spoken unto you, that when their hour is come, you may remember them, how that I told you. And these things I said not unto you from the beginning, because I was with you. But now I go unto him that sent me; and none of you ask me, Where do you go?

But because I have spoken these things unto you, sorrow has filled your heart. Nevertheless, I tell you the truth: It is expedient for you that I go away; for if I go not away, the Comforter will not come unto you; but if I go, I will send him unto you. And he, when he is come, will convict the world in respect of sin, and of righteousness, and of judgment: of sin, because they believe not on me; of righteousness, because I go to the Father, and you behold me no more; of judgment, because the prince of this world has been judged. I have yet many things to say unto you, but you cannot bear them now. Howbeit when he, the Spirit of truth, is come, he shall guide you into all the truth: for he shall not speak from himself; but what things so ever he shall hear, [these] shall he speak: and he shall declare unto you the things that are to come. He shall glorify me: for he shall take of mine, and shall declare [it] unto you. All things whatsoever the Father has are mine: therefore, said I, that he takes of mine, and shall declare [it] unto you. A little while, and you behold me no more; and again, a little while, and you shall see me.
John 14:6-16:16

In that day you shall ask in my name: and I say not unto you, that I will pray the Father for you; for the Father himself loves you, because you have loved me, and have believed that I came forth from the Father. I came out from the Father, and am come into the world: again, I leave the world, and go unto the Father. John 16:26-28

These things spoke Jesus; and lifting up his eyes to heaven, he said, Father, the hour is come; glorify thy Son, that the son may glorify You: even as you gave him authority over all flesh, that to all whom you have given him, he should give eternal life. And this is life eternal, that they should know you the only true God, and him whom you sent, Jesus Christ. I glorified you on the earth, having accomplished the work which you have given me to do. And now, Father, glorify me with thine own self with the glory which I had with you before the world was. I manifested your name unto the men whom you gave me out of the world: yours they were, and you gave them to me; and they have kept your word. Now they know that all things whatsoever you have given me are from You: for the words which you gave me have given unto them; and they received [them], and knew of a truth that I came forth from You, and they believed that you did send me.   John 17:1-8

Howbeit the Most High dwells not in [houses] made with hands; as says the prophet, The heaven is my throne, And the earth the footstool of my feet: What manner of house will you build me? says the Lord: Or what is the place of my rest? Did not my hand make all these things? You stiff-necked and uncircumcised in heart and ears, you do always resist the Holy Spirit: as your fathers did, so do you. Which of the prophets did not your fathers persecute? and they killed them that showed before of the coming of the Righteous One; of whom you have now become betrayers and murderers; you who received the law as it was ordained by angels, and kept it not.   Acts 7:48-53

And the next Sabbath almost the whole city was gathered together to hear the word of God. But when the Jews saw the multitudes, they were filled with jealousy, and contradicted the things which were spoken by Paul, and blasphemed. And Paul and Barnabas spoke out boldly, and said, It was necessary that the word of God should first be spoken to you. Seeing you thrust it from you, and judge yourselves unworthy of eternal life, lo, we turn to the Gentiles. For so has the Lord commanded us, [saying], I have set you for a light of the Gentiles, that you should be for salvation unto the uttermost part of the earth. And as the Gentiles heard this, they were glad, and glorified the word of God: and as many as were ordained to eternal life believed.   Acts 13:44-48

And we are witnesses of these things; and [so is] the Holy Spirit, whom God has given to them that obey him.   Acts 5:32

Herein I also exercise myself to have a conscience void of offence toward God and men always.   Acts 24:16

For our glorifying is this, the testimony of our conscience, that in holiness and sincerity of God, not in fleshly wisdom but in the grace of God, we behaved ourselves in the world, and more abundantly to you-ward.   2nd Corinthians 1:12

Having therefore such a hope, we use great boldness of speech, and [are] not as Moses, [who] put a veil upon his face, that the children of Israel should not look steadfastly on the end of that which was passing away: but their minds were hardened: for until this very day at the reading of the old covenant the same veil remains, it not being revealed [to them] that it is done away in Christ. But unto this day, whensoever Moses is read, a veil lies upon their heart. But whensoever it shall turn to the Lord, the veil is taken away. Now the Lord is the Spirit: and where the Spirit of the Lord is, [there] is liberty. But we all, with unveiled face beholding as in a mirror the glory of the Lord, are transformed into the same image from glory to glory, even as from the Lord the Spirit. Therefore, seeing we have this ministry, even as we obtained mercy, we faint not: but we have renounced the hidden things of shame, not walking in craftiness, nor handling the word of God deceitfully; but by the manifestation of the truth commending ourselves to every man's conscience in the sight of God. And even if our gospel is veiled, it is veiled in them that perish: in whom the god of this world has blinded the minds of the unbelieving, that the light of the gospel of the glory of Christ, who is the image of God, should not dawn [upon them]. For we preach not ourselves, but Christ Jesus as Lord, and ourselves as your servants for Jesus' sake. Seeing it is God, that said, Light shall shine out of darkness, who shined in our hearts, to give the light of the knowledge of the glory of God in the face of Jesus Christ.   2nd Corinthians 3:12- 4:6

Continue steadfastly in prayer, watching therein with thanksgiving; withal praying for us also, that God may open unto us a door for the word, to speak the mystery of Christ, for which I am

also in bonds; that I may make it manifest, as I ought to speak.
Colossians 4:2-4

Let us therefore give diligence to enter into that rest, that no man fall after the same example of disobedience. For the word of God is living, and active, and sharper than any two-edged sword, and piercing even to the dividing of soul and spirit, of both joints and marrow, and quick to discern the thoughts and intents of the heart. And there is no creature that is not manifest in his sight: but all things are naked and laid open before the eyes of him with whom we have to do.
Hebrews 4:11-13

Be not deceived, my beloved brethren. Every good gift and every perfect gift is from above, coming down from the Father of lights, with whom can be no variation, neither shadow that is cast by turning. Of his own will he brought us forth by the word of truth, that we should be a kind of first fruits of his creatures. You know [this], my beloved brethren. But let every man be swift to hear, slow to speak, slow to wrath: for the wrath of man works not the righteousness of God. Wherefore putting away all filthiness and overflowing of wickedness, receive with meekness the implanted word, which is able to save your souls.   But be doers of the word, and not hearers only, deluding your own selves. For if anyone is a hearer of the word and not a doer, he is like unto a man beholding his natural face in a mirror: for he beholds himself, and goes away, and straightway forgets what manner of man he was. But he that looks into the perfect law, the [law] of liberty, and [so] continues, being not a hearer that forgets but a doer that works, this man shall be blessed in his doing. If any man thinks himself to be religious, while he bridles not his tongue but deceives his heart, this man's religion is vain. Pure religion and undefiled before our God and Father is this, to visit the fatherless and widows in their affliction, [and] to keep oneself unspotted from the world.   James 1:16-27

Whosoever abides in him sins not: whosoever sins has not seen him, neither knows him. [My] little children, let no man lead you astray: he that does righteousness is righteous, even as he is righteous: he that does sin is of the devil; for the devil sinned from the beginning. To this end was the Son of God manifested, that he might destroy the works of the devil. Whosoever is begotten of God does not sin, because his seed abides in him: and he cannot sin, because he is begotten of God. In this the children of God are manifest, and the children of the devil: whosoever does not righteousness is not of God, neither he that loves not his brother. For this is the message which you heard from the beginning, that we should love one another: not as Cain was of the evil one, and slew his brother. And wherefore slew he him? Because his works were evil, and his brother's righteous. Marvel not, brethren, if the world hates you. We know that we have passed out of death into life, because we love the brethren. He that loves not abides in death. Whosoever hates his brother is a murderer: and you know that no murderer has eternal life abiding in him. Hereby know we love, because he laid down his life for us: and we ought to lay down our lives for the brethren. But who so has the world's goods, and beholds his brother in need, and shuts up his compassion from him, how does the love of God abide in him? [My] Little children, let us not love in word, neither with the tongue; but in deed and truth. Hereby shall we know that we are of the truth, and shall assure our heart before him: because if our heart condemn us, God is greater than our heart, and knows all things. Beloved, if our heart condemn us not, we have boldness toward God; and whatsoever we ask we receive of him, because we keep his commandments and do the things that are pleasing in his sight. And this is his commandment, that we should believe in the name of his Son Jesus Christ, and love one another, even as he gave us commandment. And he that keeps his commandments abides in him, and he in him. And hereby we know that he abides in us, by the Spirit which he gave us.

               1 John 3:6-24

He that believes on the Son of God has the witness in him: he that believes not God has made him a liar; because he has not believed in the witness that God has borne concerning his Son. And the witness is this, that God gave unto us eternal life, and this life is in his Son. He that has the Son has the life; he that has not the Son of God has not the life. 1 John 5:10-12

As rivers flowing into the ocean find their final peace and their name and form disappear, even so the wise become free from name and form and enter into the radiance of the Supreme Spirit who is greater than all greatness. In truth who knows God becomes God. Manduka Upanishad

Behold, the days are coming, says the Lord, when I will make a new covenant with the house of Israel and with the house of Judah- not according to the covenant that I made with their fathers in the day that I took them by the hand to lead them out of them land of Egypt, My covenant which they broke, though I was a husband to them, says the Lord. But this is the covenant that I will make with the house of Israel after those days, says the Lord: I will put my Law in their minds, and write it on their hearts; and I will be their God and they will be My people. No more shall every man teach his neighbor, and every man his brother, saying, 'Know the Lord,' for they all shall know Me, from the least of them to the greatest of them, says the Lord. For I will forgive their iniquity, and their sin I will remember no more."

Historical Glossary:

Abu Makki- (d. 996), from Baghdad, A hadith scholar, Maliki jurist and Sufi whose book influenced Al-Ghazalli

Abu Sa'id- (967-1049 CE), famous Persian Sufi poet whose mysticism contributed extensively to the evolution of the Sufi tradition,

Abraham- Father of the Jews and Muslims (of the descendants of Isaac and Ishmael), had faith in God, God said that all the nations would be blessed through Abraham, In Judaism he is the founding father of the Covenant, the special relationship between the Jewish people and God; in Christianity, he is the prototype of all believers, Jewish or Gentile; and in Islam he is seen as a link in the chain of prophets that begins with Adam and culminates in Muhammad.

ahamkara- Sanskrit word relating to the identification of and attachment to one's ego in a dualistic understanding of the world

al- Ghazalli- (1058-1111), born in Persia in modern day Iran, Sunni Muslim theologian and philosopher, known as Algazel to the western Medieval world.

al- Hallaj- Persian mystic, writer and teacher of Sufism, (858-922)

al-Sadiq-(702-765), considered the sixth Shia imam by Twelver Shi'a Muslims, He was a theologian and a jurist whose rulings are the basis of the Jafari school of Shia jurisprudence (fiqh); but he is well respected by Sunnis for his contributions to the Sunni scholarship as well. The dispute over who was to succeed him led to the split of the Ismailis from the mainstream Twelver Shi'a and the establishment of the Aga Khan's family line.

Analects- collection of Confucian's sayings written down by his followers somewhere between 475 BC–221 BC

Ananda- one of the principle disciples of the Buddha, name means "bliss" in Pali

Ansari of Herat- (1006-1088), celebrated Persian Sufi philosopher and writer, lived and died in Herat which was then Persia but now is Afghanistan

Archbishop Temple- (1881-1944), Archbishop of Canterbury,

Arjuna- main character in the epic Indian poem the Mahabharata, questions Krishna about the way to salvation and right living in the Bhagavad Gita right before a great battle in which Arjuna is facing many people he knows and is related to

Ashvaghosha- author of the Buddhacarita which is a verse biography of the Buddha and the Saundaramanda which is an account in verse drama of the conversion of the Buddha's half brother Nanda, One of these dramas was said to be at Kaniska's court during the Fourth Council in Kashmir during which a gathering of 499 Sarvastivadin monks complied a new canon and codified the doctrines of their school in a huge commentary called the Mahavibhasa.

Atman- "self-soul", the individualized soul which remains identical with Brahman, the Atman is an image of Brahman although in a different form,

Attar- (1142-1220), born and died in Neishapour in an Iranian province, Along with

Sanaie influenced Rumi a great deal, Wrote The Conference of the Birds,
Aurobindo- (1872-1950), Indian poet, philosopher, nationalist, mystic and guru whose followers considered him an avatar, sought to establish the Supramental Truth Consciousness Force on Earth in people so the earth would be in harmony
Bankei- (1622-1693), "My miracle is that when I'm hungry, I eat, and when I am tired, I sleep." Zen Buddhist
bardo- a state of sudden change in consciousness brought about by a shock such as death, birth, enlightenment, "intermediate state" or "transitional state", Tibetan word found and used in the Book of the Dead
Bayazid Bistami- (777-874CE), Sufi born in Bastam, Iran, His predecessor Dhu al-Nun (d 859) had formulated the doctrine of ma'rifa (gnosis) presenting a system which helped communication between the initiate and the guide. Bayazid took this a step further and emphasized the importance of ecstasy and "drunkenness" as a means of union with God. He played a major role in placing the concept of divine love at the core of Sufism. He was the first the speak openly of the annihilation of the self in God (fana fi Allah) and subsistence through God (baqa bi Allah). Taught about the Unity of Being.
Baruch- follower and friend of Jeremiah, wrote the Prophesy of Baruch still found in the Catholic Bible
Bhagavad Gita- "Song of God", part of the Mahabharata in which Arjuna and Krishna talk before battle, symbolic of man's struggle with himself to find his true self
Bodhidharma- Indian monk who came to China and founded the Ch'an school of meditation during the 500's
Brahman- Earliest uses associate Brahman with the power behind sacrifices and offerings but idea grew with the Upanishadic movement, the Infinite, Primary Cause, and Ultimate Reality and Divine Ground, the Atman is an image of the Brahman so Tat Twam Asi (Thou art That).
brahmin- the priestly class with Hinduism's caste system, the other three classes (varnas) are: rajanya- noble or warrior , vaishya- merchant , shudra- working class, peasant
Buddha- born Prince Siddhartha Gautama in the republic of Shakya in the northern regions of India, Other names for him include: Shakyamuni (Sage of the Shakyas) and Tathagata (Thus Gone). Buddha means Awakened or Enlightened. Died in 483. It was foretold by a sage when he was young that he would either lead the life of a husband and become a great political leader or he would become a great religious leader. He grew shifty staying at home and one day while out riding in his carriage he saw four sights. He saw a sick man, an old man, a dead person and then a wandering ascetic. His mind was made up and left for the ascetic life that night. He traveled with a couple of different groups and experimented with various extremes of asceticism but in the end settled on a middle path after his enlightenment under the Boddhi Tree where he sat down with single minded determination and conquered the delusion of Mara
Buddhism- religion which formed around the figure of the Buddha, broke into

sects after the Buddha's death all of which acknowledge the authority of the earliest collections of the Buddha's teachings
Bushanja- Arab mystic
Ch'ih-chueh: Zen master
Chuang Tzu- 4th century Taoist, although his works speak little of Daoism his ideas are very similar to Lao Tzu's and he talks about the Tao as the True Way
Cloud of Unknowing- spiritual guidebook written in the 14th century which focuses on love as the only means to reaching God as opposed to knowledge, The book which draws on the mystical tradition of Pseudo-Dionysius the Aeroepagite has inspired generations of searchers including St. John of the Cross and Teilhard de Chardin. The practical prayer advice contained within formed the basis for the practice of centering prayer which is a form of Christian meditation developed by Trappist monks William Meninger and Thomas Keating in the 1970's
Dai-o Kokushi- (1235-1308), Japanese Zen master
Dhammapada- Pali, translates as Path of the Dharma, Buddhist religious scripture containing 423 verses which according to tradition were the answers to questions asked to the Buddha at various times, a popular section of the Pali Tipikaka and is considered one of the most important pieces of Theravada literature.
Dharma-dhamma, Eternal Law, originally the natural condition of things, their essence and the fundamental law of their existence
dharmata- ("tathata"), translated as "thusness" or "suchness", central concept in Buddhism in which the exact nature of reality at any given time is appreciated, the Buddha referred to himself as the Tathagata ("One who has arrived at Suchness")
Dhu al-Nun- (d 859), introduced the gnostic elements (ma'rifa) into Sufism
Dogen- (1200-1253), Japanese Zen master, founded the Soto school of Zen in Japan, emphasized zazen (sitting meditation) which he considered to be identical to studying Zen
Fa-yen: (885-958), Zen master
Francis Fenelon- celebrated French bishop and author, (1651-1715)
Francois de Sales- (1567-1622), Catholic saint and influential thinker some of whose writings survive
Gospel of James- AD 150, although apocryphal and never accepted as cannon it may have the earliest attestation of the continuing virginity of Mary and it also contains the earliest exhorting to venerate her
Gospel of Phillip- book of collected sayings, does not claim to be written by Phillip the Apostle
Gospel of Thomas- gnostic gospel recording sayings attributed to Jesus found in the Nag Hammadi collection and written in Coptic, dates to the 2nd century and corresponds to a very active community of gnostic Christians in Egypt
Hakuin Ekaku- (1686-1769), one of the most influential figures in Japanese Zen Buddhism, Revived and refocused the Rinzai school, emphasized meditation and koan practice (a story, dialouge or question used in Zen practice used to provoke the "great doubt" and test a student's progress in Zen practice)
Hans Denck- (1495-1527), German theologian and Anabaptist leader during the Reformation who fiercely attacked the reformers in his writings

Hanshan- 9th century Chinese Taoist poet
Hasan of Basra- (642-728), Well known Sunni preacher, theologian, and scholar of Islam

Hsi Yun- (?-850CE), influential Chinese master of Zen Buddhism, "Essential of Mind Transmission, stressed the importance of One Mind, hsin- mind, "mind is the Buddha", rejected all dualism, Within all beings is the nature of the Buddha
Hua Hu Ching- originally compiled by the Taoist Wang Fu circa 300 AD
Hui Neng- 6th Patriarch of Ch'an Buddhism (Zen Buddhism in China), (638-713), teachings are compiled in The Platform Sutra, His status as patriarch was disputed and Ch'an divided into several lineages one of which emphasized sudden awakening and the other a more gradual process.
Hujwiri, Ali- (990-1077), Persian Sufi and scholar, contributed significantly to the spread of Islam into southeast Asia, "Revelation of the Veiled"
Iblis- arabic for Satan, fallen angel and deceiver of man, In the Quran it was Satan's pride which kept him from worshipping man which caused him to be cast out, He asked for respite until the day of Judgment to turn away all he could the true path
Ibn Arabi- (1165-1240 CE), Sufi mystic and philosopher during the Islamic Golden Age, Most notable for his explanation of Tawhid (oneness of God) through the concept of Wahdat ul Wujood (Oneness of Being), known throughout the Muslim world as Sheikh ul Akbar (the Greatest Master)
Ibrahim Adham- (718-782), one of the most prominent early ascetic Sufi saints, emphasized the importance of stillness and meditation for asceticism
Indra- Lord of Heaven and God of war in Hinduism, one of the chief deities in the Rig Veda
Idries Shah- (1924-1996), author and teacher in the Sufi tradition, "The Sufis"
Jalaludin Rumi- September 30, 1207- December 17, 1273, Persian Sufi poet, jurist, theologian and teacher, born in present day Afghanistan although then Balkh was a part of Persia
Jean Pierre de Caussade- (1675-1751), French Jesuit priest and writer, "Abandonment to Divine Providence" (also translated as "The Sacrament of the Present Moment")
Jeremiah- His writings are collected in the Book of Jeremiah as well as the Book of Lamentations but he is considered by most modern scholars to be the redactor of much of the Old Testament, went and lived in Jerusalem in the court of King Josiah and assisted in his reformation,
Jesus- Son of Mary, Son of God, Son of Man, Messiah, according to synoptic gospels and the Quran Jesus was born of a virgin, The image of God in human form. The Word of God made flesh
jinn- arabic for "demons"
Kabir- (1398-1518), mystic poet of India
Karma- "action", the belief that every act produces an effect which inevitably finds fruition, actions sow seeds, trees are known by their fruits, The Old Testament and Quran speak of it and the New Testament says that because the
punishment for sin is death and everyone sins, then everyone should be put to death

but Jesus atones for our sin. Karma is an effectual process caused by the innate nature of reality which some people live by as if a law unto itself working and acting in hopes of rewards and restraining from wrong action out of fear of punishment.

Kaya- (Pali: kama), body, The trikaya theory in Buddhism says that the Buddha actually has three bodies: the Nirmankaya (body of transformation), the Sambogakaya (the body of bliss and communication, personification of Dharmakaya) and the Dhammakaya (the body of essence).

Krishna- avatar of Brahman, drives Arjuna's chariot in the Bhagavad Gita, Metaphor for the Spirit riding with the soul and giving it guidance

Kyong Ho- (1849-1912), Korean Buddhist master, reviver of modern Korean Son (Zen) Buddhism,

Lao Tzu-author of the Tao te Ching, Old Man though happy as a child, possibly a myth or symbol, traditional founder of Taoism

Lieh Tzu-third founder and influential writer of Taoism along with Lao Tzu and Chuang Tzu.

Lotus Sutra- earliest date for this sutra is between 100BC and 100CE, deals with upayha (skillful means) in adapting teaching for audience's disposition (adhimukti). Pure Land text telling of Amitabha Buddha

Maaruf Karkhi- (750- 815), Sufi saint, Important link in the Golden Chain leading from initiates back to Muhammad,

Mahamudra- "great seal", set of advanced Buddhist meditation methods

Mahmud Shabestari- (1288-1340), one of the most celebrated Persian Sufi saints of the 14th century, "The Secret Rose Garden"

Maitreya- the Buddha to be, residing in Pure Land

mantrum (mantra)- a sound (OM), syllable, group of words or text that is considered capable of creating spiritual transformation or awakening

Mara- tempter in Buddhism, The King of Desire, has three daughters: craving, aversion, and lust

Maya- illusion covering reality according to Hindus

Melchezidek- priest of God to whom Abraham gives offerings,

Metanoia- a radical changing of mind equivocal with enlightenment, sincere repentance and an honest turning away from past sin towards the life of the new man which is becoming sons of God

Mirabai- (1498-1550), a devotee of Vishnu in the incarnation of Krishna whose poetry is still held dear

Mu- "nothing", a negation, affirmation of impossibility of describing reality in words so as to necessarily purvey understanding, Answer which Joshu gives after being asked if a dog has Buddha nature.

Muhammad- As Moses saved the Hebrews from slavery so Muhammad saved the Arabs from a long Age of Ignorance called the Jahiliyyah in which the Arabs had been polytheistic and worshipped idols although according to tradition they had at one time been monotheistic and worshipped God at the Qabba which had been established by Ishmael and Abraham after Ishmael was sent away by his Father's

wife.
Nan ch'uan- (748-834), Chinese Ch'an (Zen) monk of the T'ang dynasty
nikaya- "collection", "group", commonly used in reference to the Buddhist texts of the Sutta Pitaka, the Nikaya schools refer to early Buddhist schools
Niguma- born in 10th century Kashmir to a rich Brahmin family, Tantric Yogini (female tantric yoga practioner and teacher)
ojo- Japanese Buddhist term referring to rebirth in the Pure Land of Amitabha Buddhism
Pancha Tattva- "five" "truth", five aspects of God or Absolute Truth,
Paul of Tarsus- converted to Christianity after a vision which left him blind, became a champion for the Gentiles in the early years of the Church and traveled throughout the Mediterranean preaching the gospel and setting up churches, his letters to these churches have been collected and comprise much of the New Testament, born a Jew
Philokalia- collection of books and sayings from the early Church Fathers and saints
Pirqe Avot- collection of the sayings of the Jewish Fathers,
prajna- panna in Pali, wisdom, understanding, insight, One of the three divisions of the Noble Eightfold Path in Buddhism, The sixth of the six Paramitas (Perfections)
Prajnaparamita Sutras- Perfection of Wisdom Sutras, deals with the new wisdom taught by the Mahayanists, 4 Periods: 100BC-100CE the Ratnagunasamcayagatha and the Astasahasrika were written, 100-300 period of elaboration, 300-500 when the Heart Sutra was written, 500-1000 was a time of Tantric influence. All things appear as thoughtforms or conceptual constructs. Indispensable elements of the Bodhisattva path, paramita- perfection, prajna-wisdom
Prakriti- "nature", within Hinduism it is the basic nature of intelligence by which the universe exists and functions, primal motive force, composed of the three gunas (sattva-creation, tamas-destruction, rajas-preservation)
Purusha- "cosmic man", "Self" which permeates the Universe, within the Rig Veda he was sacrificed to create the world
Rabia- (717- 801 CE), Muslim saint and Sufi mystic, full name: Rabia Basri
Ramakrishna- February 18, 1836- August 16, 1886, was one of the most important Hindu religious leaders of India, influential figure in the Bengal Renaissance of 19th century, revered as being self-found
Ramana Maharshi- December 30, 1879- April 14, 1950, was a great Hindu mystic and saint, He lived in the sacred Tiruvannamala hill near Chennai. The core of his teachings was the practice of atma-vichara (self-enquiry).
Ramprasad Sen- (1718-1775), Shakta poet and saint in Bengal, born into a Tantric family
Rig Veda- a collection of 1,017 hymns written around 1200BC, Contains the oldest texts preserved in any Indo-Iranian language. Its core is accepted to date to the late Bronze Age, making it the only example of Bronze Age literature with an unbroken tradition. The chief gods of the Rig-Veda are the sacrificial fire god Agni, Indra, a heroic god, and Soma, the sacred potion probably made from hallucinogenic mushrooms. Other prominent gods are Mitra, Varuna, and Ushas (the dawn). Also

invoked are Vishnu, Dyas Pita (the sky), Prithivi (the earth), Surya (the sun), Vayu (the wind), Parjanya (the rain), Vac (the word), and the Vishvadivas (the all-gods) as well as various further minor gods, persons, concepts, phenomena and items. Some of the names of gods and goddesses found in the Rig-Veda are found amongst other Indo-European people as well: Dyaus-Pita is cognate with Greek Zeus, Latin Jupiter (from deus-pater), and Germanic Tyre; while Mitra is cognate with Persian Mithra; also, Ushas with Greek Eos and Latin Aurora; and, less certainly, Varuna with Greek Uranos. Finally, Agni is cognate with Latin ignis and Russian ogon, both meaning "fire".

Ruysbroek, John- (1293-1381), Flemish mystic within the Catholic Church, "Seven Steps of the Ladder of Spiritual Love"

Ryokan- (1758-1831), Japanese Zen monk in the Soto school, famous for his calligraphy and writings

Saadi of Shiraz- (1184-1283), Persian Sufi, "The Orchard", "The Rose Garden"

Sadhyas- minor Hindu gods who guard the rites and prayers of greater gods

samadhi- state of meditation (dhyana) in which a sense of oneness or enlightenment is achieved

Samsara- cycle of rebirth and death taking place because of we remain in maya

Sana'i- A Persian Sufi who lived in what is now Afghanistan during the 11th and 12th centuries, important inspiration of Rumi, wrote The Walled Garden of Truth

sannyasin- One who having fulfilled his or her obligations to their family renounces the material world and lives an ascetic life in pursuit of Holiness

Saraha- 8th century CE, one of the founders of Buddhist Vajrayana and particularly of the Mahamudra tradition

satori- awakening,

Seng tsan- 3rd patriarch of Zen in China, lived in the late 6th century

Shakti- divine feminine energy permeating the world in Tantric Buddhism

Shankara, Adi- 8th century Hindu philosopher who had a profound influence on the growth of Hinduism through his non-dualistic philosophy, Advocated the importance of Hindu scriptures such as the Veda but focused mainly on the Upanishads, Gave new life to Hinduism by emphasizing spirituality based on truth and reason instead of on dogma and ritual

Shantideva- 8th century Indian Buddhist scholar

Sheik Muzaffar- Islamic scholar and teacher, born in Istanbul in 1916

Sheik Ziaudin- Sufi author and founder

Shen Hui- Chinese Buddhist monk of the Southern School of Zen, (670-758), emphasized "sudden" teachings rather than the "gradual" teachings of the Northern School

Sheng-yen: (1930-2009), Buddhist monk and teacher of Chinese Chan (Zen) Buddhism

Shinran Shoren- (1173-1263), founder of Jodo Shinshu Buddhism, Said that because we are all defiled by greed, hatred and delusion we have no chance of gaining enlightenment by ourselves, encouraged practitioners to rely on the vow of the Buddha Amitabha to save all beings from suffering when reborn in the Pure Land

shu- emptiness in Buddhism

sila- virtue, right conduct, morality, moral discipline, An internal, aware and

intentional ethical behavior in harmony with the Dharma
Sirach- apocryphal book of the Old Testament not present in the Protestant Bible though in the Catholic canon, written 180-175 BC
skandha- Sanskrit for heap or aggregate. according to Buddhist thought they are the five elements that sum up the whole of an individual's mental and physical existence,
St. Augustine- 354-430, one of the 4 Latin Fathers and bishop of Hippo, *Confessions*
St. Catherine of Sienna- Siena, Italy, March 25, 1347- April 29, 1380 in Roma, was a Dominican layperson, at the age of seven she consecrated her virginity to Christ and at age 16 she took the habit of the Dominican Tertiaries. Had many visions and became a spokesman for peace and the poor
St. Evagrios the Solitary- (345-399), Christian monk and ascetic, teacher of John Cassian, disciple of Basil of Caesarea, first person to write down the teachings of the Desert Fathers, studied Origen and was later condemned by the Church for his belief in the preexistence of souls and other beliefs
St. John Cassian- (360-435), an ascetic Christian monk and theologian
St. John of the Cross- Juan de la Cruz, June 24, 1542- December 14, 1591, was a Spanish Carmelite friar born near Avila, worked with Saint Teresa of Avila in the reformation of the Carmelite order, his poetry is considered the summit of mystical Spanish literature
St. Jerome- 347- September 30, 420, Translated the Bible from Greek and Hebrew into the Latin Vulgate which is still the official biblical text of the Roman Catholic Church, recognized as a doctor of the Church
St. Philip Neri- (1515-1595), Catholic priest and founder of the "Congregation of the Oratory" which was a society of secular clergy, known as Apostle of Rome,
St. Teresa of Avila- March 28, 1515- October 4, 1582, a Spanish Roman Catholic mystic and a monastic reformer, born in Avila north of Madrid, her feast day is October 15
St. Thomas Aquinas- (c. 1225 – March 7, 1274) was an Italian Catholic philosopher and theologian in the scholastic tradition, He is the most famous classical proponent of natural theology. He gave birth to the Thomistic school of philosophy, which was long the primary philosophical approach of the Catholic Church. He is considered by the Catholic Church to be its greatest theologian and one of the thirty-three Doctors of the Church.
St. Victor- also called Victor the Moor, born 3rd century in Mauretania, died in 303 in Milan as a Catholic martyr for destroying pagan alters
Son of God- name given to several Old Testament figures including Adam and the sons of Adam, David, Ezekiel and also to Jesus. Muslims say that God is without a son and that the Christians have made up a lie about Jesus, but the Quran says that Jesus is the Word of God sent to mankind as a sign. It is the understanding of Jesus as somehow being the physical progeny of God which would make God physical which the Quran is against, not the idea of Jesus being a son of God in the Old Testament sense of the word which means that he abided in God and was led by God and so was the image of God.
Son of Man- name reserved only for Jesus and Ezekiel in the Bible

srotopanna- (sotapanna), "stream-winner", One who has entered the stream leading to Nirvana

Subhuti- one of the ten great Sravakas ("hearers or disciples") of Sakyamuni Buddhism, name means 'Good Existence, su: good, bhuti: existence, Best known as the disciple to whom the Buddha often speaks in texts

Sueng Sahn- (1927- 2004), founder of the Kwan Um School of Zen in Korea, in the first wave of Korean Zen Masters to teach in the West

Sufism- an umbrella term for the ascetic and mystical movements within Islam. While Sufism is said to have incorporated elements of Christian monasticism, gnosticism, and Indian mysticism, its origins are traced to forms of devotion and groups of penitents (*zuhhad*) in the formative period of Islam. The early pious figures, later appropriated by Sufism, include Hasan al-Basri (d. 801), and Rabia al-Adawiyya, a woman from Basra (Iraq) who rejected worship motivated by the desire for heavenly reward or the fear of punishment and insisted on the love of God as the sole valid form of adoration. The word Sufi first appears in the 8th cent., probably in connection with the coarse wool that many ascetics wore. Two central Sufi concepts are *tawakkul,* the total reliance on God, and *dhikr,* the perpetual remembrance of God. Al-Muhasibi (d. 857) and his disciple Junayd (d. 910) are representative early figures. The introduction of gnostic elements (*marifa*) into Sufism is often attributed to Dhu-n-Nun al-Misri (d. 859). Sufism nonetheless faced growing opposition from orthodox clerics. The scholastic and ecstatic paths further diverged with the concept of *fana,* the dissolution into the divine, advocated by al-Bistami (d. 874), and used by Hallaj in the declaration of his unity with God, which eventually led to his execution in 922. Islamic orthodoxy and Sufism were not irreconcilable, as attested by the attempt by al-Ghazali (d. 1111) to infuse conformist Muslim religious life with mysticism. The evolution of Sufism in the post-Ghazali period was influenced by Ibn al-Arabia and Ibn al-Farid. Their theoretical contributions led to the development within Sufism of a complex system of initiation and progression toward the Divine and set the stage for the emergence of organized Sufi orders. This phase of literary Sufism was also characterized by the prominence of Persian works, notably those of Shihab ad-Din Suhrawardi (d. 1191), Attar, and Jalal ad-Din Rumi and the subsequent development of Persian, Turkish, and Urdu mystic poetry. Important Sufi figures elsewhere in the Islamic world include Muin ad-Din Chishti in India and Baha ad-Din Naqshband (d. 1390) in central Asia. Sufi orders, which assimilated aspects of native religious traditions more readily than more dogmatic versions of Islam, played a major role in the expansion of Islam into sub-Saharan Africa and central, S, and SE Asia and is also prevalent in Asia Minor. Many conservative Muslims disagree with many popular Sufi practices, particularly saint worship, the visiting of tombs, and the incorporation of non-Islamic customs.

Sutta Nipata- the second of the three divisions of the Tripitaka, contains more than 10,000 suttas attributed to the Buddha, there are five nikayas or collections of suttas: Digha, Majjhima, Samyutta, Anguttara, Kuddaka

Talmud- record of rabbinic discussions on Jewish law, Jewish ethics, customs, legends and stories, which Jewish tradition considers authoritative. It is a fundamental source of legislation, customs, case histories and moral exhortations.

The Talmud has two components, the Mishnah which is the first written compilation of Judaism's Oral Law, and the Gemara, a discussion of the Mishnah. Two talmuds: Talmud Bavli (Babylonian) and Talmud Yerushalmi (Jerusalem Talmud)
Tao- The Way, similar to the Dharma and the Word
Tao te Ching- The Way of Virtue and Change, written by Lao Tzu the "old man" who composed the Tao by request of a border guard as he was retreating off into the wilderness
Tathata (dharmata)- "thusness", "suchness", central concept in Buddhism, the essential nature of reality, aspect of nibbana (nirvana)
Tathagata- "One who has thus come", "One who has arrived at suchness", Buddha referred to himself as this,
Theologia Germania- mystical treatise written in the mid 14th century by an anonymous author although possibly written by Meister Eckhart
Tilopa- (988-1069), Indian tantric
Tukaram- (1598-1649), Emphasized bhakti or devotion and said that escape from the effects of karma is only found through faith in the grace of Narayana or Vishnu who bears men's burden without consideration of their merit **Upanishads-** part of the Hindu Shruti scriptures which primarily discuss meditation and philosophy, mystic interpretations of the Vedas, known as Vedanta (the end of the Vedas), There are reputedly over 200 but Shankara only considered about 15 to be primary, Major Upanishads: Aitareya, Kauitaki, Kena, Chandogya, Taittriya, Bhadarayaka, Prajna, Mudaka, Katha, Kau_îtâki, _vetâúvatara, contain the first and most definitive explications of aum as the divine word, the cosmic vibration that underlies all existence
turya- experience of ultimate reality, oneness, enlightenment
Varuna- the guardian of *rita* (the cosmic order)
Vedas- collectively refers to a corpus of ancient Indo-Aryan religious literature that are associated with the Vedic civilization in the Ganges Valley, regarded by most historians as the oldest surviving text of humanity, the oldest text the Rg Veda dates back to 1,500 BC, the newest parts of the Vedas date back to 500 BC, the Vedas precede the Upanishads both in development and place in time, the Upanishads take ideas presented in the Vedas and provide exegesis, many of the ideas found in the Upanishads are in the Vedas although in a less developed manner, 4 Vedas: Rig Veda, Yajur Veda, Sama Veda and Atharva Veda. Basically all of Hindu literature talks of gods in a plural sense but even as far back as the Rg Veda in the myth of the Cosmic Giant Purusha there is the belief that everything in reality comes from a common source. In the myth the gods and all of the universe come from the sacrifice of the Cosmic Giant Purusha. "The lack of clear distinction between the gods probably made possible a belief in multiplicity as representing some more fundamental principle of unity" (Hindu Tradition, 10). The cosmic law governing the universe in the Vedas was *rita* which became a synonym for truth.
William Law- The Serious Call to a Devout and Holy Life (1728), together with its predecessor, A Treatise of Christian Perfection (1726), deeply influenced the chief actors in the great Evangelical revival among whom was John and Charles

Wesley although they later distanced themselves as Law's turn towards mysticism increased

William Penn- founded the Quakers, had a doctrine of Inner Light describing how God leads humans by His Word

Wonyo- (617-686), one of the leading writers and founders of the Korean Buddhist tradition, "Nirvana Sutra", "Awakening of Faith"

The Word- The mind of God, pure reality, The Light, Truth, Jesus, Logos, The Way, The Eternal Law, Mother of the Book, The razor's edge and the narrow path. Apparent to man if only he will consent to be guided. The still small voice within us all. The sharp two-edged sword which stands between man and the garden of Eden, Eternity.

Special Thanks, Bibliography, Recommended Reading, Acknowledgments and Direct and Indirect Sources

Four Sufi Classics. London, Octagon Press, 1980
Cleary, Thomas, editor. *Zen Antics.* Boston and London: Shambhala, 1993
Cleary, Thomas, editor. *Teachings of Zen.* Boston and London: Shambhala, 1998
Meyer, Marvin, translator. *The Secret Teachings Of Jesus,* New York: Vintage Books, 1984
Shah, Idries. *The Way of the Sufi.* New York: E.P. Dutton and Co., 1970
Palmer, Martin and Breuilly Elizabeth, translators. *The Book of Chuang Tzu.* London: Arkana of Penguin. 1996
Kornfield, Jack, editor *Teachings of the Buddha.* (TB) Boston and London: Shambhala. 1996
Mascaro, Juan, translator *The Upanishads.* England: Penguin. 1965
P. Lal, translator *The Bhagavad Gita.* New Dehli: Roli Books. 1994
Mascaro, Juan, translator *The Bhagavad Gita.* England: Penguin. 1962
Easwaran, Eknath, translator *The Bhagavad Gita.* Berkley: Nilgiri Press. 1985
W.J. Johnson, translator *The Bhagavad Gita.* New York: Oxford Press. 1994
WE Soothill, translator *The Lotus of the Wonderful Law*
Mu Soeng, translator *The Diamond Sutra.* Boston: Wisdom Publications. 2000
H. Saddhatissa, Curzan, translators *The Sutta Nipata.*
Donald Lopez, editor *Penguin Classics: Buddhist Scriptures.* England 2004
E.G. Browne. *Literary History of Persia.* 1998
Jan Rypka, *History of Iranian Literature.* Reidel Publishing Company. Karen Armstrong..
Buddha. New York: Penguin
Andrew Skilton. *A Concise History of Buddhism.* Birmingham, AL: Windhorse Publications
Karen Armstrong. *Islam.* New York: Modern Library Chronicles Book.
Abdullah, Yusuf Ali, translator. *The Quran.* New York: Tahrike Tarsile Quran Inc
Margaret Smith, *Rabia the Mystic and Her Fellow Saints in Islam.*
London: E.A. Burtt, *The Teachings of the Compassionate Buddha,*
New York, 1955
E Conze, *Buddhist Scriptures,* Harmondsworth 1959
E Conze, *Buddhist Texts Through the Ages,* New York 1964
H.C. Warren, *Buddhism in Translations,* New York 1963
F.L. Woodward, *Some Sayings of the Buddha,* London 1974
T.W. Davids, *Dialogues of the Buddha,* London 1921
I.B. Horner, *Middle Length Sayings,* London 1959
Narada Thera, *The Dhammapada,* London 1954
G.E.H. Palmer, Philip Sherrand Kallistos Ware, *The Philokalia,* London: Faber and Faber 1983
JR Carter and M Palihawadana, *The Dhammapada,* New York and Oxford 1987
H Saddhatissa, *The Sutta-Nipata,* London 1985
Norman KR, *The Group of Discourses,* Oxford 1992
Peter Brown, *The Body and Society,* New York: Columbia University Press 1988
Andrew Louth, *The Origins of the Christian Mystical Tradition,* Oxford: Clarendon Press 1981
Juan Mascaro, translator, *The Dhammapada,* New York: Penguin 1973
Chogyam Trungpa, translator, *The Tibetan Book of the Dead,* Boston and London: Shambhala 2000
Diana Y. Paul, *Women in Buddhism,* California: University of California Press 1985
William Theodore de Bary, *The Buddhist Tradition,* New York: Vintage Books 1972
Elaine Pagels, *The Gnostic Gospels,* New York: Vintage Books 1979
John E. Rybolt, *Sirach,* Minnesota: The Liturgical Press 1970

Robert Van de Weyer, *Chuang Tzu*, London: Hodder and Stoughton 1998
Teachings and Sayings of Chuang Tzu, New York: Dover
Andrew Harvey, editor, *Dhammapada*, Vermont: Skylight Publishing 2002
Paul Reps and Nyogen Senzaki, editors, *Zen Flesh, Zen Bones*, Boston: Tuttle Publishing 1985
N.J. Dawood, translator, *The Koran*, New York: Penguin 1999
James Fadiman and Robert Frager, *Essential Sufism*, San Francisco: Harper 1997
Reynold A. Nicholson, *Selected Poems of Rumi*, New York: Dover 2001
Swami Ambikananda Saraswati, translator, *The Uddhava Gita*, Berkeley: Seastone Press 2002
Brian Walker, translator, *The Hua Hu Ching*, San Francisco: Harper 1992
Andrew Harvey, editor, *The Essential Mystics*, San Francisco: Harper 1997
Thomas Merton, *The Way of Chuang Tzu*, New Directions Publishing 1969
Huston Smith, *The World's Religions*, San Francisco: Harper 1991
Kazuaki Tanahashi and Tensho David Schneider, *Essential Zen*, San Francisco: Harper 1994
D.C. Lau, *The Tao te Ching*, New York: Penguin Books
DT Suzuki, *An Introduction to Zen Buddhism*. New York: Grove Press 1964

To whom it may concern,

"A Mirror of Light" is a comparative anthology of world religions composed in a manner which reflects the spiritual journey every man (to some extent or other) is on. Not that every man is simultaneously a Jew, Christian, Muslim, Buddhist, Hindu Taoist, etc. in an outward sense (meaning they participate in all of the traditions of these religions). Rather, this book pertains to the spirit of these religions, for it is only when someone understands the spirit that a true understanding, an understanding that is in spirit and truth, is present. The law (representing an outward understanding) kills a person, for it becomes a superficial bond of false understanding to which a person chains themselves; life is found only through understanding and abiding in the spirit of the law, for it is the spirit of the law which both gives the words in the texts of the religions represented in this book meaning and the person who dwells in this spirit the ability to truly understand and find life.

www.ingramcontent.com/pod-product-compliance
Lightning Source LLC
Chambersburg PA
CBHW032026290426
44110CB00012B/692